TEACHING MIDDLE SCHOOL LANGUAGE ARTS

Incorporating Twenty-first-Century Literacies

Anna J. Small Roseboro

ROWMAN & LITTLEFIELD EDUCATION
A division of
ROWMAN & LITTLEFIELD PUBLISHERS, INC.
Lanham • New York • Toronto • Plymouth, UK

LIBRARY
FRANKLIN PIERCE UNIVERSITY
RINDGE, NH 03461

Published by Rowman & Littlefield Education
A division of Rowman & Littlefield Publishers, Inc.
A wholly owned subsidary of
The Rowman & Littlefield Publishing Group, Inc.
4501 Forbes Boulevard, Suite 200, Lanham, Maryland 20706
http://www.rowmaneducation.com

Estover Road, Plymouth PL6 7PY, United Kingdom

Copyright © 2010 by Anna J. Small Roseboro

All rights reserved. No part of this book may be reproduced in any form or
by any electronic or mechanical means, including information storage and
retrieval systems, without written permission from the publisher, except by a
reviewer who may quote passages in a review.

British Library Cataloguing in Publication Information Available

Library of Congress Cataloging-in-Publication Data

Roseboro, Anna J. Small, 1945–
    Teaching middle school language arts : incorporating twenty-first-century
    literacies / Anna J. Small Roseboro.
        p. cm.
    Includes bibliographical references and index.
    ISBN 978-1-60709-630-6 (cloth : alk. paper) — ISBN 978-1-60709-631-3
    (pbk. : alk. paper) — ISBN 978-1-60709-581-1 (electronic)
    1. Language arts (Middle school). 2. Creative writing (Middle school).
    3. Educational technology. I. Title.
    LB1631.R634 2010
    428.0071'2—dc22

                                                            2009050185

∞™ The paper used in this publication meets the minimum requirements of
American National Standard for Information Sciences—Permanence of Paper
for Printed Library Materials, ANSI/NISO Z39.48-1992.

Printed in the United States of America

To my husband, William Gerald Roseboro, whose support made this book possible, to early career educators willing to accept the challenge of a lifetime, and to veterans like Akiko, Carleen, and Jane for teaching middle school students for over four decades.

CONTENTS

FOREWORD

Amazing Grace

Carol Jago

If you don't know where you are going, any old way will do.

—Lewis Carroll

I started teaching middle school because I didn't know what else to do. Though born into a family of teachers, I had always said "Not me!" when asked if I planned to take my degree in English and teach. But a combination of crippling student loans and a dearth of other plans pushed me toward the education department at the University of Southern California. After what I recall as the briefest of interviews, the advisor told me to show up the next day at Lincoln Junior High to start my student teaching. I arrived expecting to take a couple of weeks getting my bearings, but the master teacher was out sick and his substitute told me to start teaching.

It was not an auspicious beginning. There were no textbooks, no standards, and no curriculum that I could find, just thirty-six eager, fresh-faced eighth graders waiting for me to do something. I shudder to remember the lessons I offered my young charges, students who most certainly deserve a refund for their first semester of eighth grade. But I was trying hard: typing up short stories on purple dittos, writing discussion questions, grading papers, and going through the motions of what

I thought English teachers do. Of course I struggled with classroom management, but the bigger problem was that I didn't know where my instruction was supposed to be heading. A line from *Alice in Wonderland* kept echoing in my dreams, "If you don't know where you are going, any old way will do."

Those students from long ago deserved better than what I was able to offer. If only I had a mentor like Anna Roseboro to ease my way into the classroom. If only someone had handed me *Teaching Middle School Language Arts: Incorporating Twenty-first-Century Literacies* to help me plan a coherent year of learning for them. The middle school scenario I describe is unfortunately more common than educators would like to admit. Data on teacher attrition demonstrates that we are a profession that eats its young. Between 40 and 50 percent of teachers leave the profession in the first five years. Anna Roseboro's book can help to turn these numbers around by helping new teachers be successful right from the first year. It also provides a much-needed tonic for experienced teachers who may have lost their way and are wondering if there isn't an easier way to make a living.

Teaching Middle School Language Arts lays out a plan for approaching a school year that is both student-centered and standards-aligned. Anna Roseboro's lessons employ a gradual release model designed to offer strong support and extensive guidance in the first months of the school year and then, week by week, month by month, greater opportunities for independent learning as students acquire the skills and habits of mind needed for twenty-first-century literacy. Roseboro answers common questions new teachers have, providing practical answers of the kind only someone who has spent a lifetime in the classroom could offer. Covering everything from choice of texts to the arrangement of desks, *Teaching Middle School Language Arts* presents a pedagogy grounded in sound theory and effective practice.

Rather than fighting middle school students' buoyant natures, Anna Roseboro revels in her students' enthusiasm. In lesson after lesson she demonstrates how a wily teacher can use young people's energy for educational purposes, capitalizing on their eagerness to know one another and know more about the world around them. She also shows how to put their love of talk to work. Calling her lessons "benevolent athletic training sessions," Roseboro artfully leads her charges in the direction she wants them to go. There is no doubt in her students' minds who is the coach. At the same time, they seem to draw strength from this knowledge.

I was particularly struck by the manner in which Anna's instructional plan treats every minute of classroom time as golden. Again and again Anna limits the time students have to work on a project, plan their writing, or prepare for a presentation—sometimes using a timer to drive home the message. This technique sends students the message that their work has urgency. There is no time to waste. We have stories to read and papers to write and so much, so much to tell one another.

But how can a young teacher manage all that middle school energy and talk? My first classroom was located on the second floor just above the principal's office. I received more than one note from Mr. Steinman's secretary querying the noise level and wondering why the furniture had to be moved quite so often. Anna offers readers not only explanations about how putting students' desks together facilitates the collaborative process (I wish I had had this defense in hand thirty years ago) but also helpful hints for students. She tells her charges when working in pairs to use "six-inch voices."

Teaching Middle School Language Arts can be a valuable resource for both new and experienced teachers whatever the particulars of their school or district curriculum. Anna Roseboro sagely advises teachers to "focus on the resources available in your anthology rather than on its deficits." We can't make excuses for not teaching well. Whatever our resources, we need to serve the children who have been entrusted to our care. Anna urges teachers working with middle school students "to challenge them to think deeply, critically, and broadly—but also charitably—toward those who are different, whether in the classroom or the literature."

I do not know a single teacher who doesn't want to be more effective in the classroom. Most teachers are eager, often desperate, to help students become better readers and writers. They agree with the pundits and politicians who insist that success in school and in the workplace depends upon literacy. They sweat to make this happen. But if media reports are to be believed, our schools are full of underprepared, uninspired, and relatively unqualified individuals collecting full-time pay for part-time work. Such reporting is dispiriting, particularly for teachers who know they could be doing a better job, but don't know where to find the help they need.

Of particular interest to teachers of middle school "digital natives" are the many examples of twenty-first-century technology applications included in this text. The average student spends six hours a day plugged into a digital communication device, often several simultaneously.[1] Linda Stone, a former Microsoft executive, describes this habit of mind as "continuous partial attention."[2] No wonder teachers have difficulty making students attend to their lessons. Fortunately Anna Roseboro has powerful ideas for engaging preoccupied youngsters in their learning.

What I never guessed those thirty-odd years ago when I faced my first group of middle school students was how seductive teaching could be or how the work itself could be so rewarding that I would never want to leave the classroom. In *I Want to Thank My Brain for Remembering Me*, Jimmy Breslin writes, "Grace appears when you don't expect it and have asked for nothing. It comes out of the mists to help people at their work. Grace comes to those who teach." Every good teacher knows what it feels like to be on the receiving end of this gift of grace. It doesn't appear on the check stub, but is the best payment of all. Thank you, Anna Roseboro, for sharing this grace, your grace, with us.

Carol Jago has taught middle and high school English for thirty-two years and directs the California Reading and Literature Project at UCLA. She is president of the National Council of Teachers of English.

PREFACE

Teaching at the Intersection of Old and New Literacies

Quentin J. Schultze

Normally the preface is written by the author of the book. In this case, I served as manuscript collaborator with the author, Anna J. Roseboro; discussed her manuscript; and helped to craft sections on technology. Encouraged by Anna, I learned to appreciate anew that teaching language arts is a highly demanding calling that requires historical understanding and a moral vision. Like students and parents, we educators feel the stress of modern, high-tech, hypercommunicative lives. We also witness firsthand some of the social drawbacks of too much media technology and too many means of communication and miscommunication.

As Anna's book suggests, teaching occurs at the intersection of ancient and modern literacies—ways of communicating primarily for comprehension.[1] Every instructor is a medium, or a go-between, who teaches at the intersection not only of text and student but also of traditional and contemporary cultures. Educators introduce students to older and newer knowledge, skills, and technologies.

The ancient–new intersection often leads to conflicts among educators and between educators and the communities that they serve. Who decides which new pedagogies, content, and technologies are to be used in the classroom? What do we give up when we adopt a new method or medium? This tension goes back at least to Plato, for whom the word *poetry* referred to all language arts but especially the most popular forms of artistic expression. Plato feared that the poets promoted undesirable passions, failed to pursue truth, and wasted students' time with impractical instruction.[2]

The National Council of Teachers of English's (NCTE) definition of twenty-first-century literacies begins, "Literacy has always been a collection of cultural and communicative practices shared among members of particular groups. As society and technology change, so does literacy." NCTE adds that literacies are "inextricably linked with particular histories. . . ." The ancient Greek rhetorician Aristotle would have loved that—know your particular audience's backgrounds.

The first and most lasting mass media were—and still are—mass languages. Languages were the original viral media, millennia before online social networking. We live in the age of twenty-first-century literacies not merely because of the emergence of new media technologies but also because of the ongoing influence of previous media such as speech and writing.

Probably because of the rapid pace of today's social and technological changes, most educators realize that literacies are dynamic; they change with languages, cultures, and technologies. Reading a paper text is not the same as reading a digital one. When media change, so do the ways that people teach and learn. This is why the academic subject of greatest educational impact in any culture is likely to be language arts—the arts of using language codes to create, maintain, and transform knowing. Every discipline depends on texts and language codes. In the sciences, for instance, the physical world itself is a text interpreted by changing scientific ways of knowing emerging with new technologies such as radio telescopes and subatomic microscopes.

As Anna's book shows, moderation, the "mean" between excess and deficiency, is essential in the teaching of new literacies. We should steer clear of both utopian language that promises too much and dystopian language that offers too little. Anna wisely avoids one-sided rhetoric.

In my view, technological moderation includes

selecting appropriate media for a given task,
considering whether particular media are sustainable, and

identifying what is realistic, not merely what technology's champions and detractors say is or is not possible.

In other words, when it comes to the study and practice of literacies, we need to ask time-honored questions. We constantly have to figure out what it means to fittingly adapt rather than naïvely adopt or reject particular media for new as well as old educational purposes.

As this book suggests, the human body itself is a multimedia technology. It's the gold standard for human communication, including teaching. The expressive capacity of the human body offers a baseline for assessing all new means of communication.

Two of the major movements in education during the last thirty years demonstrate human beings' basic multimedia nature: (1) embracing the variety of learning styles, and (2) inviting all cultures to the educational enterprise. These developments challenge us to view multimedia code-switching as an extension of human senses through older and newer media. Good education is shared code-switching among multimedia teachers and learners. We learn from the blogger as well as the bard.

I believe that the most foundational literacy that we teach across all media is listening. Listening is the practice of using all of the linguistic codes at our disposal for the purpose of becoming acquainted with reality—or at least human interpretations of reality. Listening is the art of knowing, not just hearing. Listening leads to wisdom—the deepest form of knowing. The opposite of a wise person is a fool. The fool knows only superficial bits of reality; she or he lacks a deeper, long-term relationship with the subject. The fool is a clueless person who listens primarily to self.

Anna has listened empathetically to students, parents, colleagues, and artists. The result is her lifelong love of teaching language arts. Now as a wise book author, she shows us how to fall in love with the pursuit and teaching of knowledge for the sake of students. We benefit by listening to her.

At its best, language arts instruction invites students into rich, multimedia communion with persons and cultures, with those nearby and far away, with people who lived before us and now live among us on earth.

We learn with students and colleagues what others have thought, believed, and done; how others have told and still tell us about themselves through various art forms; how we can identify with their life stories; and ultimately how we can share our own stories with others.

Some of this knowing is highly practical, such as writing a complex sentence, reading poetic alliteration, establishing a speech thesis, or memorizing vocabulary. Other aspects of language arts focus both explicitly and implicitly on character-building, heart-opening, mind-sharpening practices. These are among the many deeply held human literacies that have existed across time and through geographic space.

Why does there seem to be so much nasty, rude, and tasteless communication especially in high-tech communication such as blogs, e-mail, phone texting, and video downloading? One likely factor is the high level of code-switching required in modern life. Another one is anonymity, which includes the use of fabricated names or no names at all in blogs and YouTube video postings. Some people rely on such anonymity to attack other people and organizations. In any case, we end up with new forms of age-old problems such as gossiping and bullying.

How can twenty-first-century educators teach age-old civility in new media settings? We can do this partly by modeling civility in the ways that we use the range of media. Anna's book delicately demonstrates that how we educators communicate invariably becomes part of what we communicate. Intentionally or not, we all model communication. When we enter the classroom or teach online, we teach first and foremost via the ways that we conduct ourselves.

Our professional lives are multimedia parables. We language arts educators are living texts. There is something refreshingly old and new about that vision. Thanks to Anna for gently reminding me that the one thing that we can count on in our educational callings is that instruction occurs at the intersection of old and new literacies. May her wisdom stir us to listen well, with graceful hearts and open minds.

Quentin J. Schultze, Ph.D., is professor of communication and the Arthur H. DeKruyter Chair at Calvin College. He has written many articles and books on communication, culture, and technology. He is a recipient of the Presidential Award for Exemplary Teaching at Calvin College. He mentors former students across North America.

ACKNOWLEDGMENTS

Colleagues who have collaborated with me and the students who inspired me when I taught in Michigan, Missouri, New York, Massachusetts, and California, especially those from the Bishop's School.

Colleagues from the California Association of Teachers of English, the Greater San Diego Council of Teachers of English, the San Diego Area Writing Project, and the Michigan Council of Teachers of English.

Quin, for faith in this project.

Reviewers: Alison Bodenstab, Alison Fastov, Hal Foster, Robert Infantino, and Shayna Swafford.

Contributions to annotated book lists by Bethany J. Kim.

Poems "Strawberries" and "The Pond" used by permission of the poet, Nancy Genevieve.

Poetry T.I.M.E. cartoons used by permission of the artist, Linda Hargrove.

Student writing used by permission of students named.

INTRODUCTION

If a child can't learn the way we teach, maybe we should teach the way they learn.

—Ignacio "Nacho" Estrada[1]

Few careers in education are more exciting and rewarding than teaching middle school English language arts. Sure, some of your friends shake their heads and maybe even feel sorry for you when they hear about your work with adolescents. Unless they have worked with this age group, however, they won't understand your enthusiasm. You and I get to spend our days helping young adults develop the reading, writing, speaking, listening, and study skills they will need for success. Our work is challenging but also a lot of fun; we get to share our love of language and literature, speaking and writing—and to cultivate such love in our students. We not only must know, understand, and love the language arts content, but we must also know, understand, and love our learners in all of their remarkable diversity.

TEACHING AND WRITING ABOUT TEACHING

When a candidate for National Board Certification for Early Adolescent/English Language Arts, I reflected seriously about what, why, and how I teach. When others heard talk about that experience, they enthusiastically requested more explanation. From those conversations and from feedback to workshops presented at local, state, and national conferences and conventions, it became clear that I have valuable experience to share with my colleagues. So began the writing, putting into words some of my rationales, ideas, lessons.

In other settings, during receptions for new teachers held as part of the annual convention of the California Association of Teachers of English, I recognized how thirsty novice teachers are to learn about the solid, structured lessons that successful experienced teachers use. Concern that those starting out in the profession without the benefit of local mentors, that many states offer emergency credentialing to college degrees to satisfy the rising demand for new teachers especially in growing ethnic communities, and because most states can ill afford special courses for such new teachers, I felt compelled to record and share my experience. Many such novice teachers begin enthusiastically but soon face tough standards and accountability; while eager to do a good job, they are not sure how to serve their early adolescent students well in an increasingly multicultural, assessment-driven, twenty-first-century technology environment.

GROWING PROFESSIONALLY

None of us can become an effective middle school teacher on our own. We need active mentors. We need professional colleagues and wise administrators. We all must continue to grow professionally throughout our years of service. Why? Pedagogies change. So do students. Of course, so do standards of and standards for assessment. When it comes to middle school, the technological environments that our students live in are shifting continuously. It is critical that we constantly learn from one another how to tap into these cultural and technological dynamics. We have to admit that the differences in our ages, even generations, are factors in making such adaptations successfully. As Quentin J. Schultze says in the preface, we teach at the constantly changing intersection of old and new.

I have benefited for decades from formal study, involvement in professional organizations, conferences, and workshops, reading journal articles, advice from generous colleagues, and years of experience on which to ground my lesson planning. Consequently, the lessons in the book are informed by the philosophies and theories from a variety of sources as well as my four decades of experience as an English language arts teacher. Publications by the National Middle School Association and the National Research Council have proven invaluable. Chris Stevenson asserts that middle school curricula must be challenging, integrated, and exploratory.[2] His perspective goes along with Howard Gardner, who "proposed the existence of seven relatively autonomous intelligences: linguistic, logical, musical, spatial, bodily kinesthetic, interpersonal, and intrapersonal."[3] Both views are reflected in lessons described in this book.

SERVING STUDENTS ARTFULLY

These and many other currents in educational research have shaped my daily pedagogy. The writings of Louise Rosenblatt and Fran Claggett inspired me to incorporate assignments to accommodate many of Gardner's multiple intelligences. Rosenblatt encourages educators to allow students to respond to the reading in their own ways—that students should rely on their prior knowledge to help them make sense of the literature.[4]

This approach to reading and interpretation of literature frees us from the burden of focusing with students only on what the book means. It gives us permission to let the literature speak to the students, and it helps us to trust the students' own responses about what it says to them in their own cultural contexts and developmental stages. Nevertheless, the "literature" does have to be taught, so you need to plan lessons that require students to ground their responses in the texts to show their grasp of the knowledge, understanding of the concepts, and acquisition of the skills. Otherwise they can stray too far afield during class discussions or while writing about the literature.

Here are theory-based lessons to help you plan units for the range of students you teach. Specific assignments for the course of a school year take into account the myriad ways that adolescents can be taught and assessed based on their specific age and maturation as well as their individual learning styles. I readily admit that such a variety of lessons are developed this way to maintain interest myself because I thoroughly enjoy learning from my students. You too can find that each time you offer to your students the option to demonstrate their understanding of literature and life you gain greater insight into the literary works you are studying together. You also form a deeper understanding of the students and their ways of looking at text and at the world around them.

Artistic diversity goes beyond linguistic modes of reading, writing, and speaking. You can discover in this book that such diversity can help a wider range of students to shine before their peers, building self-esteem among some of those who need it most. Yet, at the same time, such variety saves you time. Generally speaking, written assignments take more time to grade even when they may not be as conducive to assessing particular types of learning.

LOOKING FOR THE CURRICULUM?

Unless you have taken a college course in or are a devotee of young adult literature, chances are you are not familiar with much of the literature that you are being asked to teach. You may discover that the literature in your own middle school curriculum is very different from that which you read as a student. My advice? Do not worry about your lack of background in the literature. While it is important for you to read all the literature in the curriculum, it is not crucial for you to know all of the academic literature in the texts you are using. Most middle school curricula require students to learn about different literature, how to read it, how to recognize its structure, and how to talk and write about it intelligently. The schools often are less concerned about the specific titles used in a class as they are about students' ability to read and understand any kind of writing—fiction and nonfiction, in print or online. Therefore, it is important to develop a range of strategies for teaching any kind of literature so that you can adapt to the reading lists in schools or districts that employ you.

DECIDING ALTERNATIVE WAYS TO TEACH AND ASSESS

Reading is not the same as comprehension. Once the students have read the assigned stories, plays, articles, essays, and poems, you have to determine how well the students understand them. Fran Claggett, a pioneer in the use of graphics in teaching literature, recommends that teachers employ art—either via graphics to help plot out the structure before or after the students read, or assignments for which students may use art to show what they know.[5] Today the word *graphics* seems anachronistic. So do the terms *visuals* and *media*, let alone *audiovisual*. In this, the twenty-first century, students are more versed in digital, computerized media. Yet the basics of literature as art and story have not changed. There still is skillful use of language and imaginative use of arrangement. Therefore, lessons in this book incorporate old and new media to show students a work's traditional devices, such as structure and plot lines, images, and symbols. With proper guidance students can use their artistic interests and digital talents to demonstrate their comprehension of specific works of even the most traditional literature.

What I also like personally about using art is the fact that I am not an artist, so my students get to see me at my mediocre best. They seem more inclined to risk being vulnerable when they see me somewhat un-artfully expressing what literature means to me. Students see they can produce something better because drawing definitely is not one of my strengths; they often are more adroit at working with PowerPoint design and the newer digital media from podcasts to video.

In other words, seek to reduce your students' insecurities and strive to design lessons that build their confidence and develop their strengths. Let students use music or dance to express the mood of a literary work or characters in those works. Invite your students to act out scenes, partly to assist kinesthetic learners and partly to give all your energetic adolescents an opportunity to get out of their seats and move around. When auditory and visual learners see the work of their peers, they too are learning at a deeper level.

All of this is to say that language arts learning is more than demonstrating competence in traditional linguistic modes of reading, writing, and speaking. Notice as you read that the assignments in this book give more students an opportunity to shine individually before their peers, by employing the range of their own multimedia abilities to specific language arts learning. Several of the assignments are designed to provide a variety of assessment opportunities that are not nearly as time-consuming to grade as a written assignment, yet are equally revealing and authentic.

TEACHING PRESERVICE TEACHERS AND GRADUATE SCHOOL STUDENTS

When I moved from California to Michigan and became an adjunct education professor at a state university, I noticed that preservice students eagerly latched on to the study of literacy assessment. They impatiently leaned forward to hear about instructional practices useful in guiding developmentally appropriate learning. These students recognized through their internship assignments in classrooms of local schools that being able to provide instruction is only half the responsibility of teachers. The other half is choosing or developing assessment tools that demonstrate what students are learning and then designing subsequent lessons based on the data revealed in these assessments.

After working the year in the classroom, graduate students found it beneficial to spend their summer examining research and theories, differentiated instruction, and assessment practices appropriate for the literacy needs of their students and crafting curricula to meet these needs. When it comes to assessing for twenty-first-century literacies, however, none of us can be well versed in the research, because it is still being done, but we do our best based on what it is we are trying to measure and what our measurements tell us about our students. Some of the lessons that follow can stretch you, maybe even pull you further along than you thought possible into the world of teaching with technology. That is fine. We teachers have to be students ourselves, learning by doing and assessing.

UNDERSTANDING WHAT IS APPROPRIATE FOR MIDDLE SCHOOL

Perhaps the notion that most influences effective instruction for middle school students is that they tend to work well in groups, yet you must design such group lessons to maximize individual student learning. In the early weeks of the semester, you recognize the importance of using more teacher-directed instruction, demonstrating manners, modeling lessons, and giving students opportunities to develop a set of behaviors for successful group activities throughout the year.

For this reason, a rule of thumb is student choice, teacher control. This may be another way of applying Lev Vygotsky's notion of the zone of proximal development or what Pearson and Gallagher call the "gradual release of responsibility."[6] You are responsible not only for planning lessons that provide opportunities for students to learn in different ways from different sources, but also for designing lessons that deliberately lead to meeting the standards set forth by your specific school, district, and state in ways that students become increasingly independent learners.

Bethany J. Kim, an early career teacher who contributed to the list of supplemental book titles found in the chapters on literature, says that one of her greatest challenges as a new middle school teacher is appropriately and effectively assessing her teaching and then maintaining the right classroom atmosphere. In a sixth-grade charter school that focused on building character as well as strong academics, Bethany found it difficult to set the right tone at the beginning of the year. Student choice began to swamp teacher control. When it came time for formal assessment, she realized that it would have been better to phase in the student choice more gradually during the first semester. She loved the students and the students loved learning from her, but she had not tied the pedagogy to assessment as well as she would have liked. That need not be a problem for you.

KNOWING WHAT YOUNG ADOLESCENTS ENJOY

Young adolescents enjoy talking and often learn well from each other. As *Turning Points 2000: Educating Adolescents in the 21st Century* puts it, "Cooperative learning . . . can be a successful technique both to teach content and to raise self-esteem among all students particularly those whose native language is not English."[7] Adolescents are very sensitive to perception of their peers. "A Safe and Healthy School Environment"[8] requires cooperative learning and project-based learning in order to enhance relationships among different social and ethnic groups. This is why it is good to structure frequent lessons that give the students permission to do what they love to do: to talk to one another. The key words here are structure and talk.

Once the students begin working together, simply circulate among the groups, listening in, giving assistance as needed, and you begin to discover in an informal but intentional way what ideas they have grasped, what areas need further instruction, and whether or not the students are ready for more formal assessment to demonstrate individual readiness to move on to the next level of instruction. Tryon Edwards writes that to "thoroughly to teach another is the best way to learn for yourself."[9] As often as appropriate, include assessments where pairs and small groups of students can use the new technologies, even if they are more familiar to your students than to you. By teaching each other how to "do" language arts via newer as well as older media, students teach themselves and often the teacher as well.

While students prepare together for group or student-led discussion, they are also reviewing the lessons in more depth than they might have if they were working solely on their own. Students are then able to participate in the necessary preconditions for quality: content, collaboration, and choice. When the researchers finally determine the educational value of "new" media, they might conclude that along with all of the other benefits for twenty-first-century literacies there is an age-old truth: collaborating on projects can produce mutual learning.

APPLYING NATIONAL WRITING PROJECT CONCEPTS

After becoming a writing fellow of the San Diego Area Writing Project, I began incorporating the National Writing Project's strategies into my lessons. In particular, I followed the project's sequence of fluency, form, and correctness and soon noticed that both my students and I were more enthusiastic about learning. Sequencing lessons this way gives students the time to write frequently, to conduct peer editing, to revise, to edit, and to publish in a variety of ways for a variety of audiences. The lessons in this book are similarly flexible. Here are suggested assignments for different purposes, such as to explore, to explain, to expand, and even to entertain.

The lessons described in this book also show ways to reduce the time-consuming burden of grading each piece of writing for correctness. Following the recommendations in the lessons, you begin to recognize how beneficial it is to read some students' writing or view their media projects just to discover whether your young students comprehend a particular text or just what they think about a particular topic. As a result, you can enjoy the freedom to read or view some assignments only for the ideas presented.

These kinds of writings and media productions become no-stress assessments. As you determine what students think, know, understand, and are able to do you begin to adjust your instruction based on what you have observed and read. When the students realize that every word they write or image they project is not to be evaluated for correctness, your otherwise self-conscious young teens become more fluent. They are willing to write more often; and they also appreciate that you give them some choice about what writing, print or electronic media, they wish to submit to peer editing, evaluation, and publishing.

BALANCING STRUCTURE WITH CHOICES

While offering students lots of choice in their reading, writing, and responding is important, the key to becoming an effective teacher is to establish structures and routines on which the students can depend. These structures and routines foster important habits: using time efficiently; maintaining useful notebooks for test and exam preparation; reading and writing efficiently; and participating cooperatively in small-group or full-class discussions, using technology with a critical eye and creative bent. The good habits help students learn the basics of language and forms of literature, including essays, novels, poetry, and drama. When students know the daily class requirements and routines, they have something against which to rebel without rejecting it completely. As Anne King declared in a presentation titled "You Are Not Going Crazy, This Really Is Normal Behavior," once adolescents know the boundaries, they frequently challenge them, but they usually comply.[10]

Experience has shown that even though middle school students love to try the system and to test the rules—just to see how teachers respond—they also appreciate the predictability. For some of the students, a dependable pattern gives them a sense of control and power. They know what to expect and how to perform in the midst of their own physical and emotional changes.

For these reasons, the lessons for the first semester are designed like benevolent training sessions in an athletic program, providing opportunities for participants to learn the rules of the games and to develop the knowledge and skills to be successful. The effective, experienced teachers you observe only seem to handle this training period effortlessly; such veterans know how to offer student choices within a fair, but firm, classroom structure.

REMOVING THE SCAFFOLDS

As the school year progresses, you can step aside and become more of a coach than an instructor. If all has gone well, students already know the kinds of reading, writing, media, speaking, and listening skills that they must learn. You can then increase the number of choices to practice these skills more independently and to demonstrate their growing knowledge and skills even more creatively. As you move on in the semester, the students soon learn how to act and what to do because they develop the habits of mind as well as the confidence and competence to handle the tasks set before them. Happily, they begin to enjoy the learning; when adolescents feel secure, they are able to function more effectively, bringing joy to all involved.

While I tend toward student choice over teacher control, my goals are always student-centered. What is it that the students want and need to know and do by the end of the school year? What kind of nurturing environment must be developed and experiences offered to assure that students reach these goals? For a young adolescent and for a novice teacher, this may mean a little more visible structure than would be evident in the classroom of a veteran teacher. So, while I recognize that many approaches to teaching can be effective, the ideas I share are those that have worked well for me and the new-to-middle teachers I have mentored.

In this book, then, are comments both about my experience teaching young adolescents and descriptions of specific lessons you can use throughout a full school year. These lessons are structured to get to know the students and introduce the course's main concepts. You can see that the assignments permit the students to demonstrate their understanding of literature through writing, speech, music, and art in print and electronic forms. You can find interdisciplinary lessons that encourage students to use knowledge they are learning in social studies, science, music, and art. Some lessons are designed to increase student's understanding and ease with library and online research while meeting the language arts standards you are required to address. You can see inserts recommending twenty-first-century applications and showing samples of students' responses to lessons described.

ACKNOWLEDGING PHYSICAL AND EMOTIONAL CHALLENGES

The primary challenge in teaching middle school is that physical, emotional, and social issues often overwhelm and distract students. Both your male and female students can be manically mischievous one day and dismally depressed the next.

Be prepared by designing lessons to keep them excited about learning to use the receptive and expressive language arts that can help them succeed personally and academically. You could view yourself as a ship's captain whose charge is to chart a course that provides safe passage through the tumultuous preteen and early teen years. As the captain, you recognize the need for balancing structure and choice. As the year goes by you develop a clearer vision of where you are going and how you may get there. You learn what students need to know and be able to do. You also discover that they prefer to contribute to the journey. You may even begin to envision the curriculum as the ship, the units as the decks, and the lessons as the rooms. Within the ship, upon the decks, and inside the rooms, there are choices the students can make.

As you become more acquainted with your shipmates, you find yourself adapting and adopting strategies that best keep them and you engaged, moving progressively from port to port. Eventually more and more of your students complete the journey ready to step on the firmer, more solid ground of the high school territory with self-assurance and proficiency, prepared for whatever challenges await them.

ADAPTING THE LESSONS AND IDEAS IN THIS BOOK

An equally significant teaching challenge in middle school is the fact that the literary works in the curriculum vary greatly from school to school. Few teachers arrive in their middle school classrooms having studied all of the literary works they are expected to teach. So rather than being a manual for teaching only specific texts, this book provides general background for teaching each of the primary genres taught in middle school. It is likely that your reading lists differ from those addressed explicitly in this book, but you can adapt the approaches in this book to the literature and skills you are asked to teach. The lessons in this book are designed to

- Be inviting and vigorous
- Help students connect their own lives to the literature
- Challenge students to think deeply, critically, and broadly
- Help the students write clearly, correctly, and creatively
- Encourage students to work independently, in pairs, small groups, and as a whole class
- To expand their understanding of themselves and their world
- Develop ways for students to express themselves in a variety of modes by reading, writing, and discussing a variety of genres of literature and issues in life
- Use digital technologies effectively for research, writing, and communication.

In order to accomplish these goals, look here for ideas to help with introductions to the elements of fiction, literary terms, and poetic devices; ideas for teaching specific literary genres; and assignments for writing, learning vocabulary, using appropriate grammar, giving public speeches, critically viewing and using electronic and print media. Provided are sample lessons, student study aids, rubrics, and lists of resources, along with practical ideas for engaging students with digital media.

For the veteran educators looking to revive or revise their instruction or the novice looking to rev up for the first year of teaching, here are proven ways to manage grading and assessments, and strategies for students to reflect and assess their own work. Throughout the book, note connections to the language arts standards of the National Council of Teachers of English and International Reading Association, which reflect curriculum standards in most states. Although specific standards change occasionally, they still address the basic goal of applying traditional literacies to new literacy contexts. According to the National Council of Teachers of English,[11] twenty-first-century readers and writers need to

- Develop proficiency with the tools of technology
- Build relationships with others to pose and solve problems collaboratively and cross-culturally
- Design and share information for global communities to meet a variety of purposes
- Manage, analyze, and synthesize multiple streams of simultaneous information
- Create, critique, analyze, and evaluate multimedia texts
- Attend to the ethical responsibilities required by these complex environments

CONNECTING TO TWENTY-FIRST-CENTURY LITERACIES

For these reasons, several chapters have highlighted boxes with suggestions for using tools of technology to help your students to develop the knowledge, skills, and understanding of these twenty-first-century literacies. To incorporate opportunities for your students to learn and hone their skills, choose from these options:

- Blog It—invite students to create or participate in journaling on a website

- Picture It—take photos and project on document cameras or add to a PowerPoint presentation
- Play It—add sound to an electronic file or just play a tape or CD
- Podcast It—use computer software to record and play interviews and student creations
- Record It—record on tape recorder or using computer software
- Search It—look for information on the Internet
- Send It—send an e-mail or post student work on a website or list-serv
- Shoot It—use the digital camera
- Wiki It—create online communities for students to post and edit their own and others work
- Wordle It—use computer software to make word clouds or collages

These simple ideas give you jumping off points to create assignments that interest you and your students. On the companion website for this book are other ideas. See teachingenglishlanguagearts.com.

Some of the chapters include examples of student written responses to assignments and comments on what those writings reveal about student learning. They may help expand your insight and prepare you for what to expect as you accept the challenge and come to value the privilege of teaching English language arts to young teenagers.

REACHING THE ULTIMATE GOAL—
ENJOY TEACHING

To support you in your early years and sustain you along the road, to enable you to remain an engaged, enthusiastic, and effective teacher of English language arts in the middle school, here are ideas to develop and present lessons that meet students' emotional and intellectual needs while challenging them to complete increasingly complex tasks. When students are learning and you can document that learning through appropriate assessments, both you and your students enjoy more of your times together. It is my goal with this book to offer you practical and proven practices that bring you the kind of pleasure in teaching that I have experienced these past thirty-plus years.

1

NETWORKING SOCIALLY AT THE START OF A SCHOOL YEAR

Getting to know you, getting to know all about you.
Getting to like you, getting to hope you like me.

—Oscar Hammerstein[1]

Even in the age of electronic social networking, in-person relationships are the most meaningful for teachers and learners. The classroom itself is a "site" for social networking among increasingly diverse students and teachers. Twenty-first-century learning is still grounded in social connections. The best way to nurture such connections is to design low-tech interactions.

The following opening of the school year projects show how to get your eclectic, energetic young teens working together so you can assess how well they are reading, writing, speaking, and listening already. Equally, the daily activities help your students get to know one another and you, both online and in the classroom. The five-day collage making activity is based on group and personal responses to a shared reading and works well with an older, more stable class. The one- or two-day scavenger hunt using the course anthology is more fitting for shorter class periods during the first week and works well with a younger, less-experienced group of students that includes those who are new to the school or who may be using a literature anthology for the first time.

RESPONDING TO A SHARED READING: SMALL-GROUP COLLAGE ON BOOK OR STORY

If your students have read a specified book over the summer, you are in luck. You can use a few opening days of the semester to have students work in small groups to make collages that reflect various perspectives on the summer reading. You can even organize groups around the elements of fiction: character, setting, conflict, plot, theme, and literary devices.

If your students have not already read a common book, assign them to read a short story, silently or aloud together in class. You might even ask for volunteers so you can begin to identify some of the eager or hesitant readers. Another option is to assign them to read a short story for homework. Gary Soto's "Seventh Grade" is a great choice.

In either case, think of the first week of language arts classes as the staging ground for the semester. As you get to know individual students, you can map out personalized approaches to general student activities.

A collage is a design created from lots of words and pictures. When assembled on the poster board, the collage has a message about the book or story. Each group is responsible for finding pictures and cutting out words and letters to create a collage focusing on one of the following: main characters, setting, plot, conflicts, themes, others.

The idea here is to get students involved in an activity that enables them to get to know one another and enables you to get to know each one.[2] Assemble the following:

poster board
scissors
glue sticks
magazines
colored markers
envelopes
index cards
a timer (kitchen timers work well)

blank sheets of address labels (e.g., Avery 5160)
a clipboard

These lessons are designed for a fifty-minute class period but you can adapt them as needed to fit your schedule. See Teacher Resource A for a sample collage assignment based on *The Circuit* by Francisco Jimenez, a novel assigned for summer reading.

Day One: Groups Conceive Their Collages

Students need instructions, especially on the first few days of class! They want to know what is expected. Therefore, project on a screen or post instructions somewhere in the classroom where everybody can refer to them—or print out a copy for each student if it does not overly clutter their desks or work surface. Inform students that while they are working together you may be roaming around the room, listening in, enjoying their observations. Inform them that there are no right or wrong answers. Consider giving each group a name based on a literary term—or let them select their own names from a list. Be open and helpful. Define the literary terms as needed. Answer students' questions about the assignment.

Finally, distribute name tags—or tags for them to write their own names with the markers, perhaps color-coded for each group or literary term. Set the kitchen timer to ring ten minutes before the class period ends so you have time to collect supplies, clear up the room, and reflect on what they have been doing and give the assignment for the next class meeting.

Once they begin working, it is time for you to begin observing and listening. The clipboard and mailing labels are for you to jot down notes about specific students. If possible, write on each label words that particular students say during group activities. Listen for their pithy comments, not lengthy quotations. Jot down particular words, phrases, or short sentences that can help you to structure future lessons. Note whether students understand and use literary terms or synonyms that make sense. Indicate positive/negative language toward group members. For example, "You've got that right, Lindsay." "You dummy! Don't you know what conflict means in a story!"

Box 1.1.   Project It! Making Time for Time

Language arts is all about culture and communication. Since every culture has its own sense of time, using a timer in class is an opportunity to address how meaningful time varies from place to place. Project on the screen, while the students work, an image of one of the websites around the world that counts local time on a digital clock, preferably a twenty-four-hour clock situated on a website in a language other than English. Note the time you begin and the time you end the session.

Also, make short notes about specific students. Who is talkative? Who is articulate? Pensive? Easily distracted? Who is having the most fun? Who likes asking tough questions? How are the various groups and members "doing" in their groups: forming, storming, norming, or by the end of the allotted time, performing?[3] Who is involved in these group-related activities? Be sure to avoid looking like a mere disciplinarian. Smile.

The kitchen timer is visual as well as aural. It can help to get you and the students into the rhythm of time-crunched class sessions. Students, right at the beginning of the school year, need to start thinking about completing projects on deadline. So do you. And the classroom needs to be cleaned up on time, especially if a colleague has to teach in the room shortly after your class is over. The timer also signals time for cleanup. Tell your students that when a timer goes off at the end of class you need their help in straightening out the room so that they can mess it up the next day. They smile. (See box 1.1.)

At the end of the class session, ask the students to bring in pictures from magazines or printed out from websites that can be used to represent people, places, events, conflict, and literary devices in their particular piece of literature. Be sure that you have your own supply of images on hand for those unable to bring pictures or magazines to the next class meeting.

Day Two: Groups Compose Their Collages

Briefly repeat instructions for the assignment, tell students how long they have to create a layout for their collages, and set a timer to signal the last ten minutes for cleanup. Since some of the collages are not likely to be finished, provide envelopes for groups to store their unused pictures.

Invariably, during this second class meeting, some groups wish they had the images that other groups are using or discarding. So if day one was not overly chaotic, you encourage covetous groups to swap a few pictures. Still, be careful that cross-group racket does not replace intragroup collaboration. You can always institute a couple of one-minute swap sessions to limit as well as encourage picture trading—call it "Picture Jeopardy." If possible, download the TV show theme song from the Internet and play it while students make their changes. Once the music stops, swapping ends, and groups return to work with the pictures they have on hand.

Next, begin testing the validity of your observations about students from the previous day. See if the behavior you observed the first day continues, changes, improves, or devolves. Also start looking for additional information about your crew. Who comes prepared? Who acts like the "artistic coordinator"? Which students seem to be more concrete or philosophical in group discussions? Which classmates invite in group members who may have been on the periphery of the discussions? Do any students seem overwhelmed, suggesting that you might need to provide additional encouragement and support as they board the ship for another school year? Remember to jot down brief comments made by particular students, such as "Can't you do anything right?" "I like that picture."

Day Three: Groups Complete Their Collages

By now, students are wondering what they have gotten themselves into—through no choice of their own! They might be wondering if this class is going to be a lot of fun as well as a lot of work. It is time for them and you to face the reality of school deadlines, including those for collaborative work. Students do have to demonstrate what they have learned. So, keep smiling but also start acting like the benevolent taskmaster you really are.

First, refresh their memories about the assignment. Tell them that the collages have to be completed that day. Finally, joyfully deliver the news that during the next class meeting, the groups are to give oral presentations based on their collages—and that each student is expected to contribute. Even your overachieving groups with already-completed collages now have plenty to do. A few of your students might be thinking uncomplimentary thoughts about school and especially about you. As Huckleberry Finn put it, "All I say is, [teachers] is [teachers], and you got to make allowances. Take them all around; they're a mighty ornery lot. It's the way they're raised."[4]

Hand each student a 3 × 5 index card. Inform the class that each group should jot down a couple of comments answering questions about its collage, such as "What does a particular image or group of pictures signify to you with respect to the story?" and "What does the collage reflect about different parts of the reading?" Again, emphasize that there are no right or wrong answers. These presentations are not graded. Stress the fact that you are looking for creative responses to the reading. After all, this is language arts.

Undoubtedly a few students become preoccupied with the stressful fact that they have to make an oral presentation already on the fourth day of class, when they are still anxious about their relationships with their classmates and teacher. Some students are relieved to know that they get to present in groups. Remind them that they can refer in their presentations to the ideas that they have already jotted down on their index cards. Even just a few key words or phrases should help each student follow through with her or his part of the presentation.

Day Four: Students Individually Convey Their Group Thoughts

Provide ten or fifteen minutes at the beginning of the period for groups to meet briefly to determine their intragroup speaking order and to recall what each member is going to say on behalf of the group. Ask a member of each group to write the speaking order on the class board so that each group can see when it is going to present to the rest of the class.

To aid in smooth transitions between presentations, ask students to arrange the poster boards on the chalk or marker tray in the order of the presentations, but with posters facing away from the audience. When group members rise to share their collage, one of them can turn their board to face the audience. When the group finishes, the board turner should place their board behind all the others.

If the room has space, invite the class members to sit on the floor close to the collages so students can see more of the details on the collage. In most cases, individual pictures are too small for most to see clearly if they all remain in their seats. For now, smaller than optimal collage details are acceptable since the purpose of making these posters is primarily to provide opportunities for students to work together and for you to get to know more about them, rather than to require polished speeches with equally professional looking visuals.

After the presentations are made, you can also display the poster boards for a few weeks giving group members more opportunities to examine other groups' posters up close. If the resources are available and the classroom is equipped, digitally photograph each collage and project the resulting images on a screen on day five or to show other classes who have a similar assignment. The digital photos also could be posted on your class website for families to view at home.

Day Five: Students Individually Compose Their Reflections

At the beginning of class, with the group posters in sight or projected onto the screen, ask the students to prepare to write a short reflection piece about their experience in class during the first four days. While you take attendance and review your label notes about students— associating your notes with their faces—they can be writing their first journal entries for the course. They get to metacognate (think about) their responses to the collage-creating experience. Here are sample prompts.

- What did you have to consider about your story before creating a collage?
- How did you decide which picture worked better than others for your collage?
- Why did your group organize pictures and words a particular way?
- What would you have done differently if you were working alone?
- Why do you think this is a useful activity to start the year?

Box 1.2.   Project It! Using Word Clouds

Numerous websites create a word cloud or word collage based on words entered by a user. Ask each group to enter ten to fifteen words that describe the images in its picture collage. Then project the resulting word collages and compare each image collage for the respective groups. Which collages are more meaningful to each group? Why? Students soon see that the result is more than words and that interesting and revealing results occur when students create together.[5]

- What did you learn about yourself as you worked on this collage?
- What did you discover about your reading skills while working on this collage?

Ask students to write neatly while assuring them that their personal reflections are not to be graded like exams or evaluated as though they were formal papers. Then collect and simply read the journals, thinking about what you learned as you observed them working together and as you read what they have written about the experience. These students' journal entries are now baseline writing samples—not for grading, but for future comparisons along with additional samples forthcoming in students' own journals. (Also see box 1.2.)

SCAVENGER HUNTING IN THE COURSE ANTHOLOGY

Most middle school students are oblivious to the vast resources available in language arts anthologies. Some students are unaware that an anthology is a treasured collection of words—literary passages and art work—similar in language to the idea of a collection of flowers.

As you explain the concept of anthology to your students, ask them to mentally store an anthology image in their minds by picturing a bouquet of a variety of beautiful, fragrant flowers. If you have access to fresh-cut flowers, bring in a vase full of different varieties and colors and label the vase "anthology." Meanwhile, ask students to prepare for a scavenger hunt inside their anthology. They will likely look at you askance. That is simply curiosity and is just what you want to create.

Of course, it is best to avoid pressing students into feedback about the various social, ethnic, and national groups represented in the book. No anthology is completely diverse or thoroughly unbiased. Focus on the resources available in your anthology rather than on its deficits.

Planning the Hunt for Pairs of Students

Some publishers may include a scavenger hunt handout with their textbook resources. If yours does not, you can easily prepare fifteen to twenty questions with clues to help students know where to find various elements—using the helpful journalistic method of asking the five W's and an H (who, what, when, where, why, and how). You may be surprised at how much you learn yourself, if this is your first time using this particular textbook. Here are helpful categories:

General Content
- Who is the author or publisher (explain the difference)?
- What does the title mean or suggest about the contents?
- When was it published—and when were various pieces written?
- Where is the table of contents? How is it organized?
- Where is the index? How is it organized—and why?

Graphics and Graphic Design
- What is on the cover? Does it make the book seem interesting? Inviting?
- Is there an introduction? If so, what is in it? Are the introductory pages numbered in Roman or Arabic numbers (iii or 3)?
- What kinds of design elements are included (lines, colors, text boxes, drawings, photos)? Is the artwork acknowledged? Ask students to find the name of the artist of a particularly interesting piece of artwork. (This information may be found in a separate

index or is simply identified in a special font within the complete
index to the anthology.)

Organization
- How is the table of contents organized? By genre (category of artistic composition, similar to types of flowers, like roses), theme, time, nation, or country? Chronologically? Other?
- Use the table of contents to find . . . an author who has a name beginning with the same letter as your [student's] name. Is the work a short story, a poem, or a play?
- Use the index to find a short story title that includes words beginning with letters of your first name and your partner's last name.
- How is each literary work introduced? (Devise a question that sends the students to this reader aid.) Some anthologies include background information on the author, historical period, genre, or literary device featured in the particular story, poem, essay, or play.
- Where in the book is information about authors of individual works or the editors of the anthology? (Send the students to a particular page to learn something unique about an author whose work you may teach later in the school year.)
- Does the anthology have questions following the text of each literary work, after several related pieces, or at the end of a unit? (Send students to one such page and ask them to list the kind of questions found there—such as facts or interpretative responses, maybe even connecting the literature to their own lives.) Some anthologies include vocabulary and grammar links to useful websites.

Supplementary Resources
- If there is a glossary of literary terms, ask students to locate and read the definition of a term that may be new to them but that you plan to teach them during the year—for example, onomatopoeia, pantoum, or limerick. Middle schools students like the unusual sounds of these words.
- Does the anthology define vocabulary? If so, ask students to find the definition of an interesting new word—maybe in a story they may soon read.

- Or is vocabulary defined in footnotes or side notes? If so, devise a question that requires students to use this resource.
- Does the anthology include grammar or writing resources—why or why not? (Question: Why would the publisher put such resources in a book about literature instead of in a book about writing?)
- Are there lists of suggested readings? Website links? Other resource references?

Time to go hunting. The student pairs now can complete the hunt by exploring the book for answers to the questions and then listing three to four literary works they hope the class is to study during the year. Circulate, listen, and learn. As you hear them talking about what they notice in the book and hear the stories they mention, you begin to sense what interests them. (See box 1.3.) When possible, modify your lessons to include works that seem to draw their attention. Each pair of students also could come up with a couple of challenging scavenger questions to stump the panel of other classmates once the preliminary worksheet is completed.

If students take their textbooks home, assign the last question as homework. This gives individual students a reason to review the book on their own and possibly introduce the book to parents or guardians. You might even ask the students to show their book to other family members and ask them which pieces of literature they have read or would like to read.

Box 1.3. Survey It!

If you have an online blog or school website with a "polling" feature, create a list of the readings and ask students to vote for their top choice to read first. When you present the results to class, ask students what seemed appealing to them about the top choices. Was it the title? Familiarity with the author? Length of the piece? Peer influence? Then explain that anthology entries are not popularity contests as much as hard, imperfect decisions that publishers and educators make about the educational as well as artistic value of a work.

CONCLUSION

Finally, end first week of class meetings by reviewing with your fellow crew members some of your personal objectives for the school year that may include helping them to

- Increase their appreciation, understanding, and enjoyment of reading
- Improve their understanding and use of the writing process
- Become more at ease when speaking in front of a group
- Increase their knowledge and use of sophisticated vocabulary
- Review and extend their knowledge of correct grammar
- Discover more ways that twenty-first-century technologies can help them learn

Keep in mind that the first week of class needs to be both task-oriented and relational. While introducing students to the work, be sure to help them get introduced to each other and to you.

Middle school students are some of the most creative people on the planet. Half of your job as teacher is to keep from squelching their bubbling personalities and literary imaginations. They love using language to express themselves. They especially enjoy telling stories. They probably have been telling their families stories about you and your class. Now you get to tell them about how stories work. That is the focus of the next few chapters.

(2)

UNPACKING THE STORY AND UNDERSTANDING THE GENRE

The best of my English teachers taught us literature because they wanted the art of it to expand our minds and help teach us new ways of seeing the world. I was taught to both see a work of literature as a way to understand the time it was written, and the people who produced it, and to find the parts of that work that spoke to me in my time and place.

—Sybylla Yeoman Hendrix[1]

This chapter explains how to introduce students to the basic elements of fiction by reading stories, analyzing plot structures and characterization, and eventually coaching them to compose their own short story to submit to a school journal or to publish online. Notice that the approaches work well for lessons teaching short stories, novels, poetry, and plays. But, equally, know that as students learn the language of literature and come to appreciate how the elements work to construct stories, your young teens also come to see themselves and the world in new ways. Your challenge is to teach the language of literature without diluting that appreciation.

INTRODUCING THE ELEMENTS OF FICTION

Here is a way to get your middle school students started. They need a journal, such as a spiral notebook. This study aid could be taken home daily, but if more appropriate for your school setting, set up boxes or bins to store them on classroom shelves. Then students can pick up their journals at the beginning of each class meeting and return them at the end. To help maintain order, label the bins or boxes with the class period number and sections of the alphabet by last names.

Ask students to set up their own journal section for short stories by folding a page in half vertically, forming a half-page bookmark titled "short stories." So begins their own story in this unit—the turning of their page (not a bad metaphor!). Every new life story is a chance to begin again.

Then ask students to write on the next, clean page in their journals the current date in the upper right-hand corner, and as you introduce them, the elements of fiction on the top line. Remind the students that all writers start with blank pages even if they use computers. Few students ever think about the fact that most of what they read for your class was first written on paper, typed on a typewriter, or word-processed on a keyboard.

Next, point out to your students that writers use proven techniques to engage readers—just like musicians use notes, chords, and rhythms. Writers do not just write to quickly express themselves—like many bloggers do. Knowing the different facets of fiction helps writers write, and readers read. In fact, understanding the structure of literature can assist in all kinds of human communication, from interviewing for a job to making a movie.

Demonstrating Authors' Cursive Prose

Chances are that the personal correspondence and manuscript drafts of a few of your anthology authors are available in university archives. Also, it is likely that one or more handwritten pages from their writings have been digitally scanned and made available online. Using appropriate search terms such as "personal papers" and "manuscript," use

Google Images to search for a sample manuscript page for one of the better-known anthology contributors. Then project the page in class or print out a sample to show students that novelists, playwrights, and essayists really did write by hand. You might also ask students whether "typesetting" or personal script communicates better. Generally speaking, script is more expressive and typesetting is easier and less tiring to read.

Make It Personal

If you are comfortable doing it, start this unit on unpacking stories by telling your own story about something that happened in your life—something students find humorous, unusual, or particularly revealing about you. Be a bit transparent to engage the students. Then ask a couple of students if they like listening more to stories or lectures. Students usually admit that they like listening to stories more than lectures. Moreover, they acknowledge that they prefer lectures that use stories to illustrate points, rather than lectures that just give information. Hmmm.

Normally it is best to teach those literary terms that are covered in your student textbook. If the text does not define terms, you can use those below, or write your own. The definitions for a given term are about the same, but if you would like a refresher on some of the different definitions, use Wikipedia, which generally includes different definitions and a brief history of each of the terms.

Each of the following lessons follows the same basic order:

- Teach the literary term (an element of fiction).
- Assign for reading a story that clearly illustrates the term.
- Encourage students to pay attention to how the story reflects the elements.
- Invite students to read for fun so they do not focus so much on identifying the elements that they fail to enjoy the story.

Consider assigning students to read several stories quickly, since multiple examples can be more effective than one. Below are ways of teaching each of the major elements of fiction.

LESSON ONE: PLOT

1. Ask students to turn to the short story section of their journals. Explain first of all that stories are about characters faced with solving a problem, confronting a conflict. The first term is *plot,* the series of events that make up a story. Plot usually includes an exposition, triggering action, rising action, climax, falling action, and resolution.
2. Draw a diagram of a plot line on the board or use one prepared on a poster or for a projector. See your class anthology or an online source for sample plot line. (See figure 2.1.)

Adding Plot Line Sound Effects

Talking about a plot line is not nearly as engaging as telling the story itself. Therefore, it helps students if you make your plot line lecture into a story by adding appropriate sound effects. After all, over 50 percent of the emotional impact of a movie is the sound track. If you have software like PowerPoint, create a diagram of a plot line (see step 2) in which each step in the plot appears on the screen with appropriate

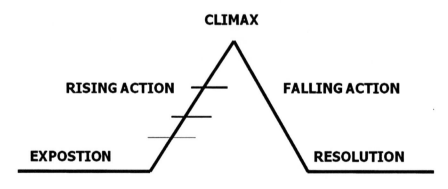

PLOT is the series of events that make up a story.

Figure 2.1.   Plot Line

sound effects. The "transition" feature in PowerPoint allows you to vary the effects and their loudness. This activity can also serve as a course project using images. Consider the sounds a roller-coaster car emits as it begins, ascends, lurches at the top, descends, and then slows at the end of the ride.

3. Fill in the parts of the plot line as you explain the purpose of each part:
   - *Exposition*: Introduces the main characters, the setting, the conflict, and the point of view. (Ex = out, position = places. Exposition = places out for the reader . . .)
   - *Triggering action*: That story point when the main character decides to do something about the problem.
   - *Rising action*: A series of events during which the main character attempts to solve the problem introduced in the exposition. Usually there are three attempts:
     - the first very simple,
     - the second more difficult, often requiring the help of another character, and
     - the third most complex, often requiring the main character to make a moral or ethical decision.

     If students are familiar with classic fairy tales, ask them to consider how often this three-part rising action occurs—"Three Little Pigs," "Goldilocks and the Three Bears," "Three Billy Goats Gruff," and so on. Ask for examples of stories with which they may be more familiar in their culture or language—perhaps from movies or TV shows.
   - *Climax*: The highest point of suspense in the story, when the reader, viewer, or listener wonders whether or not the main character has gotten into such trouble that he or she cannot get out. But, then the turning point occurs and the reader can see that the problem can be solved or (tragically) that the character has given up or been permanently overcome.
   - *Falling action*: The issues raised during the rising action begin to fall into place, the complications of the rising action seem to unravel, and the action begins to wind down. Some texts call this the denouement (day-noo-mon).

- *Resolution*: The action stops and the readers see that the main character either has solved the problem or given up (not all stories have happy endings).

Close the session with the reading assignment, asking students to identify the plot parts in the story you assign.

If you are teaching with block-scheduling you can use the additional time to start or complete a short story so students can begin identifying the plot. Reading a story aloud and asking students to raise their hands when they recognize an element is a way to focus their attention on the elements and is also a no-stress assessment for you to determine whether they "get it." But be sure to stop reading at a critical plot point, to entice the students to continue reading the story themselves just to find out what happens next.

LESSON TWO: CONFLICT

In fiction, conflict is the problem the main character(s) must resolve as a result of a struggle between opposing forces. The main character may face internal conflict, a struggle for dominance between two elements within a person, or external conflict, or conflict against an outside force—often both. See Teacher Resources on this book's companion website for sample graphic images to suggest different kinds of conflict, teachingenglishlanguagearts.com/.

Once you introduce the topic of conflict, students should be ready to work in pairs for ten minutes to identify plot elements in the story they have just read. They can work together, referring to the definitions that they wrote in their notebooks and identifying specific examples from the text. Since sharing desk space is a psychological reminder to students that they are sharing what they are learning, it is appropriate to encourage the students to collaborate by pulling their desks together and learning from one another. Circulate during discussion to learn

- What students recall about the previous day's lesson and from the story they just read

- What needs to be retaught or clarified before continuing the lesson
- Who has and has not done the homework

Next, lead a classroom discussion of student conclusions for fifteen minutes. This discussion/response format reveals to the students that there is often more than one right response to a question, especially in the study of literature. Also, it allows you to determine students' understanding of the material and readiness for formal assessment. Finally, this format is excellent practice for writing fully developed essays. Students should follow this format in their responses:

- State their opinion: "I think that the climax of 'The Three Little Pigs' is when the wolf comes down the chimney."
- Support their opinion with an example from the text: "On page three it says, 'Finally, the wolf got so hungry that he jumped down the chimney.'"
- Explain how the chosen passage illustrates the definition of the term: "This seems like the high point of the story because the reader really wonders if the pigs will be okay. Also, the action of the story starts to fall after this event."

Internal conflict occurs when a character struggles within himself or herself to decide what is the right, moral, or safe action. It is something like the cartoon of the devil and angel sitting on opposite shoulders of a character, trying to persuade the character to take certain actions. External conflict occurs when the main character struggles against forces outside of himself or herself. The students may need to be reminded that even an animal or alien protagonist demonstrates a humanlike struggle. (See figure 2.2.) Examples of external conflict are

- Person versus person—when the struggle is with another character
- Person versus nature—when the struggle is against a force of nature: weather, thirst, illness, or topography (desert, mountain, rolling rapids)
- Person versus society—when the struggle is against a group of people acting as one: a team, racial group, pack of peers, political party, social club, ethnic tribe, and so on

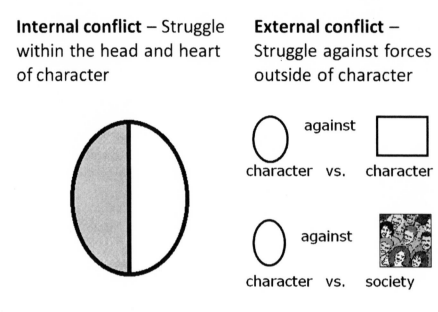

Internal conflict – Struggle within the head and heart of character

External conflict – Struggle against forces outside of character

against

character vs. character

against

character vs. society

CONFLICT IN LITERATURE - 1

Figure 2.2. Conflict I

- Person versus technology—when the struggle is against a machine, like a car, tractor, tank, or computer in science fiction
- Person versus the supernatural—when the struggle is against a ghost, an alien, the gods, or a Supreme Being (See figure 2.3.)

Ask students to identify the conflict in the story they have just completed by using P.I.E.: make the *point*, *illustrate* it with examples from the literature, and then *explain* the link between the illustration and the point. Students use "because" statements to clarify their answer, illustrate it with an example from the text, and explain why that example fits the definition of the term they have just studied.

Assign another short story to read for homework. If time permits, read aloud the opening passages. This often is enough to get students hooked so they are more likely to complete the reading on their own. Ask the students to draw a plot line that represents the relative length of time it takes for each section of the story to unfold. Some stories have long expositions and precipitous falling action and minimal resolutions.

Internal conflict – Struggle within the head and heart of character

External conflict – Struggle against forces outside of character

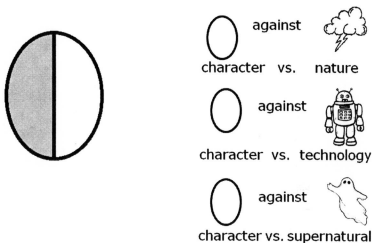

against

character   vs.   nature

against

character   vs.   technology

against

character vs. supernatural

CONFLICT IN LITERATURE - 2

Figure 2.3. Conflict 2

Let the shape of the plot line show that relationship. "The Most Dangerous Game" by Richard Connell is an excellent choice for illustrating the types of conflict and an interesting plot structure. Ask students to label the incidents in the rising action. This can be fun for them and you to see how consistent they are in identifying those events of plot.

LESSON THREE: SETTING

The setting of a story is the time and place in which the action occurs. In a short story, the setting is particularly limited—sometimes just a single day or a few hours and a single location. Here is a suggested schedule for engaging students in a review of what you have taught and an introduction to this other basic element of story structure:

1. For ten minutes, review the elements of plot and the story the students read. Ask them to work in pairs to identify the elements and the kind(s) of conflict.

2. Conduct a ten- to fifteen-minute, full-class discussion for students to share observations about the story.
3. For the remaining time, guide the students through these new definitions:
   - Setting in terms of time
     Time of day: dawn, morning, afternoon, evening, night
     Time of year: winter, spring, summer, fall
     Time of life: childhood, teen years, adult, old age
     Time in history: prehistoric, medieval, Elizabethan Age, future
   - Setting in terms of place
     Area of place: inside, outside, porch, roof, basement, or cellar
     Locale: city, country, mountains, sea, valley, forest
     Continent: Africa, Asia, Europe, North or South America
     Galactic: Earth, another planet, another galaxy
4. Finally, assign a short story to read and ask students to pay close attention to the ways that the author establishes setting. Ask them to consider how the setting makes them feel or how it creates a mood. Wait until the next period to remind them of the typical impact of daytime versus nighttime when good or bad things happen, or rural versus urban places, when the characters are relaxed versus tense.

If students are permitted to write in their textbooks, ask them to draw rectangles around words or phrases that reveal setting and then write "T" in the margin for "time" and "P" in the margin for "place." If the students are not permitted to write in their books, ask them to keep notes in their journal or use sticky notes. This active response to reading affirms for students what they are learning or what they need to ask about during the next class meeting.

LESSON FOUR: CHARACTERS—ACT I

Fictional characters (1) play roles in the story and (2) are developed to different degrees. The main character or protagonist usually solves the problem set forth in the exposition of the story. The antagonist is the opposing person (personal) or opposing force (impersonal). Authors create static or dynamic, flat and/or round characters, and reveal characters' personalities and motivations through direct and indirect means. As before, here is a schedule for the day's topic:

1. Have the students work in pairs for fifteen minutes on the homework, discussing ways the author used setting in the previous day's story.
2. Conduct a P.I.E. class discussion, encouraging the students to use the literary vocabulary and to back up their views with specific passages from their texts.
3. Introduce the topic of characters. Show or reproduce the diagrams of conflicts.
4. List the main characters on the board and use them to review the basic literary terms already introduced.

Be sure to remind students to write lecture-discussion notes in their journals to supplement the definitions. As needed, remind students to write a particular definition or other material in their journals—even hinting that a specific key concept might be on a quiz or test.

Some notes about characters:

- The *protagonist* is a human or other humanlike character who struggles to overcome conflict. A story's suspense develops as a reader gets to know more about the protagonist and the ways the protagonist responds to obstacles.
- The *antagonist* is the opposing force (external forces include another character, a group, nature, technology, or even supernatural forces; internal forces include conscience.
- *Characterization* describes how authors reveal characters' personalities and motivations. Authors reveal such traits and motives directly or indirectly.

Here is a direct, expressed motive about the character "Claude": "Claude is a popular guy but is feared by most of the students in the school." If the author merely has other characters steering clear of Claude, then readers soon infer that characters in the story are afraid of Claude even though the readers are not told so directly through a statement by the author.

After introducing or reviewing the material about characters, ask the students to identify the kinds of characterization the authors have used in stories read so far. Give your youngsters time to find specific examples in the text to support their responses. Encourage students to talk among themselves as they search for text clues. Once again, circulate among them, listening to their reasoning and gaining insight into their level of understanding. At the end of the session, summarize the terms and assign a new story.

LESSON FIVE: CHARACTERS—ACT II

Character development is complicated and involves an additional day of study. Explain how some characters develop and change during the course of the story. One option is to ask students why people do something right or wrong. The point would be that everyone is complex; every person acts on the basis of mixed motives. Real "characters" are not simple. In this regard, more complex fictional characters are like

Characters: People who are faced with solving a problem in a story. (Could be animals acting as humans.)

Flat: one dimensional, predictable, one-sided character

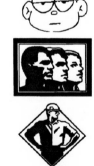

Round: one reader learns more about as story progresses

Static: does not change as the story progresses

Dynamic: changes as a result of involvement in the conflict

Figure 2.4. Characterization

readers—and readers are like them. Show or reproduce the diagram on characters and explain that for fictional purposes authors use a range of character types (see figure 2.4):

- *Dynamic* and *static* characters: Usually the protagonist is a dynamic character who changes as a result of attempting to solve the conflict. Most minor characters are static; they change very little or not at all.
- *Round* and *flat* characters: Round characters learn more as the story progresses but might not change (like a balloon that grows larger as it is blown up but does not change its basic nature). Flat characters are usually one-dimensional (like a paper doll), static, and often stereotypical (e.g., the pudgy best friend, the sidekick, the shy and bespectacled nerd, the bully, and the fairy tale's evil stepmother; see box 2.1).

Since this is the good stopping point for introducing new literary terms, review each one using all previous stories for examples. Then assign a more challenging story with more fully developed characters and a more complex plot. Edgar Allan Poe's short stories often fit this description, but may be challenging for younger students or inexperienced English readers. Later lessons are designed to introduce more literary devices.

This would be a fine opportunity to differentiate your instruction. Set up groups of four or five students based on common interests or

---

Box 2.1.   Play It! Using Cartoons to Illustrate Stereotypes

Thanks to YouTube and similar video websites, there are thousands of downloadable, copyright-free cartoons available for classroom use. The old Warner Bros. cartoons, in particular, have wonderfully illustrated simple plot lines and relatively simple characters that tend to be entirely good or evil. They demonstrate static, flat characters who have to be the same at the beginning and end of every episode. Caution: some early cartoons are extremely stereotypical with respect to gender, ethnicity, and race.

reading levels. Based on what you have learned about your students so far, assign the groups to read different stories from the anthology. If appropriate, two groups can read the same story. During the next class meetings, those who have read the same stories could meet in small groups to discuss their findings using the vocabulary of literature they are learning. Again, observe, listen, and take notes of who is confident using the new terms; who finds accurate examples to validate their claims about the story; who is encouraging and supportive; who sits and listens first but responds with comments that show they know what is going on; who hasn't a clue? All this anecdotal information can help you plan the next set of lessons tailored to meet the needs of the students you currently are teaching.

WRITING ABOUT SHORT STORIES

Once you complete this series of lessons it would be a good time for a stress-free writing assessment that follows up on students' discussion about the stories. Continue your focused observation as students work independently, then in small groups, and finally as a whole class. Here is an idea to help guide students in summarizing a story in three to five sentences using the basic journalistic questions: Who, What, When, Where, Why, and How. First model for the students a way to glean this specific information from a story:

- Who? List main characters—protagonist and antagonist.
- What? List seven to ten verbs that identify plot events. For example, choose a common fairy tale (or movie). Ask the students to list verbs, using only the verbs for "Little Red Riding Hood," "Goldilocks and the Three Bears," or a different but well-known tale.
walks
sees
peeks
tastes
sits
sleeps
awakens

fears

flees

- When? When does the action occur—or from when to when?
- Where? Where does the majority of the action take place?
- Why? Why do the protagonist and antagonist act the way they do— what drives or motivates them to act? Students may need help with the vocabulary of motivation. You could offer ideas like fear, love, hate, power, greed, jealousy, sense of adventure.
- How? How do the main characters accomplish their deeds— physically, mentally, both?

After you introduce students to the basic reportorial story categories, use the fairy tale or cartoon plot to write a three- to five-sentence summary with the students so they get the idea. Then you can be ready to assemble students into brainstorming groups to gather facts (in eight to ten minutes) about one of the stories they just read for class. Two groups can work on the same story, as needed. Tell them that they are to report their findings to the rest of the class. When someone from each group reports to the rest of the class, point out that groups sometimes identify different W's or H's in their reports. Be open with students about the fact that different interpretations can both be correct because stories and their characters are often complex—unlike simplistic TV commercials or cartoons with stereotypical characters. (See box 2.2.)

After group brainstorming, permit students to work independently to write their own summaries for ten minutes or so. If time permits, conclude the period by having one student from each group read his or her summary aloud while the rest of the class decides whether each reader has included all six requirements. What's missing? Who can add the missing information?

Box 2.2.   Search It!

Pique students' interest in writing story summaries by showing them one or two Amazon book listings—maybe even a blurb for a currently popular young adult fiction book. Note how the blurb uses the W's and the H but usually refrains from giving away the denouement (no "spoiler").

This reportorial activity provides a good appraisal of the class's readiness for a test or quiz on literary terms and story elements. If the students are ready, give them a test or quiz in a day or so. If not, take a couple of days to work with simpler stories and to practice identifying elements and using text evidence to support opinions and observations. See your own anthology or see Teacher Resources on this book's companion website for a sample quiz on literary terms.

APPLYING NEWLY LEARNED SKILLS— BOOK REPORT #1

At the end of the first quarter is a great time to have students independently apply what they are learning about the elements of fiction, but in a work they are reading on their own. If it is not realistic to expect your students to complete a book outside of class, allot twenty minutes daily for the next couple of weeks for students to read in class. To make efficient use of class time, set up a schedule so that all students study grammar for about two-thirds of the period. Chapters 3 and 11 have ideas for teaching grammar, directly or indirectly, as part of your writing instruction.

You can make that determination based on the grade and skill level of the students as revealed in the writing you already have seen them do on prior assignments. See Teacher Resource B for ideas for a first-quarter book report. This book report asks students to make connections between the story in their self-selected work of fiction and the stories they have studied together in class. It also includes a speech component to get students acclimated to giving more formal speeches later in the school year. Informal speaking activities conducted early in the semester can help students develop confidence for longer class speeches.

CONCLUSION

The key to introducing narrative theory in middle school language arts is to use examples and illustrations from stories that engage the students, keep the students reading, viewing, listening, and sharing stories. Use stories from the class text along with downloadable media files, especially short video clips. Keep in mind, this introduction or review of literary terms is designed to ensure that your students have the vocabulary with which to talk and write about the way fiction prose and poetry are shaped.

The short-term goal is to have a common word base and academic concepts of the grammar of fiction and a concrete understanding of these elements of literature. The longer-term goals are to prepare your middle school students with knowledge and skills that can serve them well when they reach high school, perhaps go on to college, and maybe eventually participate in neighborhood book discussion groups they decide to join as adults. Right?

3

EXPLORING TRADITIONAL AND CONTEMPORARY GRAMMARS

It is no longer an advantage to speak English, but a requirement!
Just speaking English isn't so impressive anymore—unless you speak
it really well.

—Heather Hansen[1]

Language is a glorious art, a phenomenal means of communication, and linguistic diversity is a gift to humankind. At the same time, there are always more formal, mainstream versions of languages that are symbols of what it means to be educated. In so many areas of life skillful use of languages leads to success in the workplace and in society in general. In this chapter you'll find reasons for incorporating discussions of culturally sensitive grammar and writing into the study of fiction.

In a diverse world full of different idiolects and dialects, students increasingly need to know how languages work so they can "code-switch" in personal, professional, and public life.[2] Fiction is one of the best ways to introduce students to Standard English usage so that they become more fluent in "good grammar" even as they become more amenable to other grammatical styles. So, think about the ideas in this chapter as you plan lessons to help raise awareness of grammar—that set of rules that govern the structure of oral and written speech—and design activities to help your students understand and value knowing when to use Standard English grammar to achieve academic and professional success.

CHOOSING THE RIGHT GRAMMAR

Few students use perfect grammar and some teachers do not use it either, but both groups recognize when others do not use grammar correctly. In fact, some students are shocked that a Mark Twain or a Toni Cade Bambara, author of "Blues Ain't No Mockingbird," do not seem to write "good grammar." Even though they, as your students may, come from communities and families with linguistic variations, students generally expect learned prose to sound the same—formal and correct, and students see school as a place for more elevated language, not necessarily as the real world as they know it outside of the classroom.

For some students who did not grow up learning Standard English, school is a place where a different language is spoken, read, and written. This, then, may be a good reason to teach English dialects the same way language teachers teach English speakers to learn Arabic, French, or Spanish. In order to encourage speaking the specific language, some instructors tell students that once they cross the threshold of the classroom, they are to communicate only in the language they are learning. This is pretty drastic for an English language arts class, but worth considering in a modified form.

Of course, when middle school students talk among themselves in small groups, there is no need to stop them from speaking their dialects, but in full class discussion, urge them to code-switch to Standard English. This practice can serve them well outside the classroom when they find themselves in situations where it is personally or professionally advantageous for them to speak Standard English.

Your young teenagers become amenable to grammar lessons when they learn that you are teaching them a form of speaking and writing that is useful to them, not only in school, but also in the broader college, business, and civic life. True, Standard English is not all there is to the real world. Still, it is essential for students of all linguistic backgrounds to learn when and where, why and how to code-switch among linguistic variations. The real issue is not who speaks or writes "properly," but instead how well someone can communicate effectively with other people. Because middle school students can understand this, you do not need to avoid the issues of language, culture, power, and privilege. Use the issues as teaching topics that hit home for many students, even for those from superficially homogeneous communities.

Students discover that some successful authors break the rules of Standard English. The students wonder why a "great" author can break the rules while a student might be poorly assessed, or marked down, for using the same nonstandard code. The answer is straightforward: students need to be able to switch from one to another linguistic variation depending on the setting. Most school writing is the setting for using Standard English.

Authors, too, learn code-switching in order to communicate well by lending authenticity to characters that would seem phony if they used only Standard English grammar. Except perhaps in semifictional autobiography, writing fiction requires character-building code-switching. Authors of young adult fiction who write well in other dialects include Rudolfo Anaya, Toni Cade Bambara, Sharon Draper, Rosalinda Hernandez, Zora Neale Hurston, Barry Milliken, Walter Dean Myers, Alberto Alvaro Rios, Juanita Sanchez, Gary D. Schmidt, Amy Tan, and Wing Tek. So, yes, teaching fiction is a propitious time to teach about both Standard English and the use of the dialects students may speak, hear, or read in their literature.

Showing your students ways that published authors use dialect to create valid and interesting stories is another reason to end a short-fiction unit in which you can ask students to write their own stories. When they focus on their own writing while also thinking about others' prose, your normally impatient students become more conscientious about revising their own work. They realize that they have to think about their characters and readers, and especially about communicating with the reader as authentically and respectfully as possible. These young writers then realize they have to get it right on behalf of the people they are writing about, not just for themselves.

Fortunately many students are already learning some code-switching by writing for digital media. They learn "texting" on a cell phone or online. They learn about writing blogs, somewhat similar to journaling. Some write "fan fiction" on popular websites, trying to imitate their favorite writers. In other words, middle school students tend to be published code-switchers already, even if they do not think of Facebook or MySpace and other social networking websites as publications with their own styles and rules. Moreover, whether they like it or not, students realize others are interpreting and evaluating what and how they write.

Video Journaling

If you have access to a class-based listserv for your students, try this simple assignment about code-switching and linguistic variations. Send the students a one-sentence message for translation into phone texting or online messaging. Select the sentence from one of the readings the class has not yet read—and don't tell the students in advance where the sentence came from.

Then copy and paste in a list the students' text translations on a sheet of paper or a projection slide to show to the class. Discuss two things: (1) the variations (idiolects) in students' translations, and (2) the difference in coding by the original author and the students. Why don't most novels use texting? When would it be appropriate—such as for dialogue by a specific character who texts? Finally, read to the students the full paragraph from the original author's work. Question? What does each version communicate about the writer and his or her opinion of the reader?

Some students, inspired by fiction, decide to incorporate dialect or syntax that reflects the oral language of a specific ethnic group or geographical region. If other authors can do it, they reason, why can't they? Why shouldn't they at least try? If it is appropriate for their story, by all means give them the freedom to try it. But they need to know that it is easy to offend those for whom a dialect is their own. The easiest place to start is writing within one's own dialect. Even then, here is the key: students need to understand that when they write in their own voice—the voice of the linguistic group with which they identify—they are making a choice with consequences for them as well as their readers.

PRACTICING STANDARD ENGLISH

If the students you teach speak different dialects of English, you could set up a schedule for them to practice Standard English. In the first semester of the school year, after you have introduced the idea of dialects and reasons to be fluent in Standard English, you could set aside one day a week for speaking only in Standard English once the students cross the threshold into your classroom. The second semester, you could add a second day a week. If students are acquiescent, during the final quarter or marking period of the school year, add a third day. As students become more fluent reading and writing Standard English in the classroom, they gain more confidence and use it when the need arises outside of the classroom.

Occasionally, for practice in journal writing, you could require them to use specific Standard English grammatical structures and more of the sophisticated vocabulary they encounter reading the fiction and nonfiction you assign. There is no need to grade these entries; they are just for practice. Simply read and comment on their journal entries. In all cases, do what you can to ensure that students' own languages and dialects are never disparaged.

SELECTING THE RIGHT TEXTBOOK

Linguistic codes get even more complicated and potentially political in education when it comes to textbooks. Who gets to dictate language, and presumably culture, by mandating textbooks? Many school districts and school sites select their own grammar books and some even choose literary texts that include grammar sections.

Textbooks are big business, so publishers pitch their books to school boards, state associations, individual administrators, and teachers. Their marketing includes all kinds of special features and selling points, including access to password-protected websites with both downloadable resource materials and links to other publically available, but sometimes difficult to discover, resources. Textbook sellers are becoming multimedia resource providers.

In other words, there are many different language arts texts from all of the major publishing houses and experienced educators are not likely to argue adamantly for the use of one book over another. Depending on the teacher, the parents, the community, the school, the state standards, and the like, each textbook has its own advantages and disadvantages. If you have a choice, select a textbook with the most accessible explanations and examples so that your particular students can learn both how language works and how to use language effectively and fittingly in a diverse world.

Introducing the Grammar Text

If your textbook can help you accomplish this goal, it is a viable teaching tool. But do not assume that students understand the purpose of the text, or that the text itself is adequate to engage students steeped in multimedia experience when you first distribute the book to students. Address the first issue by showing them how the book is organized, what it contains, and what it's for—a resource and a guide.

Few students appreciate or use their texts fully because no one has taken time to teach them how to do so. This is especially true with the anthology you may use. You probably noticed this if you had your students conduct a scavenger hunt within that text as described in chapter 1 of this book. If appropriate, adapt that hunt to this text.

Address the second issue by considering not only the insights and activities in this book, but also the digital resources provided by the publisher. You are the professional in the classroom who knows the students and their specific needs. Even if some of the resources are impractical or excessively time-intensive tools, you still might find a few student-engaging gems. (See box 3.1.)

Box 3.1. Search It! Video Journaling

If you have not already done so, spend some time exploring the world of online publishing. Facebook, MySpace, and Xanga include natural writing in students' own "young adult dialects." Fan fiction is a fascinating look into what young people care about, and how they think good authors write. Visit fanfiction.net and its sister site fictionpress.net (intended for pieces of writing that are about real people or original characters). You don't need to read specifically what your students are writing on these sites to discover what students are writing.

HONORING LA DIFFÉRENCE

Inevitably the issues of dialects in reading, writing, and discussion arise when teachers require that students use Standard English texts and require Standard English–based assignments. Sometimes parents get the impression that teachers disrespect students' native tongues or linguistic variations—even students' multilinguistic competence. Who says that Standard English is more academic, more worthy of being taught? Invite your students to ask adults they know about experiences they have had with language. Often these stories substantiate your claims better than anything else. Consider reading and talking about the poem "The Phone Booth at the Corner" by Juan Delgado.[3]

Why speak Standard English? That is a good question. Consider what you experienced in your own college or postcollege education training. Recall your exposure to the scholarly lingo, the "educationese." The American aphorist Mason Cooley once said, "An academic dialect is perfected when its terms are hard to understand and refer only to one another."[4] That is what some parents and students think about what is being taught in the schools. The language can seem like "school lingo," especially when it comes to the study and use of grammar. But it should not be limited to school speaking and writing.

Proficiency in speaking and writing Standard English is the ticket to career advancement in many professions. For this reason, educators have the responsibility to help students acquire this language even while honoring students' "heart" languages, the language with which they are most comfortable and consider their own. By so doing, effective teachers model what it means to respect others' languages and cultures.

In the ancient world, this was the basis for hospitality—making room for the stranger who is different from us and our culture. You can teach and show honor by respecting the students' ability to communicate effectively in their own codes. When you do this, you may realize that you also are a stranger. Why? Because one's standard grammar and mother tongue are different from the linguistic norms of others. By practicing linguistic hospitality students and teachers learn what it is like for others to be strangers and all come to recognize one's own "strangeness."

SEEING AND HEARING THE VALUE OF
LANGUAGE ARTS—A PERSONAL STORY

The occasion to demonstrate the value of speaking Standard English occurred when a friend invited me to present in classes at the Youth Tutoring Youth Program in Rochester, New York. This community project offered high school students an opportunity to learn the skills necessary to tutor elementary and middle school students in after school programs. During the week prior to my visit, my friend Nettie sang my praises. She told students that I was an experienced teacher who also had had a successful sales career. Student expectations were high.

When I arrived, dressed rather casually, I quietly sidled into the classroom without saying a word until I was introduced. Then I began speaking in slang, using the street English vernacular similar to the dialect of that community. The students looked at each other askance, puzzled that my preestablished ethos (thanks to my friend!) did not match the image I conveyed in my appearance and speech. As part of my monologue, I fumbled with my papers and exclaimed, "Oh darn it! I cain't find my notes." I fled the room as if to retrieve them from somewhere out in the hall.

The students burst forth with comments to each other and with questions to my friend. "She don't sound like a teacher, do she?" "I thought you said this woman is educated!" "She don't look like it!" "Where'd you get her from?" "Teachers ain't supposed to sound like that!"

My friend let them talk for a few minutes. I stood outside the classroom door; quickly removed the vest that clashed with my blouse, straightened my skirt, and with briefcase and notes in hand, reentered the room. This time, I walked more erectly to the front of the room and addressed the class in Standard English and then invited them to repeat their comments made after they first saw and heard me.

When asked why they were surprised, and even disappointed, in my appearance and speech, the students acknowledged the disconnection between their preconceptions and my presentation. They eventually admitted that, based on their teacher's description of my educational background and experience, they had expected me to speak "better" English. They realized and soon grasped the fact that just as they had

---

Box 3.2.   Record It! Picture It! Illustrating Code-Switching

Code-switching is visual as well as aural, and depicted as well as written and printed. One of the best ways to highlight each of the various code-switching grammars or media is to hold one medium constant while you vary the others. For instance:

1. Ask students to read silently a paragraph with vernacular dialogue from one of the text readings.
2. Play a recording of the same paragraph made by one of your friends who speaks that vernacular or dialect.
3. Show students a photo of the person who made the recording.

Along the way, stop after each step and ask the students who is "speaking"— what they think they know about the voice behind the text.

---

made assumptions about me based on my appearance, grammar, and articulation, others could make the same assumptions about them. Point made.

The form of English that one speaks is important. The manner in which one speaks and writes Standard English makes a difference in the way one is perceived by others. These students had witnessed firsthand the practical value of code-switching and were ready and open to learning another way of speaking. Lesson learned. (See box 3.2.)

CONCLUSION

Language arts are about life and the human condition. Professionals, like you in language arts education, are called upon to teach the multimedia grammars of code-switching. The job is not to promote particular cultures or languages over others, but to make sure that students are competent in Standard English and basic code-switching from nonstandard idiolect to standard and back. You are called upon to show appreciation of your students' languages as well as the particular language arts skills you bring.

You do this because you recognize that knowing and understanding language is practical; language is an art as well as a skill, a means for all human beings to be able to understand and be understood, to serve others and be served by them. Language essentially is at the center of who we are as people, cultures, nations, ethnic groups, communities, religious groups, and the like.

Studying language as it is written and spoken helps students to understand communication and to practice it more ethically and effectively. You see, it is primarily through visual and verbal language that your students can begin to understand what separates people and what unifies them. Honoring linguistic abilities, then, is a major component of honoring those shared differences. Through the lessons you design, you show your students that all humans share this amazing ability to switch codes in the midst of the very differences that confuse and divide people. And, as an educator you can model respect, thus teaching your middle school students to honor differences.

4

DISCUSSING AND WRITING SHORT STORIES: WHERE STORY MEETS GENRE

To read without reflecting is like eating without digesting.

—Edmund Burke[1]

Some of your students may have heard of literary terms such as *first person* or *theme*, but chances are your young teens just experience stories without thinking about who is talking to whom about what. Once they begin discussing and writing about literature, however, students soon see that learning the literary language leads to better understanding and eventually to an appreciation for how stories work. Short stories are great teaching mediums for literary devices because they provide compact, manageable examples.

This chapter offers you options for presenting or reviewing the definitions of literary terms adolescents are expected to know and use by the time they graduate from middle school. Depending on the elementary schools from which your students come, some may be very familiar with the terms; others may be learning the terms for the first time. Therefore, it would serve you well to conduct some kind of informal assessment to determine that level of knowledge and confidence of use.

Having completed lessons about literature already like those offered in chapter 2, the students probably are curious and eager to begin exploring more subtle aspects of fiction. But it is always a good idea to conduct an interim no-stress assessment, just to assure yourself that students are ready for more.

One quick and easy assessment is to have students turn to the list of literary terms in their anthology and ask them to put a plus sign next to terms they know and could explain to another student; put a check mark next to terms they recognize but are not sure how to use in conversation or writing, and a minus sign next to words that are completely new to them. If writing in their texts is verboten, print out a list of the terms on paper on which they can write. Include all the terms you plan to teach for the school year. This has a dual purpose. Seeing the whole list lets them know what they are expected to know by the end of the year; marking the terms they know shows them what they have already learned.

As you circulate among the students, peeking at their marking, you get a sense of their level of familiarity with the terms. If you notice lots of plus signs, commend the students for the knowledge they already have, and then move more rapidly through the lessons, using the ideas presented as a refresher; on the other hand, if you see more checks and minus signs, you know to move with deliberate steps through the lessons. As you discover increased student confidence, in their oral and written conversations, just pick up the pace and move on. You are the one in charge, the professional in the classroom who knows what your students know and what they need to learn. Until students can show they know; you have more to teach.

LESSON SIX: POINT OF VIEW

Point of view (POV) is the perspective from which an author tells a story. The various points of view include the following types:

- First Person POV: The author writes as though he or she is a character inside the story. The author, writing as the character, uses first person pronouns and comments on his or her thoughts and feelings about the incidents in the plot. For example, if Charles Dickens had written his classic story about Scrooge as though he,

Dickens, were the character Scrooge, the reader would know only what Scrooge sees and hears, thinks and does. With the limitations of first person POV, the reader would not know what has gone on in Tiny Tim's house before Scrooge arrives.

- Objective POV: The author writes the story as though he or she is outside the story: limited to listening and observing what characters say and do—like a reporter. The author uses third person pronouns (he, she, they—not we or I) to report the speech and actions of the characters in the story. The objective POV offers a broader perspective than first person POV because the author stands outside of the story and can observe characters in different settings. The characters can speak in the first person, but the author is reporting on their speech.

- Omniscient POV: The author writes the story as though he or she is outside the story but can see inside the hearts and minds of the characters inside the story. The author not only listens and observes what characters say and do, but also relates what these characters think and feel, like an all-knowing Supreme Being. The author not only uses third person pronouns, but also words like *thinks*, *feels*, *imagines*, and *worried* to show the inner thoughts and feelings of the characters. This is the broadest POV because the author gets inside the heads and hearts of the characters and can comment on their thoughts and feelings as the story progresses.

- Limited Omniscient POV: An author limits the revelation of thoughts and feelings to just one character, often the protagonist. To understand this, imagine being able to read the mind of one of your friends, but not the mind of a different friend. This is the way Dickens wrote *A Christmas Carol*. The reader knows what Scrooge is thinking and feeling, but can only infer that information about other characters based on what they say and do. (See figure 4.1.)

Showing Point of View with Four Geometric Shapes

As you draw a circle on the board, identify it for the students as the author, a rectangle to represent the book (story), a triangle for one character, and a square for a second character.

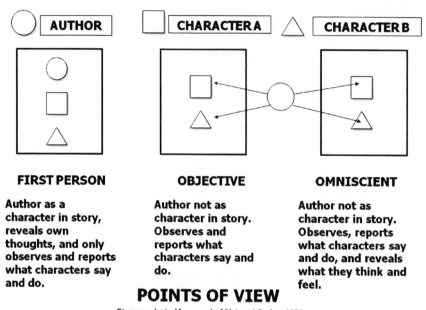

Figure 4.I.   Points of View

- For First Person POV: Draw the rectangle and to the left, a circle. Next, inside the rectangle, draw a triangle and square. Add a circle inside. Then, draw an arrow from the circle outside the circle to the one inside to show the author is writing as a character inside the story.
- For Objective POV: Draw the same rectangle, with circle outside and a triangle and square inside. Draw an arrow from circle to edge, but not inside the triangle and square to show author is writing as an observer.
- For Omniscient POV: Draw the same graphic as for Objective, except this time draw arrows from the outside circle to inside the triangle and square to show this author also can reveal what characters think and feel.
- For Limited POV: Use the same diagram, but arrow pierces only into the triangle, to show author reveals what only one character thinks and feels.

Have students copy the diagram in their reading journals as a reference for later. [2]

After reviewing previously taught literary terms with students, help them identify each author's point of view in the works the class has already read. Ask them to consider how each author's story would have been different if it were told from another point of view. What would the readers be able to know and when? What impact does that perspective have on the story? Student comments usually vary but should indicate the limitations of first and objective points of view and perhaps the different level of suspense created with omniscient point of view.

Writing Assignment for Understanding Point of View

Challenge students. Ask them to imagine that a minor automobile accident has occurred at a busy intersection during the lunch hour. State objectively that Car A failed to come to a complete stop at the intersection and rear-ended Car B, causing it to enter the intersection and hit a pedestrian crossing the street. No serious injuries occurred. Diagram the crash in PowerPoint or on the board, but give only the facts, like a reporter. Set your timer to ring ten minutes before the end of the period so you have time to sum up the lesson and give the homework assignment.

1. Divide the students into story-related personae:
   driver of Car A or B in the accident
   driver of any of the other cars stopped in the intersection
   the pedestrian who was struck by Car B
   one of three pedestrians who observed the accident
   TV reporters in their station's helicopter who happened to be flying over from a fire in the next county
   (Of course, you can use a different situation depending on what interests your students: an accident at a horse show, a robbery in a shopping mall parking lot, a brawl on school grounds, or a scuffle in the cafeteria.)
2. Invite the students to write, in first person POV, a one-paragraph description of what happened from the perspective of their chosen or assigned persona.
3. Have them assemble in groups of five (representing each of the personae) to read their paragraphs aloud within their groups.

Box 4.1.   Shoot It! Helping Students Picture Point of View

Perhaps no contemporary media genre illustrates point of view better than the news. Modern news is not just factual; someone has to decide what to report, how to cover it, who to interview, what to include in the final copy, and images or sounds. During the week that you're introducing the concept of point of view, ask interested students in groups of two or three to cover a school sports event with a digital camera, using no more than three photos and thirty seconds of copy to summarize the game.

As long as at least two groups participate you'll be able to compare the points of view of different reporter-editors as they read their copy and show their images to the class. Hint: Don't tell them in advance whether to use any particular first person or objective copy in describing the event. See what they come up with on their own.

---

4. Then, ask students individually to describe the same accident from limited omniscient POV, choosing another person who observed the incident. This time, have them read their paragraph to a partner.

About ten minutes before the class period ends, invite volunteers to read aloud to the class their writing from either perspective or point of view. Encourage the students to articulate what they learned from doing this exercise. They are likely to mention that the details seemed different depending on the position of the speaker in relation to the accident. They probably notice that using the omniscient POV provides more information for the reader and reveals bias in a character that can influence the readers' opinion of the events that occur in the story. (See box 4.1.)

LESSON SEVEN: THEME

Theme is the universal message of a story—what some textbooks call a story's central meaning or idea. To be universal, themes must reveal what is true about human nature or the human condition regardless of time or place. Life itself is an adventure in learning, but the best literature focuses on the themes that help us to understand life in all times and places.

Consider this helpful guide to universal theme: Would the fictional characters respond in similar emotional or psychological ways if the situation in which they found themselves were set in a different time or place? If so, the story probably addresses universal themes. Here is a way to approach the topic:

1. Begin the class period with a review of the last story read. Ask students to write a half page in which they summarize the story using the five W's and H concept. For this time for H, indicate how the author chose to tell the story, from the point of view.

2. Add the definition of *theme* to the key terms you already posted on the board, overhead transparency, or projection screen. Displaying a word wall of the terms is another way to reinforce learning and remind students to use the terms in speaking and writing. Seeing the list grow throughout the school year shows them how much they are learning. The list also is there for them to see when they are talking or writing about literature.

3. Explain the significance of the plot for determining theme. Ask students to pay attention to incidents in the beginning, middle, and end of the plot, especially the conflicts the protagonist faces and the responses to the conflict and attempts to overcome it.

4. Mention that a theme should be expressed in a complete sentence; otherwise the idea is probably just a topic, not a real theme. Write this sentence with blanks left where there are parentheses, "*When* (indicate the situation the main character is in,) *people* (indicate the response)." For example, "When little girls are hungry, they are tempted to steal" ("Goldilocks and the Three Bears").

5. Ask the class to state possible sentence themes in previously read stories.

6. Give them time to reflect on the stories, flip back through the textbook, and jot down their ideas.

7. Remain open to new insights since some students might come up with themes that you had not considered. But, require students to support their observations with text evidence from the stories taken from the beginning, middle, and end of the stories.

DRAFTING A SHORT STORY

As students learn the basic elements of narrative fiction they are better prepared to write well-structured stories of their own. Some students are eager to begin whether or not they understand plot, point of view, and theme. Their early drafts should give you a good sense of what elements of fiction to review along the way.

Beware: Since some students are not keen about this assignment, allot just enough time for all students to draft a brief story—not so long that you cannot maintain enthusiasm for the task. Be observant as you coach the students through this process and adjust the teaching pace as needed. Initially, plan to spend two weeks.

Hint: Tell students that it might help them to tell the story to themselves, in their heads, before writing. If they can describe to themselves in a few sentences a story with a problem to be resolved, they probably have a story. Stress the ideas of conflict and resolution so they create stories that have real plots rather than just series of incidents. You also could set up pairs of students and encourage the partners to tell their story to each other. Or, assign the students to try their story out at home or with their seat partner on the bus.

Idea: Consider a brief class discussion in which students create a basic plot outline.

- Ask for a protagonist.
- Ask for a setting (any setting!).
- Ask for a conflict likely involving an additional character.
- Ask how the conflict might be resolved.
- What attempts would the protagonist probably make to solve the problem?
- Who cares? This is the toughest question, but one that pushes students to create more interesting stories with some intrigue.

Be visual: To help visual learners, diagram the plot on the board or screen as you create the story. In other words, do your best to ensure that students are thinking "story" before they begin writing their stories.

The lesson: Let interested students draw their ideas, including plot lines and character "sketches," before they try to express those creative thoughts formally in another medium. However, keep in mind the limits of PowerPoint for visual learners.

When humans think visually, they imagine how to associate images with one another using their own experiences. For instance, when we think of what we would like to accomplish we imagine ourselves doing the things necessary to complete the task. Even if we make a list of the steps, we imagine ourselves doing verbs in the list (nouns like *store* imply actions, such as "go to" or "buy").

Many visual learners prefer to picture their creativity concretely in a medium; they will draw pictures and symbols, even when creating a list, adding underlines and uppercase letters, or combinations of cursive handwriting and block letters. Visual learners think in terms of special connections, too—arrows, boxes, circles, personal sketches, and the like.

The fact is high-tech visual tools can be too restrictive for relatively simple visual tasks. For instance, visual learners usually prefer paper and pen to PowerPoint when it comes to brainstorming. PowerPoint is difficult to use for freehand drawing and doodling. However, a technology like PowerPoint can help visual learners express their ideas effectively to others, but usually only after they have expressed it on paper, first. For many visual learners, thinking creatively with PowerPoint is inefficient if not totally aggravating. So, let students draft in the medium that works best for them.

Two to three weeks is usually sufficient time for student story drafting. Students who are interested in pursuing this kind of writing should be encouraged to revise and polish their stories for submission to the school's literary magazine or online publishers.

Grading during Story Composition

> Don't get it right.
> Get it written,
> Then get it right. [3]

Each day that you expect the students to come prepared with work on their stories, consider rubber-stamping the last page written and record check marks in your grade book to indicate that the students are completing the drafting assignments. It really is too early to begin evaluating the quality of their work. Why? Because these early drafts are like practice sessions or training drills. For sports, it is the scores of the games that go in the record book to determine the success of the season.

Now is the time for you to serve as the students' model and coach. Your attitude is important and it is more empathetic if you draft a story yourself as the students are drafting theirs and offer yours for comment, too. Model making appropriate journal comments or suggestions, offering positive statements even as you point out a weakness that needs to be addressed: "Great idea for a setting." "Do you think you have enough conflict?" "Is that enough description of the protagonist so that readers could get to know her better?" "This section suddenly changes the story's point of view. Do you want to stay with first person so the reader doesn't get confused?"

Whenever you respond orally or in writing to students' creative work, you run the risk of unintentionally deflating their enthusiasm. Often you can get at story problems simply by asking questions. If a student needs more direction than what you can provide with general questions, try more directive questions: "What do you think about rewriting the scene so it seems more realistic—something that might actually happen?" "How do you think adding some thought shots that tell or show what the characters are thinking can increase the suspense?"

Recording daily check marks in your grade book provides support for student progress, letting them know that writing is a process and that drafting is a step that counts. If, during this drafting period, you have to report to parents or an administrator about students' performance, you can rely on the comments you have made in the journals along with any other notes you make about students' active involvement in the daily assignments.

Helping "Storyless" Students

Sometimes students have difficulty coming up with a story to write. What to do?

1. Ask them to model a story they already have read for class, but with characters and settings that are familiar to them.

2. Have students bring to class pictures from online or print publications and then write stories to accompany these images. For example, a week before beginning the story writing assignment, assign students to bring in three pictures, one of each that meet the following criteria:
   only one person in the picture
   a group of people in a specific place
   scenery only—a place, with no people

You should discourage the students from choosing pictures of easily identifiable persons, such as movie stars or sports figures, to reduce the temptation for the students to limit their imaginations and have their story characters become exactly like celebrity personae.

Organize and store the pictures in three labeled envelopes until it is time to start the stories a few days later. It is good for students to forget about the article, magazine, or setting from which they took the pictures, so ask them to bring in the pictures about a week before you plan to use them. This time lapse also allows opportunities for those who may not have access to magazines at home to come before or after school to search through the box of magazines you may keep in your room or for students to print out pictures from a neighborhood or school computer.

Here's a way to set up this prewriting assignment based on pictures:

1. Before the class arrives for the first day of story writing, write prompts on the board or another classroom medium. Consider projecting them from PowerPoint slides.
2. Arrange the pictures in the three categories, face down on a tabletop.
3. Ask students to prepare by placing paper and a pen or pencil on their desks.
4. Invite students to come forward by rows to randomly select one picture from each pile before returning to their seats. You might even play a lyric-free song and ask students to march up to the music, pick up the pictures, and return to their seats before the tune concludes.
5. Give students two minutes to look at the pictures they have and decide which one they would like to write about. They should

return the rejects to the table so others might use them. Complete the selection in ten minutes or so. Then urge students to keep what they have and see what happens. Few students fail to come up with a workable story.

6. Set a timer for five minutes for a quick-write—nonstop writing until the timer goes off.

7. Encourage students to write as though their chosen picture illustrates the story they are drafting.

8. Suggest that students begin writing either in the first person as a character in the story or as an omniscient writer who reveals the thoughts and feelings of the characters.

9. If students cannot think immediately of what to write, direct their attention to the posted instructions or distribute a handout with the following prompts:

   • If using the picture with one person, write as though you are that person. Write about:
     why you are in this place
     what happened just before the picture was taken
     what's on your mind

   • If using the picture of a group of people, choose one of the people and write in that persona. Talk about:
     why you are here with this person/these people
     how you feel about the others
     what happened just before the picture was taken

   • If using the scenic picture of a place, make this the setting of the story and describe it using such strong, vivid images so that an artist could draw the scene using just your writing. Reveal:
     the time period (day, season, historical period)
     what happened just before the picture was taken
     what is going to happen in this place

When the timer goes off, invite the youngsters to reread their prose and circle any ideas that might be developed into a story that has characters in a specific place, confronted with and attempting to overcome some specific conflict. Remind them that short stories usually take place in a short period of time, often within a single hour, day, or week. Give your young authors-to-be the remainder of the period to expand on the ideas evoked by this quick-write.

As the students continue writing, encourage them to include at least three increasingly difficult obstacles to overcome. Remind them that in a successful story the protagonist solves the problem in a logical way or decides that there is no solution and after valiant attempts to solve the problem, ceases the struggle. Discourage the use of "and then he woke up." Push them to consider alternatives that lead to a thoughtful, insightful, and even surprising but satisfying conclusion.

By this time, most students are excited about developing their stories, so you can assign them to continue drafting their story for homework or to leave their quick-write and notes in their classroom folder so they came resume writing the next class meeting. In the interim, encourage them to listen to the rhythm of conversations to tune their ears to writing realistic dialogue. You should not be surprised when many students return to the next class meeting full of ideas of how to continue their story.

MAKING MINILESSONS TO ASSIST STUDENTS ALONG THE WAY

Flesh Out Characters

Use direct and indirect characterization. If students need models, refer them to characters in readings that they have already studied. Ask them to pay attention to the way the authors revealed the characters' personality and motivation. As with fan fiction, modeling a favorite author can effectively jump-start students' writing. Remember the annual Hemingway imitation contests?

Build Suspense

Ask students to

- Circle the sentence in their story that indicates the conflict the protagonist is facing. No such sentence? Time to add one!

- Put a rectangle around the sentence in the story that identifies the antagonist.
- Draw a plot line of their story to verify that their protagonist is faced with a believable problem and is making logical choices while facing increasingly complicated obstacles in an attempt to resolve the conflict. Remind them of the image of a roller-coaster ride.

Encourage students to revise their work so that their stories flow to a suspenseful climax. They should include the thoughts of the protagonist as he or she considers the final step to solving the problem because the final attempt often is an internal conflict during which the protagonist struggles with issues of right and wrong, and safe and unsafe, advantageous and disadvantageous choices.

Complete the draft for homework: word-processed copy for class in two days. If this homework assignment is not a realistic expectation for the students you have, arrange time for them to use the school computers for a couple of class periods. Encourage them to use the rubric the class creates or that you provide to evaluate the draft of their own story.

PRACTICING PEER RESPONSES

Professional writers have editors who read their drafts and offer suggestions for revision. Before sending their manuscripts to a publisher, many professional writers ask friends or colleagues to read drafts or the writers participate in a writing group that gives them useful feedback. Allay their skepticism by letting your fledglings know that no one publishes fiction without editors who check everything from storyline to grammar. No writer is that good.

Now is the time for students to serve one another as helpful, encouraging peer editors. Establish either writer-editor partners or small (three to four students) writers' groups within the class. The partners or groups can review each others' drafts and make suggestions. The purpose is to give positive feedback in tune with the basic rubrics the students have already created. Make positive statements: "What a vivid descriptive passage. I can also see the wind blowing across the meadow." Offer encouraging suggestions: "Wow, have you thought about telling what the character is thinking right here?" Professional writers frequently have brittle egos. So do amateur writers of any age.

Students usually have good ideas for improving stories. However, in order to keep the peer comments on track, provide the criteria they are to consider on a printed peer response sheet with a rubric. A rubric in chart form should include those statements about what constitutes an effective story. You may create your own or invite your students to help develop these criteria statements. Many writing rubrics include statements about content and creativity, organization and flow, as well as quality of vocabulary and correctness relating to mechanics, usage, and grammar. Your budding authors then can share the assessment standards and presumably the stories with parents or guardians too. A number of teacher websites, such as Rubistar, have templates and programs for creating and modifying rubrics to meet the specific requirements of a variety of language arts assignments.[4]

Once the students understand the rubric, let them try it. Provided you have given each writer enough time and feedback to do his or her own revisions first, the peer review process should go smoothly and helpfully. Here are two ways to conduct either the partner (or small group) or workshop editing sessions:

Option A: Editing in Pairs—Desk-Touching Exercises

Ask students to pull desks together to work in pairs. Touching desks suggests sharing a common work surface, physical permission to collaborate. Or if your room is furnished with tables, you may have students pull their chairs together so that the conversation between two students can be private, without distracting or disturbing their other tablemates. The rest is gloriously simple but effective:

- Remind students to speak in six-inch voices so only their partners can hear them as each one reads his or her story to the other one. Let the partner hear how the story sounds as narrated by the author. If there is an odd number of students, serve as a partner yourself using the story you have been drafting along with the class.
- Encourage students to listen for consistency in point of view and verb tense.

- Then, as students respond to authors, let the authors take a few notes on their own drafts.
- Once the comments are concluded, allow time in class for authors to begin making corrections and revisions as they see fit. Assure them that their stories are their own works; they do not have to make the suggested revisions. But they do need to address grammatical issues and should correct other problems that may cloud communication.

Sometimes it is necessary to modify your teaching timeline based on what you overhear during the desk-touching exercises. If the majority of the students sound as though they need another day of writing before sharing in groups, extend the due date. Keep students on task by making your presence felt and coaching their understanding as needed.

Option B: Editing in Groups—Writers' Workshop

Once the students have worked with a partner and revised their stories it's time to workshop their stories in a format recommended by the National Writing Project.[5]

1. Ask students to group themselves into three circles (ten to twelve students)—A, B, and C.
2. Instruct them to pass their drafts to a volunteer group leader in the circle.
3. Collect the stacks of papers and redistribute group A papers to leader B, group B papers to leader C, and group C papers to leader A.
4. Set a timer for two minutes.
5. Once the leader passes the stories to group members, each student should read as much of the story as possible until the timer goes off. Then pass that draft to the right.
6. Repeat reading and passing papers to the right until all but one of the drafts has been read.
7. Distribute the second copy of the peer response worksheet and ask the students to write the name of the student writer and complete that sheet for the last draft they receive to read.

8. Encourage students to talk among themselves about the general strengths they see in the set of drafts and what problems they recognize they have made themselves and should be corrected to improve the next draft.
9. Take some time now to have a general class discussion and list on the board what seems to be working in the stories so far and what are the main areas on which students need to focus their attention during revising.
10. At the end of the period, return the draft and peer response sheet to each author and assign a revision to be due in two or three days.

Before the final draft is due, take the time to review the grading rubric with the students so they can once again assess their own work before you grade it. The fewer grade surprises, the better. When students have a clear idea what is expected of them, they are more likely to meet those expectations.

You may decide to schedule a second read around session when the students have finished their stories and are ready to submit them for publication outside the school. In this case, if this has been a generally positive and supportive group of students, you could ask them to rank and rate the stories of their peers. If so, you may find it useful to use Teacher Resource C as a guide to set up an assignment that suggests that students work with papers with no names on them and from a different class period. This gives students a little more anonymity and makes for more objective reading.

Student Guidelines for Final Drafts

1. Print final drafts double-spaced on white paper with one-inch margins, using a ten- or twelve-point font. Times New Roman, Arial, or Bookman are most readable (avoid unusual fonts).
2. Drafts should be three to five pages long.
3. Add a title sheet with the story title printed without quotation marks, your full name, the class and time period it meets, the teacher's name (spelled correctly!), and the due date arranged neatly on the page.

4. Use the picture from the first classroom exercise as an illustration with the final draft, if desired. Or include an original drawing or a computer-generated image. Be sure to give credit if using an image from a website (write the Web address in small letters under the image).

5. Submit all of your work on the story, stapled together. Include a handwritten note on the bottom for each section: Draft 1, Peer Response, Draft 2, First Plot Line, and Final Draft. Include any other sections that show evidence of your process. The packet is visible and tactile evidence of what it takes to write a good story.

6. Celebrate! When all of this work is organized and stapled together for submission with title page, do something fun.

Do follow through with a full class celebration—like an authors' reception or a book-publishing party in class. Invite students to bring in "neat to eat" treats. You might even randomly select stories to read aloud to the class yourself or to invite the author to read—as dramatically as they would like to do. Let the authors embellish their reading if they are comfortable. Join the fun by reading something that you have written. (See box 4.2.)

The final-final step for some students might be publishing their story on campus—in print form or online on your pages of the school website

---

Box 4.2.   Blog It! Publishing Online Fan Fiction

A newer way to encourage students to publish is to offer credit for students' contributions to online fan fiction.[6] These "works in progress" are essentially readers' own writings designed either to extend novelists' printed prose or sometimes to comment upon novelists' works using "drabbles" (short, one hundred-words-or-less vignettes that rely on characters or settings from the original works).

Fan fiction is like blogging (web "logging," or commenting on subjects and experiences). Fans write on special fan fiction websites rather than on their own blogs or social networking pages on Facebook, MySpace, and the like.

or in an off-campus printed periodical or one of the websites that publishes student work. Carefully choose from the myriad sites now available on the Internet. Avoid those with inappropriate advertising and those that do not provide for privacy of students' personal information. Consider offering students credit simply for submitting their work. It is a big step for some of your adolescent writers. And do not be the least surprised when one or two students who submit their work each year have it selected for a print journal or anthology. This simply encourages others to try the next time.

Your librarian may agree to display in the library a loose-leaf binder with the stories your students write. Obtain a white binder with a clear pocket cover and slip in a student-designed or computer-generated cover. Then, add a table of contents of the stories arranged alphabetically by author. Students who view the collection are not likely to mark or deface the book; students tend to respect peers' work and enjoy reading it—especially the older students who remember when their writing was similarly displayed.

CHOOSING AND REPORTING ON A SELF-SELECTED SHORT STORY COLLECTION—BOOK REPORT #2

Each quarter, build in time in the schedule and assign students to read a book they individually select. For the second quarter, offer them the option to read an anthology of short stories by several authors or a collection by a single author. See Teacher Resource D for a sample handout for this assignment based on student-selected collections of short stories.

Unless you are a language arts–teaching magician, you do not have class time for students to peruse the library on their own. You have too much curriculum to teach. But you can schedule a meeting or two at the library for students to learn from the librarian about some of the possible titles or series. You and the librarian can preselect collections that are appealing and appropriate for middle school students. You can ask the librarian to reserve the preselected books on a special cart or shelf during the weeks of the assignment so replacements are still on hand should students decide to change books.

Finding Books for Boys

Encourage students to read additional books by the same author or on the same topic. Usually school librarians rejoice at occasions to give book talks and to help students find just the right novel. If you would like to stay abreast yourself and be able to make recommendations to your students, you may want to check out the *ALAN Review*, which includes the article, "Cool Books for Tough Guys: 50 Books Out of the Mainstream of Adolescent Literature That Will Appeal to Males Who Do Not Enjoy Reading."[7] The *ALAN Review*, published by the Assembly on Literature for Adolescents of the National Council of Teachers of English, sponsors an annual conference that usually follows the NCTE Annual Convention. Whenever you have the opportunity, attend one or both. These professional organizations provide a wealth of information and inspiration for the middle school teacher that is difficult to find in any other single setting.

While in the library, encourage students to peruse several books, check out one or two books that seem interesting, and even begin reading in one of the collections if there is still time before the class period ends. Assure the students that they are free to change books after a couple of days if they have tried but have not gotten into the reading by that time.

Then, validate the students' outside reading via the book report assignment. The first quarter includes the oral report based on their summer reading or on their self-selected book read during the weeks the class was studying grammar. In this second quarter, when they have studied short stories and have begun writing structured paragraphs in response to their reading, consider assigning a written book report that draws on that knowledge of literature structure and provides practice writing about a book they selected.

Here is the literary catch: this second book report requires students to recommend stories from their collection to characters in the stories they have read for class. Students get to imagine how they would encourage a fictional character to read a work of fiction. What fun! In other words, they have to know both the audience character and the one in the short story on which they are reporting. How revealing! Imagine writing a recommendation to Tom Sawyer or to Stanley in Louis Sachar's novel

Holes! Of course, students must include specific information from each literary work to demonstrate that they understand both.

Encourage them to write P.I.E. paragraphs stating their opinion or position, illustrating them with examples, quotations, or facts, and then write sentences explaining or expanding and showing the link between those examples and their position statement. In other words, they demonstrate that they understand what interests both character A from a story studied in class and character B from a short story they have chosen from the short story collection, and what each would like and why.

If appropriate for the class, add a section to the assignment where the students also write about their favorite story from their chosen collection. Why did they like it? In this case, too, they have to demonstrate knowledge of the story as they explain their enthusiasm for it.

The P.I.E. structure is like the structure used in many textbooks:

topic sentence
some examples
concluding sentences

But with the P.I.E. image the students see the purpose of each of the sentences and visualize the value for them to state their own observation, opinion, or position. A pie needs a filling to be worthwhile. Using P.I.E., your students write richer, more personal paragraphs and ultimately better developed essays.

It is important for them to know that you not only want to hear what they have to say about a topic, but also expect them to defend or explain their ideas. There is an added bonus of assigning this kind of substantiation. When they are required to return to the text for evidence, students develop a deeper appreciation for the stories they have chosen for the assignment. They no longer write unsupported feelings about a story. They also feel more certain because they are standing on the evidence of their text.

Student Response to Quarter Two Book Report Prompt

Seventh grader Cressy returns to the literature studied during the short story unit. In one section of an essay she attempts to include all that she has learned about writing summary sentences and P.I.E. paragraphs—in just a few sentences:

> Two people both have goals to consume food, Hannah, in *Sixteen Short Stories by Outstanding Writers for Young Adults*, in "I, Hungry Hannah Cassandra Glen," by Norma Fox Mazer, and a youth in *World Literature*, in "A Glass of Milk," by Manuel Rojas, both people who have a goal to consume food, and both reach their goal. To start off, Hannah, a girl whose mom is not in the greatest position considering money, wants food and doesn't get a ton of food, so she and a buddy, Crow, go to a funeral, because when it is over, at the after-party, there are all sorts of delectable foods she devours, and it is like Hannah, the very main character, is telling this in first person POV, taking place in the town that Hannah lives in, the other man character is Hannah's very good bud, Crow, and the conflict in getting the food, and Hannah a goal to consume food. [Whew!!!] Switching to "The Glass of Milk," a youth after being booted out of a boat, and in the town he was put in, doesn't have any money, so this is a problem, he feels the need for food, and would like to consume food, but at first, the problem about accepting food or money from others is "timidity and share" (page fifty-seven), and then, he wants food so much he decides to consume, no matter the consequences, and reaches his goal. He, like Hannah, also has a goal to consume food. These two people are alike, for they both have a goal to take in food, and in the end, they both reach their goal. They are alike in these ways.

Although her sentences run on, Cressy clearly is on her way to understanding and writing about literature. To encourage writers like Cressy, invite them for a conference to discuss ways their next writing could include pertinent information without rambling. By the end of the school year, as they learn to reduce repetition and use varied sentence structures, their writing, like Cressy's, will show significant improvement.

CONCLUSION

Students having the opportunity to practice writing a genre they have been reading develop a deeper appreciation for what it takes to write a good story. When they write about stories they have read using the language of literature they are learning, the students extend their understanding of why some stories work and others do not. Equally important, when students read widely, they have a peek into the way people in different times and places confront the conflict in their lives. The students often see new ways of addressing problems they encounter in their own lives. While that is not the primary purpose of teaching literature, it often is a positive by-product.

Finally, offering students an opportunity to publish their writing locally in your classroom or library, or more publicly in a printed periodical or electronic magazine, you validate that what they have to say is important enough to revise and edit, to polish and share with others.

SHORT STORY COLLECTIONS TO RECOMMEND FOR SELF-SELECTED READING

The Friendship and The Gold Cadillac by Mildred D. Taylor

These two short stories by Mildred D. Taylor explore what it was like to grow up black in America during the 1900s. *The Friendship* is about the consequences that occur when a black man calls a white storekeeper by his first name. *The Gold Cadillac* follows the journey of a black family as they travel into the south in a brand-new car—a seemingly insignificant journey that turns out to be strange and dangerous. These two stories work well with a study of black history.

Grades: Sixth

Caution: Language, Violence

The Gift of the Magi and Other Stories by O. Henry

These classic stories about life in the early 1900s are very accessible for middle school students. Well known for their surprise endings, O. Henry's stories are typically pleasant and entertaining. This collection includes the popular *The Gift of the Magi* and nine others. Particularly touching is *The Last Leaf* in which a woman connects her fate with the leaves falling from a tree.

Grades: Seventh through eighth

Caution: None

Guys Write for Guys Read edited by Jon Scieszka

For this anthology, John Scieszka collected dozens of stories and illustrations from popular authors who write for boys. Scieszka's goal was to provide a wide variety of very short stories in order to help boys identify what types of things they like to read. The selections include personal anecdotes, short stories, poetry, and illustrations with descriptions, comics, and even a "Guyfesto." This is a great resource to reach a variety of boys, particularly reluctant readers.

Grades: Sixth through eighth

Caution: None

On the Fringe edited by Donald R. Gallo

On the Fringe is a serious and thoughtful collection of eleven stories about high school outcasts. Compiled in response to the Columbine shootings, the stories include characters like Brian who's considered a wimp, Jeannie who's a tomboy, Renee who decides to write about her school's outcasts, and Gene who brings a gun to class. These stories are perfect for encouraging discussion of difficult but very important topics. Even though the book is intended for high school students, middle school students definitely relate to it as well.

Grades: Seventh through eighth

Caution: Language, Sexual innuendo, Bullying, Smoking, Sexual abuse

Short and Shivery: Thirty Chilling Tales retold by Robert D. San Souci

This is a collection of thirty retold ghost stories from around the world. The tales are scary enough to hold middle school students' attention, but not scary enough to concern parents. Represented countries include England, Russia, Costa Rica, Norway, the United States, Iceland, Japan, and others. Many of the stories are new to students and teachers.

Grades: Sixth through seventh

Caution: Mild violence, Terror

A Wolf at the Door **edited by Ellen Datlow and Terri Windling**

Thirteen science fiction and fantasy writers contributed stories to this collection of retold fairy tales. The stories are meant to return to the older, more frightening and complicated style of fairy tales. Some stories change the perspective (the dwarfs from *Snow White*), some are updated (the ugly duckling as a modern girl), and some are little-known (*The Months of Manhattan*). Middle school students enjoy comparing these stories to the originals, and trying their hand at their own fairy tale retellings.

Grades: Sixth through eighth
Caution: Magic, Mild violence

The Wonderful Story of Henry Sugar and Six More **by Roald Dahl**

Roald Dahl's stories are funny, strange, and often irreverent. This collection of seven stories includes, among others, "The Wonderful Story of Henry Sugar" in which a man uses for good his ability to see through playing cards; "The Boy Who Talked with Animals," in which a little boy saves a giant sea turtle; and "Lucky Break," the story of how Dahl became a writer. The stories are fairly long and complicated and therefore could be used for a more extensive study of short stories.

Grades: Sixth through eighth
Caution: Bullying, Mild violence

Any Collection of Short Stories **by Edgar Allan Poe**

Edgar Allan Poe's short stories are both fascinating and terrifying. Try using one of his stories as an introduction to a short story unit—students become more excited about participating in the unit when they know how interesting short stories can be. Good choices are "The Cask of Amontillado" and "The Tell-Tale Heart." Poe's stories work well for studies of plot development, characterization, and symbolism.

Grades: Seventh through eighth
Caution: Violence, Disturbing images

5

CHECKING OUT A TWENTIETH-CENTURY NOVEL

In Robert Peck's award-winning young adult novel, a young boy queries his father:

"Fences are funny, aren't they, Papa?"

"How so?"

"Well, you be friends with Mr. Tanner. Neighbors and all. But we keep this fence up like it was war. I guess that humans are the only things on earth that take everything they own and fence it off."

"I never looked at it that way."

"Time you did."[1]

In this twentieth-century novel, father and son discuss how human beings create "fences," including physical and social walls between ethnic groups, generations, and individuals. It is likely that your middle school students are noticing such fences and are beginning to learn about those who live across the fences in their own lives. They are probably asking questions about gender, race, ethnicity, language, social class, disability, age, and religion.[2] Peck's moving novel offers a peek into the world of a twelve-year-old boy who wonders about the real value of socially constructed fences, some of which he wants to tear down, others that he comes to understand, if not accept. This chapter offers ideas for teaching this novel by Peck in ways that you can adapt to the twentieth-century novel you get to teach to your class.

For adolescents, peeking across the fence into the adult world can be like a trip to another culture. This boy's father, Vermont farmer Haven Peck, makes ends meet in the late 1920s by slaughtering pigs for others to eat. Why does the elder Peck earn a living that way? Do people really have to kill and eat pigs? Peck's son has to come to terms with adult reality.

Modern novels like Peck's help students discover other contemporary people and cultures. It can be frightening and confusing for adolescents to traverse childhood fences. But reading about life beyond one's fences can also be fun, engaging, and relevant to students' lives. They get to learn about both social differences and universal human experiences, and sometimes see ways to address issues they face as young adults.

As a middle school teacher, you have the honor of and the responsibility for guiding students across fences into the stories about other persons and places, helping them to engage various literary forms and themes depicting other cultures. You can inspire students to learn how to interpret, understand, and respond critically to modern literature in the context of their own multimedia lives.

This chapter explains how you can teach a modern novel for twenty-first-century literacies by delving with your students "into, through, and beyond"[3] a novel. What follows also explains how to apply these strategies to any novel—classical as well as contemporary—in ways that are appropriate for your community. In fact, each subsequent chapter builds on the previous one and discusses different strategies that you can add to your list of teaching options.

The California Reading and Literature Project recommends planning lessons to help students get "into, through, and beyond" the literature. Specifically:

Get into the novel by

- Encouraging students to make initial predictions
- Providing background information
- Identifying text-related vocabulary

Work through the novel by

- Reading aloud to the students
- Having students read aloud and silently during class
- Challenging students through active reading
- Directing students to write about the work
- Connecting the book to students' lives
- Fostering class discussion with student- and teacher-generated questions

Move beyond the novel by

- Assessing student comprehension with performance and/or product options
- Assigning projects and essays
- Getting students involved in research about the novel and its culture(s)
- Inspiring students to read more[4]

As you read you can equip yourself to teach ways that contemporary authors employ the essential elements of fiction. Here are concrete examples from Peck's novel to demonstrate how you can teach even reluctant readers the skills and literacies that they need in order to flourish in today's multicultural, multimedia societies.[5]

PREPLANNING THE UNIT

To ease your anxiety if you are teaching a novel for the first time, estimate how much class time you need to spend on the novel. Consider the following:

- Your school's homework guidelines and curricular goals
- The language arts standards of your course
- The interests, skills, and needs of your students, perhaps as reported by teachers who have had the students in English the previous year

Estimate how many pages of fiction your students can handle per day. Then plan a realistic reading schedule before launching the unit.

Record It! Video Journaling

If students are already interested and motivated, you might want to allow groups of two to three students to make video recordings of their written journals. You can ask them to write one journal entry as a group, collaborating on the content, but then delegating responsibilities for (1) final drafting for reading on camera, (2) operating the camera, and (3) editing out any retakes. Using most digital cameras, they can record video in a compressed format and burn the video to a CD/DVD or upload it to a school computer server. In some cases you might allow them to post their video journals to a school server or public site like YouTube, but only after making sure that they will not identify themselves personally on the recordings or in the accompanying text captions.

The following three tips will help them to create a more professional video journal:

- Hold the camera steady to avoid jerky movements.
- Shoot images that capture the subject from about midchest to the top of the head (the more personal, engaging image size that most TV news shows use).
- Speak from an outline on large cue cards placed close to the camera rather than read from a manuscript without appearing to make eye contact with the audience.

The ideal length for these video journal entries is about forty-five to sixty seconds. Ask students to include copies of the video script outlines in their journals.

For assessment, remind your budding video producers that video journals should display neatness, clear images, good visual grammar, editing that enables the viewer-listener to follow along, and correct pronunciation and spelling in print journals.

Remember that covering a novel is not the same thing as teaching it. Until students can understand and engage a text, you are not ready to continue. Even with a modern text, moving too quickly leads to superficial student understandings. On the other hand, moving too slowly results in missed opportunities for greater textual engagement. So determine students' critical abilities, monitor their progress, and make appropriate scheduling and pedagogical adjustments as you go.

You can help them read more deeply, critically, and efficiently as you remind them of and teach them a range of strategies to increase their reading comprehension. Depending on where they attended elementary school, your students may be familiar with some of these ideas. But, because adolescents seem to have a more positive attitude toward more recently written literature, it often is better to teach and add to these approaches for reading literature while working with a modern novel rather than with a more challenging classic novel or complex poetry.

GETTING INTO THE NOVEL

A great place to begin a unit on the novel is by having students to create a "novels" section in their written journals, and then to create subsections for the novels that you assign throughout the year. Their journal is a personal place for them to write their own reading summaries, responses, reflections, vocabulary study, diagrams, and drawings along with questions similar to those mentioned in chapter 2 on teaching the short story.

Playing Online Audio and Video Files

If quality readings of the opening of the novel are available online you might want to play one of them in class. YouTube and other video-posting websites sometimes include acceptable fan readings. These can be downloaded or played directly from the Internet in class. Avoid performance video clips that might frame the novel visually for students before they have developed their own mental pictures of characters and settings. Chances are you'll have one or two tech-savvy students who can find recordings, download them, and bring them to you for previewing.

Begin teaching journaling with open questions designed to get the students thinking and to familiarize them with this longer form of fiction. Questions might include: Do you recall a novel that grabbed you from the first sentence? How would you define a *novel*? Other than length, how do you think a novel is different from a short story or a movie? Try to create an open, exciting experience for students while avoiding any questions that would make your reluctant readers feel ill at ease.

Your opening attitude sets the tone for the class. If they know that you enjoy fiction they are more likely to read it expectantly. Of course, you want to allot time for them to read novels they choose themselves. Several titles to consider appear at the end this chapter.

Your young teens do not enjoy a book very much if they do not understand the cultural context, time period, unusual references, and difficult vocabulary. So, before you assign them to read too far in the novel, spark their critical interest in the story and give them some helpful tools to begin enjoying and discussing the text right away.

Sparking Critical Interest in the Story

You can ignite interest in the novel and elicit visual interpretation by having students do something as simple as examining the cover art of a paperback or the art included with the story in your class anthology. Give the students two or three minutes to examine that art or print individually or in small groups. Then ask them to predict and answer the following kinds of questions in their journals:

1. Based on the graphic art, what do you imagine this book is about? If there is a synopsis on the cover or first page, you might need to modify this question.
2. What have you already heard about this book—and does that word of mouth fit with your view of the artwork?
3. What do you know about the topic/setting of the book? For example, for *A Day No Pigs Would Die*, "What do you know about raising pigs, the state of Vermont, or about the origin of baseball?"

No cover illustration? First check Amazon.com or the publisher's website to see if you can find cover images for past paperback or hardcover editions. Even without a cover image, it's worth discussing the book design graphics. In this case, ask "Why do you think the publishers chose certain fonts, font sizes, colors, or word placements? What is the name of the font(s)? Why are there no graphics—photos, drawings, and so on?" Also talk about the publisher or reviewer comments—those promotions designed to convince the reader ahead of time what to think about a book. Where else do you hear or read comments about the arts (e.g., movie trailers and newspaper or Web ads for movies).

These metatextual strategies—ways of talking about how texts communicate—create curiosity about the novel. They also encourage the groups of students to own their own learning, since it is clear that they can learn from one another as well as from you. Students soon discover that it is educationally good to formulate and to express opinions (reasonable interpretations and evaluations) of texts. Finally, students who think only classic writing should be analyzed soon learn that often modern texts are meant to be examined as well as enjoyed—and that criticism can lead to greater enjoyment.

Locating and displaying images of the time period and/or part of the country also creates intrigue. Picture books, encyclopedias, and the Internet are great sources for these images.

Using Student-Produced PowerPoint Slides to Facilitate Early Discussion

As you begin your discussion with students, write on the board one- or two-word summaries of their initial thoughts and feelings about the novel. Then encourage interested students to compose a simple PowerPoint slide(s) that contains one of these short summaries using font and background colors designed to match the meaning of the summary. They can add relevant highlighting or other features that help them explain their view of the novel. Fonts and colors can "speak" to readers even though these visual images are not as literarily precise as "word language." This kind of assignment teaches media grammar, too.

A student interested in drama might want to speak the word(s) interpretively as a looping sound track for each image. The student would try to say the word or phrase in a way that adds to the visual interpretation (combining oral and visual). For example, a student could contrast his or her oral interpretation with that of common text-reading software found today on most computers. Students rarely think about how computerized "reading" interprets language (such as computer-generated digital voice messages).

Finally, students doing multislide presentations (one word or phrase per slide) can add a sound track that relates to the novel's subject or characters. Google the topic "pig lyrics" for Peck's novel. PowerPoint's player function creates a short "motion picture" that sets a prereading benchmark for later review. If students enjoy seeing these PowerPoint presentations in class, consider showing them again at the end of the unit to discuss initial versus later impressions of the novel.

PROVIDING BACKGROUND INFORMATION

While it is important to provide some background for the novel, initially it is good to let the text speak for itself. Give the students only the information that they need to understand the beginning of the story. Then, as the story unfolds, supply additional information. Even if you have to do a lot of research yourself to prepare to teach an unfamiliar book, remember not to inundate the students with all of your newly acquired knowledge. It can overshadow, even bury the book.

A host of textbooks, websites, academic books, and colleagues can help inform your own understanding of the text, but during class, dis-

Figure 5.1.   Piggy

pense, rather than dump, this newfound knowledge on a need-to-know basis. First, focus on the basic aspects of the time and place that the students need to know in order to figure out the plot, setting, and characters. Carefully selected, engaging books speak for themselves.

DECIDING WHAT VOCABULARY

Vocabulary study is a topic to consider pedagogically before and during students' reading. For example, if you did not grow up on a farm, you may lack experience of the smells and sounds needed for teaching Peck's novel set in rural Vermont. The same may be true for your students. Whichever modern novel you use for class, be sure to introduce the students to the cultural language of the text; identify the specific vocabulary that students might not know and determine how best to provide definitions or elicit definitions from them. It is perfectly fine for you to give students definitions of words unique to the book. Vocabulary they need to add to their speaking and writing vocabulary can be handled differently.

Also consider having students create their own lists of new words as they read. They should write these in their journals and indicate the page number for each word or phrase. Then you can pull twenty or twenty-five words common to their lists, supply definitions, and discuss a few of them in the context of the novel. You can also ask the students to use dictionaries or other online resources to write their own one-sentence definitions that fit the context of their reading. It is not useful to have students learn all the definitions of every vocabulary word on the list. Focus instead on the word meanings that help them understand this particular piece of literature.

WORKING THROUGH THE NOVEL

Reading to Students

Adolescents, like many adults, enjoy hearing good reading. Think about how often you and your peers purchase or borrow books on tape. So is not surprising that one appealing way to begin teaching a novel is to read portions aloud to them. This gives struggling readers a chance to learn by listening and following along. It helps English language learners, partly because it connects the sound of the language to the printed words.

Since some international students' first language uses a non-English-style alphabet, they might need practice in associating sounds with the written English letters as they work to improve just their basic reading literacy. Hearing the words as they watch the text is another way to increase this association and expand their comprehension.

Try connecting early on with students' multiple intelligences by assigning different activities for them to do while listening in class. They might sketch in their journals what is happening in the story. Or mold with clay. Or jot notes in a chart with story events. Many multitasking students prefer to listen to music while studying. Since there is no right way to read, as long as students are following and comprehending the text, engage nonaural learners with appropriate ways to formulate and express textual interpretations. Consider playing instrumental music during silent reading time. Music played in a rhythm that matches the beat of the heart at rest calms listeners and helps them to focus.

Fortunately, many novels are now available in audio formats. People of all ages listen to voice recordings while computing, commuting, exercising, and when patronizing libraries. The latter is rather ironic since until about the fourth century CE, all reading, even in libraries, was out loud.[6] Recordings of some books are available online and from reading-for-the-blind programs.

Silent Reading

Although reading aloud to students is good pedagogy, students also need to be able to learn by reading silently. You can help students to stay on schedule by providing in-class reading periods. This helps to eliminate the frustration for students unable to participate in class discussions simply because they are behind on reading. Consider writing a prompt or question on the board before students arrive. Then ask them to use the first five or ten minutes of class to peruse their reading to find text evidence in the story to support their answer or just to catch up on the reading. Walk around the room and peek at what they are writing.

As they write and you circulate among them, taking attendance, also stopping near individuals, you can add to your notes indications of student engagement in the task. Journaling in this simple writing activity focuses students on the day's topic while you complete record keeping. Observing their responses and watching them read also can help you identify students with potential difficulties. Pay attention to how long it takes individuals to complete a page of reading. If you have concerns and do not yet have the expertise to address them yourself, seek the assistance of a reading specialist or the advice of the department chair or a colleague.

Student Reading to the Class and in Pairs or Groups

Occasionally, give students the chance to read aloud with the whole class, in small groups, or to a partner. Students who dislike reading aloud particularly may need to practice in a nonthreatening setting. You can invite such students to read aloud short passages of their choosing just to you; this helps you track their progress and gives you a chance to encourage them personally. Remind students that public speaking skills are important for careers and reading aloud can help them practice their articulation—clear pronunciation of words. Students work harder at it if they know that reading aloud is a significant step toward occupational success.

Of course you have the hams, too. Many of your young teens just love to play parts from the novel and the dialogue in the text often provides exceptional ways for students to gain insight into the personalities of the characters in the novel. Some students even come to class begging to read a particular part. Encourage it, but also be sure to promote fairness by giving all interested students a turn reading aloud dialogue from the most popular characters. Assume the role of narrator if you want to ensure that the reading stays on track.

Reading Actively

It is essential for students' future education that they become critical readers. Students know that people read novels for fun, but they might not realize that adults also read much fiction simply to enrich their lives. In short, middle school students can begin to actively read, view, and listen to texts to deepen their understanding of different cultures as well as the human condition. Students benefit when they learn that active reading requires careful attention to the text, regardless of the medium—print, aural, or electronic.

One essential skill in active reading is recognizing how subparts of a larger text relate to one another. These text structures, sometimes called rhetorical structures, include descriptive, sequential, enumerative, cause-effect, problem-solution, and compare-contrast relationships within a text. Middle school students may recognize some of these structures in expository nonfiction works.

Students even employ these techniques in their own texting and blogging without realizing it. You may be surprised by the number of them who employ such narrative skills by participating in online fan discussion groups or fan fiction websites where fans publish their own stories based on the characters and settings established by print authors or TV/movie producers. Yet students do not necessarily recognize the use of these techniques in fiction even if they watch many movies or voraciously read young adult stories. Most students do not see how these structures "work" in fiction. That is one of your jobs as their teacher.

Learning to Use Text Structure

If text structures are not defined or explained in your anthology, several websites include definitions and minilessons to help you get started. Most suggest that teachers

- Introduce the idea that expository texts have a text structure.
- Introduce common text structures.
- Show examples of paragraphs that correspond to each text structure.
- Examine topic sentences that clue the reader to a specific structure.
- Model the writing of a paragraph that uses a specific structure.
- Have students try writing paragraphs that follow a structure.
- For students who are proficient with paragraph organization, do the last three steps (above) with longer chunks of text or entire chapters.[7]

Box 5.1.   Shoot It!
Capturing Vocabulary Meaning in Digital Photos

One way of encouraging visual as well as linguistic literacy is asking students to draw vocabulary-related pictures. Today students can take digital photos that interpret the literal or figurative meanings of words. Just ask them to draw a picture or take a photograph of a still scene (not video) that depicts the word's meaning. Sharing these pictures with a partner, in triads, or in small groups can reinforce their understandings of new terms. Some students may already know this strategy as "vocabulary squares."

Today photos and drawings can easily be scanned on many printers and integrated into PowerPoint presentations or posted on a class website; the drawings can be stored from year to year and later integrated into presentations by you or enterprising students.[8]

When students read fiction they enter into a story created by the author. They let the author transport them into a projected, imaginary world that shapes readers' views of the text's subject.[9] In order to accomplish this world-projecting storytelling, author's structure reveals

- Relationships among characters
- Characters' motives
- Causal relationships between characters' thoughts and actions

Because of these author-created structures—along with readers' own real-life relationships—students quickly "learn to form expectations about a [fictional] text."[10] (See box 5.1.)

Tracking Character Development

Students wonder why characters think and act in particular ways. As they read, students speculate about why particular events led to other events—like the age-old conundrums about why bad things happen to good people. Students begin mentally asking the same kinds of questions about fiction that they are starting to ask about life.

And, middle school language arts teachers can help them "to decide which strategies [or "techniques"] they should use to comprehend, interpret, and evaluate what they are reading."[11] As they learn to identify and examine the impact of intratext structures in their own reading, students engage the story as if conversing with the author and the characters.

Encourage students to write questions in their journals as they arise in their reading. Then, when each question is answered, record that, too. Include the page number(s) so they can refer to them during classroom discussion and when writing about their experience reading the novel. This personal and sometimes communal dialogue in class discussion about the text is the nature of all literacies, regardless of the medium.

So how do students move from the novel itself toward a more critical dialogue with it? The conversation has to start somewhere, but your students probably have not practiced taking notes when they see a movie, play a YouTube video, listen to an audiobook, or read fiction. Therefore, a reader-response journal can effectively initiate their personal dialogue with a text.

In this type of journal, students

- Transcribe or copy important passages
- Record their own questions about the text
- Write their responses to the text, such as *like, dislike, enjoy, wonder*
- Indicate important material for later study

Students also can journal in their textbooks with sticky notes so they do not have to recopy the text sections in their journals. Then they can copy those thoughts into their separate journal notebook while keeping the sticky notes for quick reference in their books. You might even offer them different color sticky notes to code story elements and log their reactions, especially their questions. Encourage students to visualize what is going on in the novel based on the author's direct and indirect statements. Propose that students use a specific color to note any passages that strike them as potentially effective video or audio scenes for

Symbols for Marking Text or Making Journal Notes

Consider using text-marking symbols to remind students of the kinds of things that they should be noting and responding to in the text. Here are some basic text-engaging symbols:

☺ = I understand; I knew that.

! = Wow! I didn't know that!

***= This is important. I should remember this.

☐ = New character is introduced (write name and words that identify the character, such as "George, 10 years old").

→ = Great visual image—I can picture it in my mind.

? = I don't understand. Ask about this.

Figure 5.2.   Mark Text

later recording. Drawing maps and pictures in their journals helps some students hold on to those visualizations. (See figure 5.2.)

HIGHLIGHTING ACADEMIC VOCABULARY

What about terms in the text that the students should be adding to their own speaking and writing vocabulary? What about words used in the novel that also appear in the reading and conversations your students have in other classes? And what about general academic vocabulary used primarily in school? You can help students learn the meanings of and connections among words by identifying such academic words on their vocabulary list and asking students themselves to find the definitions in print or online dictionaries. Invite students to list the definitions alphabetically on a class website or to post comparative definitions on a class wiki. The wiki itself then serves as a kind of study sheet that students can print out or download to their own computers. Many teachers find it productive to maintain a word wall to which they add new words throughout the school year. Seeing is believing. If students view the wall daily, they catch on that it is important to learn and use the words. The words that are specific to the text, though, are those for which you can provide definitions.

Reinforce the importance of students using new vocabulary words in their prose by offering extra credit for incorporating the terms in writing for other classes. For instance, ask students to show you graded assignments from other classes (such as social studies or science) in which they have incorporated vocabulary from your class, especially from the current novel. Sure, the other teachers may question the ways that your students use the vocabulary. But once the students explain that they are trying to expand their vocabulary, your colleagues are likely to support the students' work even if the vocabulary sticks out awkwardly like a sore thumb. You know the old adage, "If you don't use it, you lose it." Challenge your students to use their vocabulary regularly even if they are teased for their increased sophistication!

RELATING THROUGH PERSONAL CONNECTIONS

As mentioned earlier, textual literacy includes the ability to relate critically the fictional worlds to one's own life. These reader-to-self, reader-to-world, or reader-to-text relationships can work in two ways—as a mirror and as a window. As a mirror, novels depict familiar characters, settings, and situations. As a window, novels introduce students to unfamiliar people, places, and circumstances—including cultures, ethnicities, races, and geographies. As often as you can select novels that help to expand your students' understanding of themselves and of others, to see across and through fences.

Although the Internet usually brings together like-minded people to communicate about things they already have in common (social networking, for instance, tends to be more "intraculture" than cross-cultural), the Internet can also provide amazingly wide windows to cultures beyond students' existing life experience.[12]

USING WIKI SOFTWARE TO CREATE STUDENT-CONTRIBUTED VOCABULARY DEFINITIONS

A wiki (like wikipedia.com) is a website for developing user-contributed content, especially encyclopedic definitions. Free wiki software enables anyone to start an online wiki on any topic, and even to limit access to users with necessary passwords.

Best of all, language arts wikis provide a means for users to interact about words. Any approved user can add a new term, contribute a definition, edit or expand a definition, or even relate a definition to another word or text (such as a sentence or paragraph from the novel). Wikis save records of all changes so you can see who is contributing, what they are contributing, and whether or not you need to resubmit an entry that was mistakenly removed or incorrectly edited.

Public wikis, like Wikipedia, generate disputes over differing interpretations of the meaning of words. So be sure to set down some rules for civil engagement among students—like posting only positive contributions, respecting classmates' opinions, and thanking others for their helpful postings before critiquing their contributions.

The key to developing these diverse personal connections is helping students to recognize three things:

- First, a modern novelist's imaginative story is usually a mirror for some people even if it is not a mirror for others, such as your students.
- Second, students can discover that other people's mirrors can serve as windows for getting to know those who are different from themselves. Reading then serves as a form of hospitality like inviting neighborhood newcomers for dinner and conversation about mutual life stories.[13] Windows become venues for self-understanding as students begin to see similarities among those they read about and those with whom they live.

- Third, stories about others enable students to see what all human beings have in common, across their cultural fences. Novels express not only cultural particularities of time and place, but also common aspects of the human condition, such as fear and loneliness, joy and delight. For instance, each adolescent in every culture must eventually come of age; the process is universal even though it takes different cultural forms. Fictional windows can help students to understand simultaneously themselves, their communities, other persons, and other communities.

Often students need encouragement and role modeling to learn how to connect personally with fictional texts. Please do not hesitate to identify appropriate personal connections that you notice between the text and your own life or hesitate to encourage students to do the same. One way to inspire students to pay attention to such connections is to ask them to write personal responses to the literature they read and then to discuss those responses with their families, friends, or classmates.

HONORING STUDENT PRIVACY

Ask students to journal about their personal connections with the world of the novel; such journaling promotes discussion because students articulate in writing thoughts they can then paraphrase out loud. Just remember that some students are reticent about reading or discussing their reflections with the entire class. Respect their privacy and you can gain their trust and motivate them to read deeply and write honestly.

Consider giving students the option in class of folding down the page in their written journals if they do not want you to read their reflections. If you provide that option, keep your promise. But do inform them. If anything they write and leave open for you to read makes you believe they are in danger, to themselves or others, you are bound by law to report it to authorities.

Also warn students about posting personal information online, since privacy is a major issue in the information age. One of the reasons that social networking websites such as Facebook are so popular is that students can regulate who they allow to access their postings by approving who their "friends" are—those who can access their website.

Privacy and tact are important literary issues; openness and honesty are important to building trust in the classroom. So write in your own journal frequently, right along with your students. Doing so not only models this kind of writing but also reminds you of what it is like to reveal text-to-self connections with others. Share with your students some of the experiences you have had with your parents, siblings, and friends—and also that there are some experiences you would not, and they should not, write about online. If you respect students' privacy, they are more likely to share their journals with you—and they learn that responding to readings should be an ethical as well as an academic practice. In other words, invite, rather than insist that they share or show what they write to others.

Inspiring Class Discussion

English teachers often approach the study of a novel by giving students a list of chapter discussion questions. This can effectively ease students into the book and demonstrate the types of questions and ideas that they should be considering. But you foster better, more engaging discussions if you let students come up with their own thoughtful, life-connected, and text-connected questions.

Regardless of how you settle on the questions, try a variety of discussion group formats—pairs, small groups, and the entire class. Some students are more inclined to read their journal entries and discuss personal responses to the text if they are in smaller groups. Still, middle school students like to push the envelope, test the boundaries, and interject topics that are on the edge—just for fun or attention—so it is important to circulate among them as they read and talk about their writing. If a student offers an inappropriate remark, a moment's eye contact, a subtle head shake, or a quiet admonition from you should be enough to refocus the discussion.

Think about setting up literature circles for a few chapters in the novel your class is studying. For this approach to reading and discussing literature, you create small groups of five or six students and assign or let them draw names or numbers to perform certain tasks. These responsibilities may include

- Making connections between what the class has read already and the novel they currently are reading
- Pointing out ways words on the vocabulary list are being used
- Selecting a particularly interesting, humorous, or thought-provoking passage to read aloud to the members of the group
- Drawing a picture of a scene that is crucial to the plot or understanding of a particular character
- Bringing in a prop that illustrates an incident or symbolizes a character
- Keeping time to ensure that the group completes the tasks in the allotted time

The tasks can vary depending on the novel you have chosen. See the Internet for numerous configurations of literature circle and roles based on the work of Harvey Daniels.

TESTING THOUGHTS ON THEME

While studying a novel, students can examine further concepts of theme—the overall message(s) of a text, or what the text is trying to say about a topic. The concept of literature itself is sometimes defined by a work's universal themes about human nature and the human condition as well as by its aesthetic qualities. Themes, though, generally are statements about topics, not just the topics themselves; themes require a verb to indicate the author's viewpoint. "Life is grand" is a theme; "Life" is a subject but not a theme. "Fences make good neighbors" is a theme; "fences" is simply a subject.

Your students may have been introduced to this kind of thinking about literature in elementary school and are already familiar with a graphic organizer, an S.W.B.S.T. chart, on which they record what Somebody Wanted, But, So, and Then, to reflect the main characters, the conflict, the attempts to solve it, and then, the resolution. Using this

S.W.B.S.T. chart may be a good place to start and then move on to the sentence statements.

After you have explained to students the concept of universal theme, let them try to discern what may or may not be a universal theme expressed through the novel. Encourage students to experiment with theme statements in their own reading and journaling. What is the story saying to them? Also ask them to test or verify their ideas about themes with specific, supporting examples from the beginning, middle, and end of the novel. Students soon notice that most novels have at least two or three overarching ideas that can be summarized in thematic statements that capture most individual responses to the text.

Instructions for In-class Writing about a Novel

Develop three questions about the story, then ask students to answer one using specific references and selected quotations from five of the seven chapters read so far and smoothly incorporating those illustrative facts and words into their writing. Encourage answering the question in a thesis statement, then writing two or three paragraphs to make a hearty P.I.E. with lots of rich, meaty filling, and concluding with a summary or reflection on what they write in the body.

- P= Point—state your point or position in response to the prompt.
- I = Illustration—support your point with two or three direct references to the story. One of these can be a short quotation. "For example, . . ." (Give the page number in parenthesis following the reference or quotation.)
- E = Explain the connection between your illustrations and your point. "This shows . . ."

Figure 5.3.　Pie

One of the themes in *A Day No Pigs Would Die*, for example, is that something may die in order for something else to live. When searching the novel, students find these examples: a cow nearly dies birthing the twin calves; a crow sups on the frog; and the narrator's family eats animals they slaughter for food. Ultimately, Rob, the main character, suffers the death of his father and has to assist his mother with farm tasks, including killing his own pig so the family can have food to eat. A few students become so enamored of Rob's pet, Piggy, that they convert and become vegans—at least while studying the novel. Of course even as vegans they have to consume formerly living things. All life depends on other life.

Preparing to Assess for Understanding

Test-taking skills are important for students to learn, especially as they prepare for high school. You can serve your young people well by reviewing test-taking skills. Then format a test in a student-friendly way; your young teens not only appreciate less-stressful testing but also perform better on tests they understand. Design a "Prepare for the Test" handout that includes the test format and suggestions on how to study for each kind of question.

For example, if you plan to test their understanding of vocabulary from the book, tell them whether they need to know definitions, synonyms, antonyms, or how to use the words in a sentence. Or, if you have had students copy select passages from the book in their reading journals, you should be able to test successfully for quotations simply by reminding students to study the text material in their journals.

If you have test questions that require answers written in a complete paragraph or short essay, remind students in advance to review the structure of each one. A test prep handout can also include the number of points allotted for each section of the test. Such information saves time and angst. Students do not have to use valuable test time trying to figure out the format of the exam or how best to allot their time. On the test review day, remind students to spend the most time studying for the sections with the highest value.

RETURNING AND LEARNING FROM TESTS

Because students in middle school still are learning how to take tests and how to learn from the kinds of mistakes they make, allot a full class meeting to go over tests when you return them. On those days, also ask students to come with their self-selected reading books. If you finish your test analysis early, the students can begin or continue reading on their own in preparation of the next quarter book report. This independent reading time can be a handy time to meet privately with the few students who may have done more poorly on the assessment than you or they expected. Often it is a minor issue that caused a major loss of points.

What kinds of topics should you cover during test analysis? First, ask the students to determine the kinds of errors they've made. Did they make errors because of

- Misreading the question or prompt
- Running out of time
- Misunderstanding a concept, term, or instruction
- Studying the wrong material
- Failing to respond to the question
- Missing clues to answers in the prompt or stem of multiple choice question
- Other

Once the students determine the kinds of errors they have made, talk about ways to avoid them on the next test. Usually, the youngsters calm down when they learn that correcting one problem before the next test can help them miss fewer points the next time.

ANALYZING TESTS CAN LEAD TO STUDENT CONFIDENCE

You may want to spend time talking about ways students can develop the confidence that they are answering the questions correctly. One way is to have the students underline the verb that tells them what to do and put a rectangle around the direct object—the noun indicating what they should be looking for or working on. If they cannot write on the test/ quiz, you may ask the students to write those key words on their answer sheet. Taking a few minutes to do something physical helps the test takers to focus on what is being asked of them.

If there had been vocabulary on the test or quiz, you can look at the clues in the sentences that could have helped the students know when they had chosen the correct response. For example, some sentences may have a synonym, an antonym, or a definition in the prompt question. As students learn to look for such clues, they are more likely to recognize the correct answers.

One of your additional tasks as a teacher is to help students develop better reading strategies and more efficient test-taking skills. Taking the time to do this immediately after administering the first few tests/quizzes is sure to reap positive benefits for both students and teacher. You are happier when students do well on your assessments. You also want to learn whether the assessments you plan actually reveal what you have taught. If, during your analyses with the students, you discover they are missing questions you were sure they would be able to handle easily, you may find it necessary to revise your questions or rework the layout of the tests/quizzes you administer.

It also is important to develop tests that ask the students to show what they know in a variety of formats—multiple choice, matching, true/false, paragraph writing, or short essay. This can be done incrementally. Early in the school year, design tests that include such a variety and with questions requiring factual information in the first couple of sections, and then follow with prompts for short answer responses. Those "fact questions" trigger the students' memories, and by the time they get to the sections that require longer answers requiring them to show ability to interpret and connect the facts to other literature or life, the students usually feel confident they can handle this higher level thinking. Depending on the skills development of the students in a particular year, you can reserve fact questions on tests for interim quizzes, and focus on test questions that require full sentence, paragraph, or essay responses.

ASSIGNING PROJECTS AND ESSAYS

As you do when planning each assignment, determine what you need to know about student understanding and design product or performance assessments through which students can demonstrate that knowledge. Plan a wide variety of projects for assessing students via multiple intelligences. Let a musically inclined student write a song about the book or choose songs that appropriately reflect certain characters. Let an aspiring filmmaker produce a scene of an incident from the book.

Identify writing projects that students enjoy, especially those that tie the novel to their lives. A photographer could bring in photos of real places or staged scenes that reflect the setting or themes. A pair of drama buffs could create and perform a short reading of a key scene using simple props or wearing simple costumes. Include a brief writing or speaking component in which students must refer to a passage in the text that influenced their decisions as they worked on their project. This should suffice to demonstrate comprehension at a pretty deep level.

Below are some creative writing projects adaptable to most classes and schools. The caution when assigning differentiated assessments is to monitor how much time each project is taking and to make adjustments so that students can complete your assignments without impinging on the homework time required for other courses. Your colleagues appreciate your thoughtful consideration of them and the work they are doing with the students you share.

Constructing Found Poems

Invite students to write a found poem, using specific words and phrases they find in the book and arrange these words and phrases in a found, but original poem.[14] Students reading *A Day No Pigs Would Die* identify with the boy's physical and emotional growth. They see that he is addressing the same kinds of social fences and facing the same types of adult responsibilities that all adolescents must face. When your students finish reading and begin discussing the entire book, ask them to capture these themes in a poem using exact words and phrases written by the author, Robert Peck. Found poems can also be fun to record in audio and video and play back to the class, using the principles discussed earlier for PowerPoint presentations.

One poetic variation for this novel is a "Piggy Poem." Students write a fourteen- to sixteen-line poem about *A Day No Pigs Would Die* that portrays incidents, a memorable scene, or a favorite character. They may choose a specific poetic format, one that is structured or unstructured, traditional or new. Your early adolescents may enjoy writing

acrostics
lyric poems
limericks
sonnets
free or blank verse poems, or
shape poems.

For these kinds of poems, evaluate the quality based on linguistic precision—vivid and concrete verbs; original figurative language—hyperbole, metaphors, similes, symbols, and so on; and of course, factual accuracy with the novel. Seventh-grader Kristen seemed to be taken by the idea that although the boy, Rob, appears to be forced into becoming a man overnight, he has been practicing for that role for much of the story.

> Tomorrow he is going to be a man.
> Yesterday he was a boy.
> It is hard for him, but he can.
> He can't play anymore with a toy.
>
> This man's name is Rob.
> His father's name is Haven Peck.
> The father taught him not to sob.
> Haven did this slitting Pinky's neck.
>
> Pinky is a hog.
> But they found out she is a brood.
> We will kill her in the winter fog.
> Now she is going to be food.

It is Dad who died in May.
They were all sad.
Rob did the chores that day.
He couldn't just be a lad.
("Practice" by Kristen)

Cressy, stunned by the "D" Rob earned in English, chose that grade as the subject of her pantoum, a form of poetry described in the poetry chapter of this book (chapter 7). Cressy wrote in first-person point of view and imitated the style of dialect used in the book.

A "D" is the awful grade I had for English class.
I did not tell Mama.
Aunt Matty discovered my "D."
Aunt Matty was extremely displeased.

I did not tell Mama.
Mama soon found out, all because of Aunt Matty.
Aunt Matty was extremely displeased.
Aunt Matty was quite stunned.

Mama soon found out, all because of Aunt Matty.
Aunt Matty announced my "D" to the household.
Aunt Matty was quite stunned.
How could I, a smart boy named Robert Peck, get a "D"?

Aunt Matty announced my "D" to the household.
Aunt Matty discovered my "D."
How could I, a smart boy named Robert Peck, get a "D"?
A "D" is the awful grade I had for English class.
("D" by Cressy)

EXTENDING AND SUPPLEMENTING READING

Many educator websites provide online opportunities for students to expand their knowledge of topics addressed in the books used in language arts courses across North America. Cyberguides, for instance, are "supplementary, standards-based, web-delivered units of instruction centered on core works of literature."[15] The cyberguide for *A Day No Pigs Would Die* includes links to information about Vermont history, the Shakers, baseball, and pig farming.[16] You can find a number of cyberguides and webquests for other popular young adult novels, maybe even the one you choose to teach to your students.

CONNECTING BEYOND THE CLASSROOM

You might want to ask students to share their poetic responses to the novel with other classrooms across the nation and around the world via the Internet. If you meet teachers from other schools, counties, or areas of the country, consider a joint project. For instance, a teacher from Florida and another from California set up a "Coast to Coast" project in which students wrote to each other about the poetry that both classes were studying. The instructors posted selected works by a poet from their own state and invited the students to discuss their responses online. The resulting conversation offered the students insightful peer perspectives while affirming that students on both coasts have to learn and apply the same kinds of analytical and evaluative skills.

Consider posting an invitation for other teachers to join your class in this type of assignment based on a commonly read novel. You may decide on other twentieth-century favorites like *The Skin I'm In* by Sharon Flake or *Among the Hidden* by Margaret Peterson Haddix. Use an education site like edublogs.org or launch your own on a social network like the education version of www.wetpaint.com that has no commercial ads, or use the National Council of Teachers of English site at www.ncte.org/community. Invite other teachers who may be teaching the same novel simultaneously. If you begin planning early you are sure to find other educators willing to coordinate assignments and due dates. Collaboration is invigorating for both students and teachers.

Grading Student Responses to a Novel

Encourage formal and informal student responses to the novel. Since informal writing is more personal, students should earn full credit just for demonstrating that they have read the selected material and responded responsibly to the prompt. Formal writing, on the other hand, calls for more precise literary analysis and is graded for form and accuracy as well as content. Cressy's journal essay (Journal Entry #1) was a five W's and H summary (the journalistic who, what, where, why, when, and how) based on seven to ten verbs that describe the plot. She wrote this entry after two months of studying the elements of fiction and reading a number of short stories for which students were writing this kind of summary.

Journal Entry #1—by Cressy

> Robert cut school because he was made fun of. He found a cow who was in labor and having a calf. He is in Vermont, and 12 years old. He desperately tries to help the cow, because she is in pain and when the cow chokes, he reaches down her throat and pulls out the "goiter." She bites his arm and pulls him all around. His arm was gnawed and flesh was missing. He gets stitches and after being in bed for about a week, he goes to help his pa. Their neighbor that owns the cow thanks Robert for helping her, and given him a pig! Robert is excited. His dad informs him of the care it take to own a pig. Then they talk some more.

About a week after beginning a novel, once students have closely read and discussed exposition, your students should be ready to write personal responses, normally by answering what and why questions. Reading their personal responses helps you to learn which parts of the story interest students as well as whether students are missing important details that would then need to be addressed in class. You also learn more about the students as people—which can help with planning subsequent lessons to better meet learners' academic needs and accommodate their varied interests.

To prepare the students to write analytically, ask them to write journal entries in which they focus their attention on the elements of fiction or literary devices. Kristen chose to write about symbols and similes. She understood the former but not the latter device. Her incomplete Journal Entry #2 did not include an explanation of why each of her quotations is a symbol or a simile. Thankfully, seeing her entry before the test revealed that she needed help identifying the ways that authors use symbols and similes. After she and others had reviews in class, Kristen handled these kinds of questions well on the test.

Journal Entry #2—by Kristen

Peck uses symbols as similes. On page number 104, it says, "And during fair week, I guest it's like a big brass band that can't stop playing." Another time he uses a symbol is still on page 104. It says, "Just like a mouth I know that's got blackberry all over it." These are both symbols in the book.

Warren rambled in Journal Entry #3. But his entry revealed which incidents caught his attention and which ones needed clarification. Sometimes students ask questions in class; other times questions arise only in students' writing.

Journal Entry #3—by Warren

One of the things about this book is that it will start out with a conflict, then tell why that conflict arose. For instance, in the end of this section of the . . . There is a man that goes and digs up his daughter from her grave. I didn't really understand the whole conflict of why he couldn't dig her up. Oh, also we now have proof that Robert is a Shaker because he goes to the meetings. I'm amazed that a pig would get to be as big as twelve year old boys. Because unless they get any bigger than that I probably wouldn't believe it was unless I saw it.

CONCLUSION

As you prepare your reading list for the school year, check to make sure you have a variety of topics and genres that provide mirrors and windows to ensure that your students are learning more about themselves and the world while they are meeting the content standards set by your school. Novels from in the twentieth century fit quite well into curriculum designed to be student friendly and academically vigorous. Adapting ideas from this chapter and using the Internet to locate background information for your chosen novel help to enrich your instruction and capture your students' hopes and fears in much the way Robert Peck does in his novel about Rob and his pet, Piggy.

With your careful attention to students' multimedia, multiple-intelligence learning, they soon see that well-told stories can transcend the fences that people put up around themselves and between their communities. Your students discover that modern fiction, like *A Day No Pigs Would Die* and other novels such as those listed below, can help all readers to erect humane gateways to shared understanding of the various experiences that separate and unify us human beings.

TWENTIETH-CENTURY NOVELS TO TEACH OR RECOMMEND TO STUDENTS

The City of Ember by Jeanne DuPrau

Lina and Doon are two young people living in the underground City of Ember. At twelve years old they not only receive their permanent job assignments but begin to realize that something is very wrong with their city. As city power and supplies rapidly run out, Lina and Doon race to find a way out of Ember. A great adventure story, *The City of Ember* includes themes of government corruption, doing what's right no matter the cost, patriotism, responsibility, and when it's appropriate not to follow the rules. This book is particularly appropriate for lessons on characterization and setting. Showing the movie version leads to an interesting compare and contrast activity.

Grades: Sixth through seventh

Caution: None

Ella Minnow Pea by Mark Dunn

This novel, written entirely as correspondence, takes place on the fictional island of Nollop. The island is named after Nevil Nollop, author of the phrase "The quick brown fox jumps over the lazy dog," the only phrase to contain every letter of the alphabet. When letters start falling from the memorial statue of Nevin Nollop the town council systematically banishes them. The loss of letters is reflected in the written communications of Ella, a girl living on the island, and her companions. As more citizens leave and more letters fall, Ella struggles to save the island by fulfilling the town council's challenge—come up with a new sentence that contains all of the letters of the alphabet. A subtle tale of totalitarianism, the true joy of the book comes from watching how the citizens of Nollop manage to correspond without various letters. *Ella Minnow Pea* just may inspire your students to love language.

Grades: Seventh through eighth

Caution: None

Holes by Louis Sachar

Louis Sachar's Newbery-winning book tells the story of Stanley Yelnats, who is wrongly accused of stealing and ends up at a boys detention center called Camp Green Lake. Forced to dig holes every day in order to "build character" Stanley at first believes that his predicament is just part of a family curse. But he and his new friend Zero soon get caught up in the true story of Camp Green Lake—a tale of racism, greed, and crime. Not only is *Holes* an attention-grabbing story, it also can prompt your students to discuss the worth of each person—even if they seem like a Zero. Disney produced a well-made movie version starring Shia LaBeouf.

Grades: Sixth through seventh

Caution: Racism, Verbal abuse

Hoot by Carl Hiaasen

Today's kids are bombarded with ideas about "green" living and how important it is to save the environment. In the midst of these sometimes overwhelming environmental issues, students and teachers may appreciate studying *Hoot* as a way to launch discussion and generate concrete solutions. The story follows thirteen-year-old Roy, once again the new kid in town, as he bands together with young environmentalist Mullet Fingers and tough girl Beatrice. Together they fight to save a family of miniature owls that are about to be displaced in order to make way for a pancake house. Hiassen does not talk down to his young readers, but rather employs the same satiric writing style that he uses in his well-known adult mystery novels. Any of Hiassen's other young adult novels, all environmental stories, would make an appropriate book study.

Grades: Sixth through eighth

Cautions: Some schools or parents may be offended by the representation of most of the book's adults as stupid. Truancy.

Joey Pigza Swallowed the Key (and sequels) by Jack Gantos

Jack Gantos's award-winning novels follow off-the-wall Joey Pigza as his zany behavior lands him in one laugh-out-loud predicament after another. Joey faces many challenges including learning to control his ADHD, living with his frazzled mother and nutty grandmother, and coming to terms with his well-meaning but mostly absent father. These books are perfect for a unit on voice and rich in topics such as the effects of divorce, what it means to be a "good" kid, figuring out who you are, and relating to people who are "different." The audiobooks are read by the author and are very entertaining.

Grades: Sixth through seventh

Caution: References to smoking and drinking

The Last Book in the Universe by Rodman Philbrick

Spaz lives in a future where Earth has been devastated by the "Big Shake," geographical regions are harshly governed by "latch bosses," and people are entertained by miniprobe needles shooting information right into their brains. Now a thief working for a latch boss, Spaz has been banished from his family unit by his stepfather who feared Spaz might harm his sister during one of his seizures. Now Spaz's sister is sick and he must travel through a dangerous world to get to her before she dies. He's accompanied by Ryter, an old man who still remembers literature and is determined to write "the last book in the universe." This book prompts many big questions about the future and whether or not one person can truly make a difference.

Grades: Sixth through eighth

Caution: Some violence and disturbing images, particularly Ryter's death at the end

Time Stops for No Mouse by Michael Hoeye

This self-published gem tells the story of a watchmaker mouse, Hermux Tantamoq, whose slow-paced, hardworking existence gets turned upside down when extraordinary aviatrix Linka Perflinger comes into his shop. Hermux is yanked into a mystery that involves a power-hungry cosmetics tycoon, a crazy plastic surgeon, and a possible key to eternal youth. Hoeye's biting humor examines the true meaning of beauty and the lengths that people (or mice) go to in order to stay young. Look for later editions of the book as the first edition was published in a very difficult to read font.

Grades: Seventh through eighth

Caution: Cartoonish violence

Uglies (and sequels) by Scott Westerfeld

Tally Youngblood lives in a future world where, at sixteen, all people are given an operation to make them beautiful. All Tally wants is to get the operation and start her new life as a Pretty. Instead she is forced to act as a spy when her new friend Shay runs away to find the Smokies—a group of rebels who have chosen not to have the operation. On her journey Tally must consider what it truly means to be beautiful. Westerfeld also addresses issues of population control, environmentalism, and government power. This book is perfect for older reluctant readers.

Grades: Seventh through eighth

Caution: Mild violence, Disturbing images

6

TEACHING CLASSICAL FICTION: WHERE THE GHOSTS OF THE PAST SPEAK TODAY

"Are you the spirit, sir, whose coming was foretold to me?"
"I am!"
"Who and what are you?"
"I am the Ghost of Christmas Past."
"Long past?"
"No. Your past. The things that you will see with me are shadows of the things that have been; they will have no consciousness of us."
Scrooge then made bold to inquire what business brought him there.
"Your welfare. Rise and walk with me."

—*A Christmas Carol*[1]

A ghost. Prophecy. Time travel—long before *Back to the Future*. Spooky! But also interesting, engaging, and moving. Just the kind of off-beat adventure that middle school students enjoy. Then again, middle school students are adults in the making. They have the capacity to dig deeper than the surface narrative. Like adults, young teens have experienced regret, guilt, and hope. How appropriate that these students should read the works of authors who molded their deepest fears and wonderings into timeless works of fiction. This chapter can help you get started looking back at the classics and helping your students see what these authors have to say to readers today.

Unfortunately, your students probably do not immediately see the value in the classics. Middle school students sometimes think, "If it's a classic, it must be old!" And, in adolescent logic, if it's old, how can it be good? It is your privilege as their language arts teacher to prepare your students to enjoy what may be their most challenging and rewarding reading experience of the school year. Charles Dickens's *A Christmas Carol* is a marvelous story to begin a classroom journey into the classics.

Of course no classic is culture-neutral. Consider using *A Christmas Carol* by Charles Dickens because of its universal themes, mindful of the distinctly religious symbols and overtones. Even if you choose other novels that have remained relevant over time, such as those by Alcott, Golding, L'Engle, Lowry, Orwell, and Twain, the ideas here will be useful to you.

Perhaps the one important reason for studying a classic is to show students that, although times change, people don't. Still, it takes a different kind of preparation to allay their apprehension and ease students into understanding and appreciating the classical novel. For one thing, the classical novel is usually set in a time and place completely unfamiliar to the students. Furthermore, it likely was written for an audience with different expectations of its writers.

MAKING THE CLASSIC ACCESSIBLE

Right away, make the novel accessible. Timing makes a difference. With *A Christmas Carol*, you could plan to begin the novel in December. Many television, movie, and theatrical performances of this well-known story run in the holiday period. So, why not capitalize on the time of year? The season provides a milieu for reading the text, especially for students whose family may not observe this particular holiday. Reading this particular classic may help them understand some of what they see and hear about those who celebrate it. Another attraction for this book is that the students are surprised that the real story is not "all that long" and that they can comfortably finish it in the three and a half weeks between Thanksgiving and Christmas or winter vacations.

You may decide on another way to bridge your students to the literature you decide to teach. You may find the classic you choose works better if you begin at another time of year and correlate it with the content of course work the students are studying in history or science. For example you may decide to teach the classical thriller *Dr. Jekyll and Mr. Hyde* when students are studying an aspect of genetics in science; *Call of the Wild, Johnny Tremain*, or *Across Five Aprils* when they study American history.

Another way to ease student concerns about studying a classical novel is to prepare a study packet. When students complete the packet on their own, they experience a sense of accomplishment; the packet also provides a sense of security. The study packet does not need to be collected or graded for anything other than completeness. It simply supplements your teaching and supports student learning. In addition to, or in lieu of, a journal, the packet becomes a repository for information to study for the quarter or semester exam. Some of the individual class activities that follow are the kinds that students do in a packet, such as vocabulary work or text-to-world connections—recording current news events that relate to issues raised in the classical novel you choose to teach.

Sample Study Questions for *A Christmas Carol*

As you read the story, mark the answers to the following questions. Then, in your own words, summarize what you've learned in your reading journal.

Stave One—"Marley's Ghost"

1. How has Dickens used direct and indirect characterization to reveal the personality of Ebenezer Scrooge? (Indicate page numbers to support your answers.)
2. Who is Marley? What part does he play in setting up the conflict of this story?
3. What is the weather like in this stave? How does it affect the setting and mood?

4. List seven to ten verbs to summarize the events in the plot in this stave.
5. What questions do you have about this stave? Ask them next class meeting.

Stave Two—"The First of the Three Spirits"

1. At what time does Scrooge awaken?
2. Draw a picture of the Ghost of Christmas Past. Include as many details as you notice. Use colors if available.
3. List the places Scrooge is taken by this Ghost. What do we learn about Scrooge?
4. Who uses a candle extinguisher in this stave? What does this character do with it? What does the candle extinguisher symbolize in this stave?
5. What questions do you have about this stave? Ask them next class meeting.

GETTING INTO THE NOVEL—CREATING THE MOOD

On the first day of the unit—after the students have made a classics section in their journals—lay out the context for the novel. In the case of *A Christmas Carol*, it is helpful to explain that in nineteenth-century London, families with leisure time depended on literature for entertainment. They had no radio, television, video, DVD, telephones, or computers. Readers during this period did not expect the story to end quickly so that they could get on to something else. This is how they relaxed after a day of school or work.

Those readers enjoyed imagining what the people and places in the books look and act like; consequently, the authors wrote numerous pages describing characters' physical appearance and relationships and establishing the setting in terms of time and place. Often these early novels would be read aloud by a family member sitting near a candle, lantern, or oil lamp while the rest of the family sat nearby. The listeners may even have closed their eyes and let the words of the author paint pictures in their minds. Clearly this was a different time. If you are teaching a fantasy novel, remind students of the different world the author may create.

Overview before Reading

After distributing the books, give the students a few moments to peruse them. Ask the students to examine any included graphics. As they begin reading, students may express disagreement with the choices the editors have made to depict characters or places. Their opinions are worth a discussion, so let it happen. It means they are paying attention.

To raise interest in verifying supposition, ask the students to write down five random page numbers, then turn to those pages and read a few sentences on each. You would be creating opportunities for organized randomness. Ask them to predict the significance of these randomly chosen sentences. Young teens enjoy guessing and rejoicing when they are right!

As the students flip through the pages, invite them to point out what they see that is familiar to them. In *A Christmas Carol*, some recognize the names of Scrooge, Marley, and Tiny Tim. Many have seen television versions of this story with humans, Muppets, or cartoon characters playing the parts. This probably gives students a false sense of security— they know the story. On the other hand, the fact that the story is familiar might entice students to read the "real" one for themselves.

Is there anything unusual about the structure of the novel you have chosen? There is in *A Christmas Carol*; it is not divided into chapters, but into staves. Staves are similar to the stanzas in traditional hymns or poems. Be sure to clarify formatting differences in the book you are teaching. Some classical novels may have considerably longer descriptive passages than students are accustomed to in more modern novels. Or, there may be no chapter divisions at all!

Starting the Book

From the first paragraph, build excitement about the book. Be creative. To help create the mood when you begin reading aloud from *A Christmas Carol*, you may dim the classroom lights and ask the students to imagine they are sitting in a room lit by an oil lamp and heated by a fireplace. If your classroom accommodates such an arrangement, pull your chair into a place where the students can sit on the floor around you. Read slowly and dramatically. Ask them to visualize the story—to let the author's words "paint a picture" on the canvas of their minds.

When you finish a particularly vivid passage, ask the students to draw what they "saw." Some students may recognize this as a "sketch to stretch" visualization strategy they learned in elementary school. Drawing what they visualize is a way of stretching their imagination. Sharing these quick sketches with partners expands the comprehension of both those drawing and those viewing. It is worth taking the time to get the students involved on the first day. If you can hook them at this point, they are likely to continue reading with understanding and pleasure.

Of course, to prepare for this dramatic reading, you must practice ahead of time reading the section aloud. And, select and read just enough to give the students a good sense of the story and yet raise curiosity enough to want to continue reading on their own. While there are professional recordings of many of the classical novels and you may decide to use excerpts from them another time; it is better for the students to hear you read well. So it is your voice they hear in their minds when they begin to read on their own, reminding them that you care enough about them to prepare and read so impressively the book the class studies together.

Classical texts like *A Christmas Carol* are generally available in dramatic audio readings. In fact, some classic film clips are available free online and can be played in class just as audio clips without using the video. Complete dramatic readings typically are available through online audio distributors such as iTunes.

Play a few audio clips of a classical novel for the students so they will be more intrigued about the story. Audio requires the students to begin imagining what the characters and settings look like without preset, preconceived visual images. Audio clips can also open up initial discussion about the text's setting as reflected in the linguistic codes such as grammar and dialect.

DECIDING VOCABULARY WORK

The vocabulary in classical novels is often difficult and merits direct study. To begin, select eight to ten words from the first section of the novel. Initially, do not get hung up on teaching the words—you are better served by getting into the story right away. For now, quickly give the definitions and move on. The point, of course, is for students to understand enough words to be drawn into the story.

Include a list of suggested vocabulary words in the study packet, along with page references, and encourage the students to refer to lists during various lessons. Draw attention to the words during particular lessons by posting them in the room, particularly words students should be adding to their speaking and writing vocabulary. Reading the words, copying them, seeing them daily, and being encouraged to use them in conversation and writing all are ways to reinforce learning.

On subsequent days, as you progress through the novel, you could have pairs of students look up words in the dictionary to find the definition that best fits word usage in the novel. Then have them copy this definition in their notebooks. For this type of vocabulary study there is no need to focus on other meanings of the word. Have volunteers read the definitions of the assigned words and urge students to make necessary corrections in their own notebooks.

ACCEPTING ADMIT SLIPS

This activity frees students to acknowledge (or admit) that reading this classical novel is a challenge and that the language and sentence structure are stumbling blocks for them. At the beginning of the next class period, ask each student to write three questions he or she has about section one of the novel you have assigned. They may use their books. While they are writing, you can circulate among the students to monitor who is up to date on the reading. Also notice how quickly or slowly students can find passages. This is a hint to whether the passage is familiar or new to them. You may need to adjust your day and give time for students to catch up on the reading.

Once the students write their questions, collect them and assign the next vocabulary exercise. This assignment could be a set of ten words you have chosen from the next reading assignment. As the students are working in pairs to complete the vocabulary assignment, you should read and organize the admit slips. These questions can form the basis for the discussion of this section, and make up the rest of your class time. The point is to help the students clarify details of the story so they can continue to comprehend what they read.

Selecting Vocabulary to Enhance Academic Learning

While reading a classical novel you may wish to highlight vocabulary words that are important for students to use in their own writing. As a guideline, check the Internet for a range of academic vocabulary lists with words that students need to know for academic reading.[2] You also can find graphic organizers for a variety of ways to have students study these new words. Consider asking them to pair words for different reasons: near synonyms, antonyms, same part of speech, etymology, reminds them of something, and so on. What color does this word sound like? Be patient. Be persistent. Learning vocabulary takes time. Make it fun, but not silly. Be imaginative.

Encourage the students to keep a list of words that challenge them and then, from these lists, assemble a list that the class can learn together. Later in this chapter is a writing assignment requiring students to incorporate some vocabulary words from the novel into a story the students write themselves. Regardless of how students create a vocabulary list, if they are encouraged to use the words in speaking and writing in school and out of school, they are more likely to remember them. You may recall the maxim that if you use a new word ten times in a day, it is yours for life. Challenge the students to test the adage. (See box 6.1.)

WORKING THROUGH THE NOVEL

One way to assure that your students are engaged in the novel is to help them grasp firmly the main characters, the setting, and the conflict or problem to be solved right from the beginning. Then you are ready to dig

---

Box 6.1. Podcast It!
Using Digital Recorders for Family "Readings"

If a student's family is reading the novel along with their son or daughter—or if you want to encourage such coreading during a term—consider asking the student to record a family member's oral reading of a selected passage. Many cell phones and music players such as iPods have recording functions that enable short, quality voice recordings that can be downloaded to a computer. Technology-oriented students enjoy the recording and editing (removing and replacing misreading requiring "take two," eliminating background noise, and sometimes adding soft music). Short recordings can be distributed online or via computer networks (podcasting) as well as played in class. Remind students to credit the author and to secure family permission.

---

into serious discussion about character motivation, writing style, use of literary devices, and development of theme. You want to spark thoughtful talk and insightful writing. In this section are examples of ways to increase interest and maintain momentum in classical literature.

Conducting P.I.E. Discussions

Using the questions the students write on the admit slips, conduct a discussion of section one of the novel. Read the more common questions first and ask the students to consult their texts to find answers to the questions. To keep the discussion focused on the author's words, remind them of P.I.E. responses, where the student states the point, illustrates with a reference to a specific incident or sentence from the text, and then explains how that information in the text answers the question. Or, you could distribute admit slips, set your timer for five to seven minutes, and ask pairs or triads of students to search text and be prepared to share answers with the class when the buzzer rings.

Do not be surprised if discussion on the first section takes two or three full class periods; the language and style may be more difficult for many of the students. It is worth a little extra time to clarify the basic elements of character, setting, conflict, and point of view presented in the

Box 6.2.   Play It!
Assisting Slow Readers with Audio Recordings

If any students are struggling on their own, allow them to read along with a recorded version of the book. Your local library probably offers recorded books. If you can't find what you need, record excerpts from the book yourself or ask strong readers from your class to record interesting passages. Some students love doing this kind of project.

exposition. However, be alert to the fact that spending too much time dilutes the power of the story. Students lose interest and resist reading anymore. It is always a balance for teachers. However, the more vigilant you are to what the students know and are able to do with this novel, the more likely you are to pace it just right.

For the most part, trust the power of the writing and read quickly, and then go back and discuss. You probably recall times in your education when a teacher or professor spent so much time analyzing the story that it lost its flavor and you had no desire to consume anymore of it on your own. You, of course, want to avoid this blandness in your own teaching.

Assign students to read section two. The number of pages you assign should be based on the complexity of the novel you choose and the pace of reading you know your students can handle. Be prepared for grumbling, but do not be discouraged if it takes the students three or four days to get into the rhythm of classical writing. Instead sustain your enthusiasm; you know the richness of the novel you have chosen to teach them. Need a boost? Now may be a good time to play an audio portion of the novel, or again read another passage aloud yourself. Hearing passages read aloud gives your reluctant students a voice in their minds as they read silently to themselves. (See box 6.2.)

DRAWING TO INTERPRET DESCRIPTIVE LANGUAGE

Followiing is an example of a descriptive writing assignment from *A Christmas Carol*, but you can adjust the details based on the book you and your students are reading. You need colored pencils, pens, or crayons.

Direct the students' attention to the visual images Dickens creates with his language—vivid verbs, concrete nouns, and humorous details. Ask the students to reread the description of the Spirit of Christmas Past, and then as accurately as they can, draw in their journals what they visualize. Circulate among students as they draw, but resist the temptation to comment. Encourage, but do not evaluate. Pay attention to those who go back and reread to find the details and to those who seem to retain the image and quickly begin to draw. Neither is cause for concern. Some may be confident about what they remember; others may not. Some may not have read and are trying to catch up right then and there. Either is fine. More will be ready for the next step.

After most of the students have completed the drawings, invite two or three of them to draw their pictures on the board or on large pieces of butcher paper. Because Dickens's descriptions are so detailed, the students notice lots of similarities in their drawings. To focus attention to the language and pattern of the writing, invite students to read aloud in class passages that appeal to them. This activity stokes their interest and the students become more attentive readers once they see how well they can interpret Dickens's descriptive writing. This version of the "sketch to stretch" activity expands and extends student comprehension of what they are reading. Their drawings also help you see what they see when they read. (See drawing of Scrooge in figure 6.1.)

Figure 6.1.   Scrooge

Enhancing Understanding with Summary Writing

To deepen their understanding and to create a record of key points from the book, teach your students to write brief summaries. You may choose to teach formal summary writing or simply have students track a sequence of events. Ask the students to list the places that the Spirit of Christmas Past takes Scrooge, or in other classical novels where the action moves from place to place. After students record the locations, they can summarize in a couple of sentences what they infer about the character, what they learn about the character's life, in this case Scrooge's, at each of these places. This unfolding information about character personality and attempts to solve problems naturally leads to conversations about some of the books' themes.

Moving on to Section Three

A narrative text is more powerful when it is not dragged out for too long. So when you sense that the students are relatively comfortable with the structure and style of the text, assign them to continue reading for homework or allot in-class time for reading. Continue to read quickly and then come back and discuss elements of style and the author's use of literary devices. Remember, you are working from a complete reading of the text. You can "see" things they will not notice until they have finished and reflect on the book as a whole.

Sheridan Blau suggests that teachers enjoy tackling difficult texts for their students.[3] He compares teachers' predigesting of literature for students to the mothers chewing food for babies rather than letting children chew for themselves. His point? Don't do that. Let your students masticate for meaning. As you teach your students to analyze the literature on their own, they begin to experience the flavor of language, the joy of reading, and the thrill of discovery you have been hording for yourself.

SETTING PACE FOR READING

During section three, follow the same lesson structure as section two. Draw an important scene, summarize the events, and discuss the section. Then introduce new vocabulary. Continue assigning reading for homework or for fifteen or twenty minutes during class time. There is no need to be reluctant about permitting such in-class reading. You instruct partly by the way you allocate time for classroom activities and skill building. If it is important for students to learn to read independently, you must allot some class time to model and to help them develop that skill.

In addition to modeling silent reading, you can carefully observe the students as they read. Pay attention to their reading pace. Notice who marks the texts, uses sticky notes, or writes notes in their journal, practicing the skills that you have been teaching. Observe who reads by moving their lips or using their finger to stay focused. Neither is wrong if either helps students stay focused and reading efficiently.

The use of fingers to guide reading is a skill often taught to those who experience dyslexia or who learn speed-reading. It is not necessary to stop students from using such reading aids. Just determine who uses them so you can adapt your teaching to accommodate student needs and reading speeds. Ask for assistance from a reading specialist to help you better teach and support the youngsters assigned to your classes in a particular school year. If there is no specialist on staff in your building, ask your department chair, a more experienced colleague, or go online to learn what resources are available in your area or on the Internet.

POSING INTELLIGENT QUESTIONS

Continue to ask thought-provoking questions—those that require more than superficial reading to answer. At this stage of the story, about halfway through the book, ask students to predict the outcome. By now the protagonist recognizes that he or she cannot solve the problem alone and may be seeking the assistance of someone or something else. Soon, the protagonist may be challenged to make moral or ethical choices in order to solve the problem of the conflict.

Encouraging students to consider options and to predict ways the characters may address this problem is another way to refocus their attention on the characterization and motivation. Do the choices the characters make seem logical to the way the author has developed the personalities of these characters? If not, why not? How does this disconnect impact your students' appreciation of the story?

USING MOVIE ADAPTATIONS

Movies, picture books, animated cartoons, and graphic and comic book adaptations can promote student interest, increase comprehension, and lead to worthwhile discussions. Borrow a video from the school collection or local library to show portions of the story. View the movie ahead of time to choose appropriate scenes to show and to time the length so you can plan effective use in class. Look at a variety of adaptations until you find one that you like and serves your purpose for showing it. Characterization? Setting? Pacing? Filmmaking?

Before showing the video clip, tell the viewers the questions you plan to ask at the end. This helps the students focus on some of the aspects of media grammar—film shots, use of color, timing, screen shots, cuts, and so on. Allow time at the end of the period for students to discuss the director's or artist's choices for depicting character, setting, and action. Ask students how the viewing is different from the reading. Are they surprised, pleased, disappointed? Why? Why not?

Showing visual versions of the novel can help you avoid wounding fragile young egos. This activity gives students an opportunity to assess and even confirm the observations they have been making as they read. And, in a nonembarrassing way, viewing clarifies scenes or passages for those who may have misunderstood something. You know that classical novels can be challenging reads for today's middle school students, so arrange various ways for them to understand the plots and characters. Whether you decide to show video, DVD, cartoons, comic book, or graphic novel versions, you can be confident that each can supplement and expand student understanding and increase their appreciation for this older, classic work of literature.

If you are teaching a novel that does not have a DVD or other visual format that you can locate, you may use something set in a similar time or place; a careful selection of an alternative resource to view still can enhance the students' understanding and appreciation of the book you are studying together.

RECOGNIZING DYNAMIC AND STATIC CHARACTERS

About two-thirds of the way through the novel is a good time to reflect on and examine the static and dynamic characters in the story. Remember that a dynamic character changes throughout the novel. Usually the static, or unchanging, characters serve as foils for the dynamic characters. Ask questions to point out the different types of characters for those for whom this terminology is new or forgotten. Here are a few examples of questions about character development based on *A Christmas Carol*:

- What specific evidence is there of changes in Scrooge?
- What is most different about the interaction of this Spirit with Scrooge and that of the other two Spirits?
- What do you learn about Scrooge based on his interaction with other characters?
- Through what means do you learn most about Scrooge? Direct or indirect characterization? From what he says or what he does? What others say about him? How others respond to him?
- Which characters do not change even though they appear in several episodes?

The best literature has clear examples of how and why the characters have changed. Before calling on students to verbalize their answers, remind them to support their observations with specific passages from the text. Students can write the page numbers in their journals or use sticky notes to mark the sentences they can read aloud and explain why they believe those passages prove the point they wish to make.

Rereading these passages helps to clarify concepts and reinforce vocabulary. Hearing the language reminds students of ways authors structure sentences to create certain effects on their readers. No matter what novel you are reading together, there is plenty to talk about on this topic of character motivation and development, use of structure, and choice of vocabulary.

SUMMARIZING THE WHOLE BOOK— REFLECTION TIME

Dedicate a class period to a summary activity. This may be a time to use the same or a different video version of the book, to show the concluding scenes and ask the students to discuss their responses to the director's choices. This critical thinking about what they see versus what they read raises their awareness of the power of visual and graphic images to create different responses. You may ask students to compare what they anticipated in the beginning or predicted in the middle with what they now recognize at the end of the reading. What caused the change in their understanding?

Moving beyond the Novel

You are not finished teaching a novel until you have given students opportunities to connect what they have learned with their own life and with other fiction or nonfiction works. Making connections is not just a higher level of thinking; seeing connections demonstrates why we study rather than merely enjoy literature. One creative way to accomplish this is to have students use their own experience and creativity to write an additional section for the book, an epilogue set sometime in the future. Challenge them to model the style of the author. For *A Christmas Carol*, you could assign the students to write a stave six—Ten Years into the Future.

For whatever novel you decide to teach, the following is a set of guidelines to which you can hold the students accountable for students who write epilogues.

- Include at least three characters from the original book.
- Retain their personalities and build on details that have been presented.
- Incorporate seamlessly at least five words from the vocabulary list.

A great activity to tie up your novel study is a class presentation of these writings of episodes set in the future. Students enjoy hearing what their classmates come up with and talking about what this classical novel means to them personally.

GRADING STORIES THE STUDENTS WRITE

You can give a holistic grade for the student stories, evaluating them based on their adherence to the prompt. Ask yourself the following questions:

- Have they created a logical epilogue, including three characters that have grown from the descriptions presented in the original work?
- Are the incidents in keeping with the situations introduced by the author?
- Does the vocabulary flow seamlessly (or relatively anyway) into the text of the story? It may or may not, depending on the style and the vocabulary words the students choose to use. If the words are used correctly, go ahead and give full credit. If they all stand out like palm trees in the desert, lower the grade somewhat.

Student Responses to Creative Writing Assignment on *A Christmas Carol*

The following are two seventh-grade student responses to that assignment. Cressy wrote the first story and Amanda the second. The italicized words are words from the vocabulary list Cressy used. Notice the difference in reading for vocabulary when one of the students italicized the words and the other did not. Are the vocabulary words Amanda uses noticeable?

Stave six of *A Christmas Carol* by Cressy (with italicized words from the class vocabulary list).

Years later, Scrooge forgot all about the *spectral* creatures that he had seen. It was Christmas Eve, actually, when he remembered a *vestige* of what had happened to him years ago. He was having Christmas dinner with his nephew and family and his nephew's house when he remembered. He pondered if he should tell his nephew, or if that would cause *tumult*. With a *persevere* attitude, he determinedly decided to tell his nephew.

Scrooge waited and *loitered* in the kitchen while dessert was being made, and decided to break his news to his nephew while they after their sweet dessert. Just about when he was ready to tell, he got a strange feeling. Should he tell, or not? He decided to wait a while until the others finished, so he and he nephew could be alone. Then he would tell. While Scrooge was waiting, he decided to try the dessert, which tasted *odious* to him, or maybe he just wasn't in the mood to eat, for he had something important to tell his nephew. His now *genial*, bouncy attitude gave him the feeling that now was to time to make his move, or else he may never come to telling his nephew, and if he didn't tell, it was possible that nephew could get confused about why his uncle likes Christmas now, when he used to hate it, and his nephew's confusion could possibly take Scrooge's genial attitude away.

"Nephew, do you remember how I used to be *caustic* about Christmas, how thought it was odious?"

"Yes, I do."

"Well, have you ever stopped for a moment to think, 'Why did my *covetous* uncle change?'"

"Actually, yes, I have!" replied the nephew, who cheeks turned a ruddy red.

"I used to think Christmas was one of the most horrible things! Now I like it because three ghosts taught me about Christmas and my life. The ghosts of Christmas Past, Present, and Yet to Come. They all took me places, and I learned that on Christmas people are happy and jolly, and I should be happy and jolly, too! Christmas is a time to love, not *ruddy*. I know that now, because through the ghosts, I learned!"

"Wait, do you mean . . . real ghosts? How is that possible?"

"I'm not sure, but you have to believe me, Nephew! How else could I have changed from hating Christmas so much to loving it so much?"

"I don't know, but . . ."

"I urge you to believe that I am telling the truth!"

"You expect me to believe that ghosts came and toured you around and taught you about Christmas?"

"It may sound odd, but ghosts toured me around to many different places. I even went to your house! I saw the family playing giving, and having fun! I saw it, I know it Nephew, I was in your house!"

"How did you get in my house?"

"I'm telling you, the ghost brought me!"

"I still don't believe you!"

"Fine! I'll get proof! I'll prove to you that the ghosts are real, and they changed me!"

Scrooge slumped back, wishing he could take back what he just said. How was he supposed to get proof? "Maybe," he thought to himself, "I can talk about what happened to me the day I was changed—my whole adventure told in detail. Then he ought to believe me!"

Scrooge poured out his whole story.

I, for one, would feel compelled, for Scrooge told his story with such drama and compassion. I don't believe in ghosts, but Scrooge had a pretty convincing story.

Scrooge stopped to catch his breath when his nephew started trembling violently. The nephew's face turned paler than porcelain, for behind Scrooge, there stood three ghosts.

The next stave six was written by Amanda. Called "10 Years Later," it reflects how she is learning to integrate sophisticated reading vocabulary into her own writing.

Scrooge sat in his nephew Fred's house listening happily to the tumult around him. Fred's five, ruddy faced children playing and running around gave Scrooge such joy that he nearly hopped up and joined them. But if Scrooge had been an old man a decade before, it was nothing compared to what he was now. And although he was no longer the covetous man he had been and gave his money generously to all who needed it, he was now feeble and cane-ridden. This, however, did not dampen his genial personality and was often told he and his nephew had identical dispositions. He sold his house nine years back quite cheaply to a poor family with over a dozen children for they could fill that old house much better than Scrooge or Marley ever could. I wish I could have been there while they were moving in, for they filled the house with such love, joy, noise and bodies. I'm sure the house nearly fainted from surprise for it had been a stranger to all of that which this blessed family brought to it for most of its life. Scrooge had the moved into, well, not exactly a small house, more, an average sized house in the suburbs of the city, retired from his counting business, and gave it to his former clerk, Bob Cratchit to make up for his cruelty and underpayment of him.

Scrooge shifted to a recumbent position and scooped up his youngest great-nephew, Dean, and began reading him a book, which Scrooge had bought the boy the day before. Dean greatly resembled Tiny Tim who was now growing into a handsome young man. But not only on the outside did Tim and Dean resemble each other but also in spirit, for both were always optimistic. Scrooge finished reading to Dean and stood up to take his leave. He said good-bye to Freddy, the eldest great-nephew, gave Ann, the second eldest, a hug, and patted Jill and Mill, the twins, on the head, who were currently having a glorious tea party with their two favorite dolls. He then kissed Caroline, his niece, on the cheek, clapped Fred merrily on the shoulder, and thanked them both for having him with which they both responded it had been a great joy to have him. He let himself out of the house into the street and started hobbling home, waving cheerfully to every man, woman, and child that came into his sight.

While Amanda obviously needed work on pronoun agreement, she clearly captures the style of Dickens with the complex sentence structure and second person point of view—speaking directly to the reader as though the two of them were seated together as Dickens shared his now classic tale of transformation. She used the vocabulary words *tumult, ruddy, covetous, genial,* and *recumbent.*

CONNECTING CLASS-ASSIGNED BOOKS WITH SELF-SELECTED READING BOOKS

Here is an interesting assignment to encourage additional reading. Have the students read a collection of short stories and write an essay recommending three of the stories to three characters from class readings. (See Teacher Resource D.)

Reporting on *The New Oxford Book of Ghost Stories* by Dennis Pepper, seventh grader Warren recommended a story for Scrooge. Here is an excerpt from his essay:

Another story from *The New Oxford Book of Ghost Stories* is called Snookered. Snookered would be good for Scrooge from a book called *A Christmas Carol* by Charles Dickens. I would recommend that Scrooge read this story because then he would know that it's not just him that are visited by people that they know that have been dead. In Snookered by

Catherine Graham, the story is about a man who is playing a game of pool and finds that his friend, that had just died, was helping him win. In *A Christmas Carol*, Scrooge is confronted by his old friend Marley who had died a couple of years ago. In both, they again get to meet their old friends.

Warren identified the stories and characters from our class text. He explained why a character from our text might enjoy reading a story about a character from a book that Warren had read independently. The assignment gave him an opportunity to reflect on our course text and to demonstrate how well he understood the short story he read on his own.

CONCLUSION

Middle school students appreciate classical literature, especially if the related pedagogy and text address the kinds of universal themes that young adults are already pondering. Offer students a variety of options for accessing what may be a more challenging piece of literature, provide support with vocabulary study, read aloud yourself or use professional readers, encourage sketching and drawing, show visual versions, and invite students to connect what they read to their own lives, to what they see around them, and to other literature they have read.

While a book like *A Christmas Carol* can be especially challenging to teach in a multicultural community in which many families are not very familiar with Christmas traditions, it also may prove to be a wonderful window for those who just enjoy the writing of a talented storyteller. Whatever classical text you select, be sensitive to the cultural nuances as you explore with students the universal themes reflected so well in novels revered so long as the classics.

CLASSICAL NOVELS TO CONSIDER TEACHING OR RECOMMENDING TO STUDENTS

The Adventures of Huckleberry Finn by Mark Twain

Most students are familiar with the character of Huck Finn because of the many TV, movie, book, and drama adaptations. They may not, however, know much about the book beyond it being the story of Huck and his companion Jim as they raft down the Mississippi River. Twain wrote the book as a harsh critique of Southern culture during the 1800s. The characters and places that Huck and Jim encounter all reflect this critique. Students should be introduced to the history necessary to understand the satire in the book. If the book is too long or the language too complex for your students, you could try using just a portion of the easily segmented novel.

Grades: Seventh through eighth
Caution: Language, Racism, Some violence, Physical abuse

Animal Farm by George Orwell

Animal Farm is a simple but powerful allegory about the corruption of a socialist society. When the animals of Manor Farm oust their drunken master, they at first establish a fair and seemingly perfect society. But the slow takeover by the pigs of the farm eventually brings the animals back to the place where they started. Orwell wrote the novel in response to his experiences in the Spanish Civil War, which makes it a perfect pairing for a study of that time period. Students could be encouraged to write their own allegorical tales after reading this novel.

Grades: Seventh through eighth
Caution: Violence, Drunkenness

The Giver by Lois Lowry

The utopia of twelve-year-old Jonas's society seems perfect. There is no poverty, crime, sickness, or unemployment. Everyone is given an appropriate job and mate. It isn't until Jonas begins his training as the new Receiver of Memories that he questions his model existence. What has his society given up in order to achieve utopia? A wonderful book for discussion, *The Giver* can be paired with other books about utopian living or dystopian societies. Interested students will enjoy the sequels *Gathering Blue* and *Messenger*.

Grades: Sixth through eighth
Caution: Euthanasia

The Lion, the Witch, and the Wardrobe by C. S. Lewis

When air raids during World War II drive children out of London, four siblings end up staying with an old professor in his country house. But their adventure doesn't truly begin until they pass through a wardrobe and find themselves in the land of Narnia. There they are drawn into a classic battle between good and evil. While three of the siblings help the creatures of Narnia escape the eternal winter brought on by the White Witch, the youngest boy, Edmund, is seduced by evil. Simply but beautifully written, this first book in *The Chronicles of Narnia* is entertaining and easy to read. It's a great choice to entice reluctant readers to read the classics.

Grades: Sixth through seventh

Caution: Mild violence, Religious imagery/metaphor

Lord of the Flies by William Golding

What happens when a group of boys crash land on an island and are left to govern themselves? When William Golding asked this question it led to one of the best-known books of the last hundred years. Golding's view of human nature is devastating—the stranded boys' initial attempts to establish a fair government quickly turn to chaos and violence. Students will no doubt have much to say about the themes in this book so it could be used as a trigger for longer writing projects. The novel could also be paired with a study of other books that examine human nature (*Animal Farm, Brave New World*). Many modern TV shows and movies draw from *Lord of the Flies* (*Survivor, Lost*), which makes the book a great basis for a study of literary allusions.

Grades: Seventh through eighth

Caution: Violence, Disturbing images

The Phantom Tollbooth by Norton Juster

In this fantasy story, Norton Juster uses literary concepts to create characters, settings, and even a primary plot. Milo is bored with everything until a tollbooth magically appears in his room. When he goes through the tollbooth he finds himself in a land where he gets stuck in the Doldrums, visits Dictionopolis and meets five guards who speak entirely in synonyms, eats letters, and rescues the princesses Rhyme and Reason. The book is not only an entertaining story but provides fun ways to study dozens of language topics. Students will be encouraged to try their hand at this unique form of creative writing.

Grades: Sixth through seventh

Caution: None

A Wrinkle in Time by Madeleine L'Engle

Madeleine L'Engle is a wonderful, "intelligent" children's author who employs science and philosophy in fantastic adventure stories. *A Wrinkle in Time* is no exception. It's the story of Meg Murry—a young woman who feels different from other kids her age. Years before, her father disappeared while working on a secret government project on tesseracts ("wrinkles in time"). Now Meg, along with Calvin O'Keefe, one of the most popular boys at school, must travel through time and space to find and rescue her father. *A Wrinkle in Time* is a story about family love and finding your own unique gifts. A necessary caution about the book is that if students do not understand the science, they will probably not enjoy the book. A little extra research may be necessary before using the book with a class.

Grades: Sixth through eighth

Caution: None

⑦

TAKING T.I.M.E. TO TEACH POETRY

Words stir me
When I hear them,
When I read them,
When I write them,
When I speak them.

Words urge me
To keep listening
To keep reading
To keep writing
To keep speaking.

Let me hear you,
so I can know you.
Let me speak,
so you can know me.

Prodigiously stirring words
help me know you.
And viscerally urging words
help me know me.

—Anna Roseboro, "Words, Words, Words"

Figure 7.1.   Poetry Big Key

For some reason, young teens are apprehensive about studying poetry. They believe there is a key or secret code to understanding poetry and only teachers have the key to decipher that code. Experienced readers know that is not the case; it is a matter of understanding the genre and approaching poetry in a different way—paying special attention to poets' careful selection and arrangement of words. The lessons in this chapter are designed to provide you and your students with a set of strategies that can help them approach, read, understand, analyze, write in the style of, and write about classical, contemporary, structured, and free-verse poetry.

PREPARING TO TEACH POETRY

Borrow as many books of poetry as you can. Look for them at the school or neighborhood library, your department library, and borrow from your colleagues. If several of you are teaching poetry at the same time, you may wish to borrow a library cart so you can merge your poetry collections and move the cart easily among your rooms. To make this a really rich experience for your students, have a ready trove of poems for students to mine during their study of poetry. At the end of the chapter there is a list of collections for you to locate and add to the resources you make available for students to peruse and use.

Using a Poem to Introduce Poetry Analysis

Begin with a poem to explain the process. Consider the poem "Unfolding Bud" by Naoshi Koriyama, which you can have posted or projected in the room when the students arrive the first day of the direct instruction on poetry reading and writing. It provides a useful metaphor for the experience the students have when they read poetry. This poem seems to allay some of their anxiety about understanding poetry. You may also hand out copies, but at first, do not read the poem aloud. Instead, without saying anything more, let the students look at it for a couple of minutes. Sometimes silence gives space for student learning.

> One is amazed
> By a water-lily bud
> Unfolding
> With each passing day,
> Taking on a richer color
> And new dimensions.
>
> One is not amazed,
> At a first glance,
> By a poem,
> Which is as tight-closed
> As a tiny bud.
>
> Yet one is surprised
> To see a poem
> Gradually unfolding,
> Revealing its rich inner self,
> As one reads it
> Again
> And over again.
> (Naoshi Koriyama, "Unfolding Bud"[1])

Now, use a multiple reading format. Here is how it works. Ask the students to read the poem silently, paying attention to the punctuation and marking words or phrases that catch their attention. Next, read the poem aloud yourself. Then, ask them to do a "jump in" oral reading. One student begins reading and stops at the first mark of punctuation (comma, semicolon, period, question mark, and so on). Another student, without raising his or her hand, continues reading until the next punctuation mark.

Students are likely to giggle when more than one student begins reading aloud at the same time, but just start over and encourage students who jump in at the same time to listen to each other and read together as one voice. It usually takes three or four false starts before the students get the idea and are comfortable reading aloud this way. Other students can continue jumping in to read in this way until the end of the poem. Relax and allow the pauses between readers to be moments of resonation and reflection. False starts encourage students to pay attention to the words, lines, and punctuation, and thus expand their understanding of the poem.

This first day is a good time to talk about the value of multiple readings and why it often is necessary for this condensed form of literature. "Unfolding Bud" is a great conversation starter for this topic.

When teaching poetry, resist the temptation to ask students what the poem "means." This phrase incorrectly suggests there is only one meaning for a poem. The phrase "what it says" encourages the students to look at the individual words and respond with a literal meaning, which can be the first step to analyzing poetry. The subsequent steps include determining whether or not the poem is saying something about a bigger issue or idea and whether the poem is speaking metaphorically.

Some poets may not have begun writing their poem about big universal issues; they may have written simply to recreate a very personal incident, observation, or experience. Yet, when read by others, their poem speaks to the readers about issues quite different from the literal ideas originally intended. Often these bigger ideas do not emerge or manifest themselves on the first or second readings. "Unfolding Bud" closes with the lines "again / and over again," which suggests that poetry is somewhat different from some prose and drama in that, more often than not, multiple readings are required to understand poetry.

Alternative Reading of Opening Poem

If you would rather not use jump in reading to introduce the unit, slowly read the poem aloud yourself, allowing time for the words to sink in. Then ask a specific student to read the poem according to the punctuation, rather than just stopping at the end of each line. This second reading helps the students focus on the fact that poems sometimes include punctuation and that the punctuation serves the same functions as that used in prose. Punctuation clarifies the meaning of words organized in a particular order. It still is beneficial to have a third reading of the poem by another student who, by this time, has an idea of what the poet may be trying to express, and this student probably chooses to emphasize different words or reads at a different pace and thus offers a third level of understanding. Both jump in readings and multiple readings demonstrate the value of repetition to allow a poem to reveal itself to the readers and listeners.[2]

DEFINING POETRY:
A FOUNDATION FOR DISCUSSION

The first day of the unit is a prime time to provide the students with a definition of poetry. Use the one in your anthology or the one that follows. In either case, dictate the definition and have the students write in the poetry section they have set up in their reading journals.

Definition: "Poetry is literature designed to *convey* a vivid and imaginative sense of experience, especially by the use of *condensed* language *chosen* for its sound and *suggestive* power as well as for its meaning and by the use of such literary devices as *structured* meter, *natural cadences*, rhyme and metaphor."[3]

You may want to read the definition a couple of times, letting your voice emphasize the italicized words. Then, read it more slowly so students can write the definition in their journals. Afterward, project the definition so students can verify their writing. Why this laborious start? Hearing, listening, writing, and viewing are ways to reinforce the concept. This definition will form the basis of subsequent reflections on the form and function of poetry studied throughout the unit.

Take a few moments more and ask the students what they think the italicized words mean in the context of poetry. If no one offers definitions, direct the students to find the words in a dictionary or on their computers and to share the definitions with the class. This is a situation in which it is good to have stored dictionaries under students' desks or on shelves around the room so students can reach them easily without having to ask or disrupt others. It should not be unusual to see one or more of them reaching for a dictionary during any class meeting.

Now return to the poem "Unfolding Bud" and again ask the students what they imagine this poem is saying to them about reading poetry. What elements of the definition has Mr. Koriyama used in his poem?

To solidify student understanding, end the lesson by having the students read aloud in unison, like a Greek chorus, the definition of poetry they have written in their notebooks.

Completing the First Lesson

For homework, assign students to peruse their literature anthology or other poetry collections they have, can borrow, or find in the library, and to copy into their notebook at least one poem they particularly like. If such an assignment is not a realistic expectation for the students you have, allot some in-class time for them to peruse their anthology or the poetry books you have collected for their use in the classroom. Just ask each student to select and copy into his or her own notebook one or two poems that attract their attention. The physical act of copying a poem slows them down a bit so they can pay attention to structure and pattern in poetry, two of the distinguishing features of this genre of literature.

Your students then have a self-selected poem to refer to and share with the class later on during the unit. The value of this assignment is that it gives the students an opportunity to read a variety of poems for which they are not required to do anything more than choose one they like. And the bonus? They are likely to read twice as many poems this way than if you were to assign them a specific one to read for class the next day. The next day, simply record in the grade book whether or not each student has a poem written in the journal. The goal here is to get them reading poetry and to become more at ease with this literary form. (See box 7.1.)

DISCOVERING POETRY T.I.M.E—
A STRATEGY FOR POETRY ANALYSIS

Poetry T.I.M.E has been around for decades.[4] This idea for poetry analysis has been passed along from teacher to teacher across the nation.

> **Box 7.1. Play It!**
> **Using Popular Song Lyrics to Introduce Poetry**
>
> Encourage students to bring in song lyrics that are appropriate for sharing in class. Until you point it out, probably few young adolescents recognize that song lyrics are often poems. Having your students bring in poems and song lyrics of their choice also is a way for you to become more familiar with what current young teens listen to and find interesting. They also feel as though they are a part of the learning process because they're the ones helping to shape the lessons. Depending on the students you teach, you may wish to collect and read the lyrics first, and then use them for a lesson later in the unit.
>
> If you have time, ask students to bring in ten- to fifteen-second musical samples of the choruses for their selected song lyrics. Play a few of these as examples of poetic repetition.

You, too, may have been taught this way and find this clever acronym just what you need to organize your instruction and enhance student learning. If you choose to use it, you are likely to have former students who return to express their appreciation for having a mnemonic that serves them well on standardized and placement tests as well as on final exams in other courses. In relation to poetry, T.I.M.E. stands for title, imagery, music, and emotion. (See figure 7.2.)

Knowing this acronym can help students unlock meaning in poetry. As your students have learned in the lesson on "Unfolding Bud," poems are written in condensed language and often require multiple readings. T.I.M.E. really is a pun and refers not only to the fact that it often takes more time to read and write poetry, but also refers to elements of a poem that, when considered independently, can lead to a deeper understanding of the poem in its entirety.

The Letter *T*

Begin with *T*, for the title of a poem. If a poet has chosen a title, it often serves as a hint to what the poem is about and may indicate the emotion or opinion the poet has about the experience related in the

T - The speaker's Title
    THOUGHT / THEME

I - IMAGERY

M - MUSIC

E - EMOTION

Figure 7.2. Poetry Clock

poem. The T also could stand for the thought or theme of the poem. This is a flexible acronym and you can decide the best word(s) to use with the students you have. You may use one, two, or three of these T words. All are related to the study of poetry.

Next, draw the students' attention to concepts about the speaker and audience. Published poetry is meant to be understood. You may choose to clarify this idea and specify "published poetry" because many people write poetry just for themselves and may not care whether or not anyone else even reads it let alone understands it. Generally, though, a poet is someone saying something to someone.

That first someone is "the speaker" who may or may not be the poet. For example, you may have a poet, an elderly woman, who writes a poem in the persona of an adolescent boy. In this example, though the poet is a woman, but the speaker in the poem is a boy. Looking at the kind of pronouns used, the vocabulary and images can help the reader imagine the audience. One visual way that helps students think of poetry as a piece of writing with a message is to use a graphic design with three spaces—one large rectangle in the middle of the page and a small circle on the left and a larger one on the right of the large rectangle.

After they make this chart in the poetry section of their journals, ask your students to draw a picture of a possible speaker in the small circle on the left and in the small circle on the right, a possible audience: one person, a special person, or a group of people. Then, in the rectangle in the center, they could write a summary of what the poem could be saying and quote a couple of lines from the poem to support their opinion. (See figure 7.3.)

Demonstrate how this could work by referring again to "Unfolding Bud." Draw the graphic organizer on the board and then ask students, "Who could be the speaker?" "Who could be the audience?" Typical answers include a parent talking to a student who is doing his or her homework and who persuades the young person to hang in there and not give up just because the poem is difficult to understand after one or two readings. Some students may respond that it is a teacher speaking to an individual student or to the class as a whole.

To reinforce the ideas of speaker and audience, distribute a copy of Emily Dickinson's poem "I'm Nobody." Ask the students to read it and think of as many different speaker and audience sets as they can. The only limitation is that the sets must be supported by the words of the poem. Your middle school students may come up with pairs such as

a student new to the school talking to another student at lunch time
a new player on an athletic team
a prisoner talking to another prisoner
a new teacher at the first department meeting
a kid at the playground during a pickup soccer, football, or basketball
   game
a rock singer waiting to perform on a TV program

SAYING SOMETHING TO

SOMEONE   SOMEONE(S)

THE SPEAKER   THE AUDIENCE

1 SPECIAL PERSON

1 KIND OF PERSON

1 GROUP OF PEOPLE

Figure 7.3.   Poetry Someone Saying

an actor trying out for a part in a play
a parent talking to another parent during the school open house
a woman attending a neighborhood luncheon for the first time

If you are in the mood, act a little silly, ham it up, and reread the poem
in the voices and persona of the pairs the students suggest. Great fun!
It makes the point, too, of multiple possibilities but common meanings.
See figure 7.4.)

POETRY IS

SOMEONE saying SOMETHING to *SOMEONE(s)

○ → 🎬 → ○○

*a specific individual, kind of person, group of people

Figure 7.4. Poetry Is Diagram

The Letter *I*

I stands for the imagery of poetry. Poets use words to help create pictures, emotions, or incidents in the minds of the readers and listeners. Poets may use sensory or figurative imagery or a combination of the two. Sensory imagery appeals to one or more of the five senses: sight, hearing, taste, touch, and smell. It is through our senses that we experience the world, and many poets appeal to these senses as they recreate their own experiences in poetic form. (See figure 7.5.)

Rather than presenting this portion of the lesson as lecture, simply draw an eye, an ear, a mouth, a hand, and a nose on the board. Then, ask the students to label the drawings and give examples of words or phrases that appeal to the senses. Prepare for the lesson by looking at a variety

Figure 7.5. Poetry I = Imagery

of poems, compiling sample lines from poems that illustrate appeals to the various senses. Better yet, invite students to offer lines they recall from lyrics of songs familiar to them.

This would be a good time to ask students to look back at the poems that they selected and copied into their journals at the beginning of the unit. Set your timer for ten or fifteen minutes. Have the students pull their desks together, or turn to a table partner and then share with a partner these poems, pointing out examples of sensory images from their chosen poems. Working with poems they have chosen validates the assignment to choose and copy them into their notebooks. Invite volunteers to read aloud to the class lines that illustrate the sensory images they find.

Next, introduce figurative imagery. Many middle school students learn about similes and metaphors in earlier grades and are able to define them for the class. Some know the term *personification*; fewer know *hyperbole* and *symbol* and *allusion*. So be prepared to introduce these devices and give students definitions and examples. Here are some simple definitions of these types of figurative imagery:

- *Simile*: a comparison between two things using the words *like* or *as*. Example: The thunder roared like a bear.
- *Metaphor*: an implied comparison between two things without using *like* or *as*. Example: Raindrops the size of dimes pelted me in the face.
- *Hyperbole*: exaggeration to create an effect. Example: That fish was as big as my leg!
- *Personification*: giving a nonhuman thing the characteristics of a person. Example: The dog smiled when he snatched up the steak bone.

Occasionally a poet uses a symbol—something concrete that stands for something else: an abstract concept, another thing, idea, or event. For example a "flag" is a cloth on a stick. But a certain configuration of colors and shapes such as stars on a blue rectangular field in the upper left corner of a red and white striped cloth suggests the American flag, which stands for the nation, for freedom and patriotism. Symbols can be a great opening to talk about cultural contexts. For example, a snake or serpent symbolizes different ideas depending on the culture, the religion, or the nation. Red in some cultures is a sad color representing blood or anger; in other cultures, it is a happy color representing marriage or royalty.

An allusion is the reference to another body of literature, a movie, or an incident the writer believes the readers know. Allusions can help the writer create an image with just a few words because the writer believes the allusion automatically triggers memories, ideas, or emotions from the reference in the poem.

In Western literature, frequently allusions are made to the Bible with its Hebrew and Christian scriptures, Roman and Greek mythology, Shakespeare's writings, and fairy tales. Sometimes a reference may be made to a familiar movie like *Star Wars*, or a historical incident like the Civil War or the Gold Rush. If your students represent a broad range of cultures and national origins, select samples from the literature that are more familiar to them. Consider stories, myths, and sacred texts your students may know from literature and life in Central and South America, Asia, India, and Africa.

You could spend the remainder of the period looking at examples of poems that have strong imagery. Again, ask students to find examples of all kinds of imagery to share and compare with a partner, and encourage them to copy favorite lines into their journals. Remember, in order to find their own examples, the students read much more poetry than if you provide all the examples. Equally important is the fact that each year you teach the unit you should be learning, too. You also discover what kinds of poems interest students in each different class.

Nancy Genevieve, a poet, writes delicate images in her free verse. Students enjoy pointing out the figurative language in the poems that follow. Notice the ways that she uses metaphors and personification in her poems "Strawberries" and "The Pond."[5]

> Jeweled fruit of Kings
> Pixie capped in green
> Small perfect morsel
> Of pure delight
> Bite-size taste of heaven.

27 pints of preserves
and 15 frozen pints later,
prickly whiskered smell stuff
tempted to poke good with bad
down the garbage disposal only . . .
Perhaps, rub glass
In the sunlight
On the pantry shelves
Tomorrow.
("Strawberries")

Bubbles frozen in ice
Pearls of silence
waiting for spring.

Crystals etched in glaze
Petals of illusion,
blooming by night.
Twilight bathed in mist
flames of fading,
seeping into no more.
Evening cicadas
tune up for the night,
practicing their
lull-a-bye
for summer.
("The Pond")

Patterning Poetry—Student Responses

An assignment that always evokes positive responses and pretty good poetry is one on patterning poems.[6] Ask the students to select one or two of the poems that they particularly like either from their anthology or one of the books in your room. Next ask them to think of a memorable experience of their own. Finally, invite them to pattern the structure and imagery of their chosen poem to recreate the experience of their chosen incident. Of course, if you are writing poems along with them (and you should), you experience what it feels like to write on demand as you are asking them to do. Then, you have something newly written to read during sharing time.

For example, you could ask your students to write a short piece that patterns a ballad, like "Barbara Allen," or a lyric poem like Robert Frost's "Acquainted with the Night."

Oh, it was around Christmas time
When the marriage, it was planned.
The family and friends all came to see
Sir William wed Lady Ann.

The musicians were seated, all playing their songs
Awaiting the groom to appear.
And seated among the guests that day
Sat his former love, Lady Mear.

The minister signaled the groom to come out
To stand with best man at the right.
The minister motioned the guests to stand
As the bride marched in dressed in white.

Lady Mear, she stood with hankie in hand
Weeping for the man she had lost.
She'd been too proud to accept the ring
Sir William had gotten at cost.

The bride advanced at a stately pace
By her handsome groom to stand
Lady Mear, near the aisle, could be heard for a mile,
Shouting, "Hey Lady Ann, that's my man!"

Sir William's response to the lady's outburst,
"You had my heart in your hand.
You cast me aside. Yes, I did love you first,
But today, I'll wed Lady Ann."

So that day long ago about Christmas time,
The guests got more than was planned.
An old love turned mean in quite a wild scene
When Sir William wed Lady Ann.
(Anna J. Small Roseboro, a.k.a. Mrs. William G. Roseboro, "The Ballad of William and Ann." Patterned after "Barbara Allen," Anonymous.)

Another practice activity is transliteration—the act of converting from one genre to another. Young teens love knowing and using such sophisticated words. You could give this assignment after reading together Gordon Parks' poem "The Funeral." In the poem, he describes things that appear to have changed since he left his hometown many years ago. You could ask your young teens to write about places that seem different to them now that they are middle school students. They first write a paragraph in prose, and then recreate the incident as a poem, by condensing the language or creating word images. The move from prose to poetry reiterates the concept of condensed language or the use of sensory and figurative imagery that you talked about earlier in the definition of poetry.

The following is Kristen's paragraph, then her poem in which she experiments with hyperbole and rhyme:

> Since I've gotten older I have realized many things have changed. The school looks a lot smaller than it used to. My home used to feel roomier and it felt like it had more space. My bed even seems smaller. The walls and sealing feel closer but my sibling seem the same.

> The walls and the ceiling have started to shrink
> While I get taller and taller
> And the schools must be fooling my eyes
> They're growing smaller and smaller!
> My room is getting less roomy.
> I can't stretch out in my bed.
> I wonder what will happen?
> Opps, I've just hit my head.
> ("Changes," modeled after "The Funeral" by Gordan Parks)

A second poem that students seem to enjoy reading, discussing, and patterning is Langston Hughes's "Mother to Son." His poem begins,

> Well, son. I'll tell you:
> Life for me ain't been no crystal stair.

Here is Kristen's patterning of Langston Hughes's "Mother to Son":

> Life is not a perfect picnic
> There are many bad conditions like

Ants
And seagulls
And wet grass
And even places without a blanket
Cement
But there is no way you can give up
Or go back
You have to keep on waiting for the grass to dry
And looking for a spot to sit
And eating the food
And sometimes going in the shade
But don't give up
Keep searching for the perfect spot.
("Life Is Not a Perfect Picnic")

You may need to remind the students about acknowledging their sources. When students pattern a poem, they should indicate somewhere on the page the title and author of the poem they are modeling. This teaches them academic honesty, and also lets them know that patterning is an acceptable way to write, as they notice when reading collections of limericks, sonnets, and haiku. Same patterns. Different personal experiences.

The Letter M

M stands for music or the sounds in poetry. According to the definition used earlier, poets chose words "for their sound and suggestive power." Look at three aspects of music and poetry: rhythm, rhyme, and the sound of words. Some poets arrange their words to create a pattern of beats or rhythm. If your students are ready, teach the I.T.A.D.S., an acronym for five common poetic rhythm patterns—iambic, trochaic, anapestic, dactylic, and spondee. (See figure 7.6.) These words identify the patterns of stressed and unstressed syllables, information students surely are expected to know and use in high school.

During this lesson on music, mention to the students that I.T.A.D.S. patterns are called the "feet" of poetry. There is only one stressed syllable in each foot. Explain that a poem's rhythm, or the "meter," is named for the number of feet or beats per line and the kind of foot that

RHYME

RHYTHM

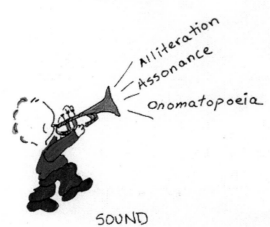

SOUND

Figure 7.6.   Poetry M = Music

is in each line. For example, a line of poetry with four feet or four beats is tetrameter (tetra is Greek for four). If the feet are iambic, the line is identified as iambic tetrameter. Have fun by asking students to identify the rhythm patterns of their own names. Anna is trochaic. Jamar is iambic. Roseboro is dactylic. What are the patterns of your name?

Moving to the Music of Poetry

Because many students are kinesthetic learners and can remember what they feel physically, you should demonstrate the rhythms of poetry that way, too. Read a poem with a strong beat while standing up and marching in place. How about inviting students to clap their hands, tap one foot, or snap their fingers to the beat?

To use that abundance of adolescent energy, have the students march around the room when you read William Wordsworth's "Daffodils": "I wander'd lonely as a cloud." Rather than wandering quietly, stomp loudly. Use your arms to sway broadly from side to side to show the rhythm of the waves in John Masefield's "Sea Fever": "I *must* down to the seas again, to the *lonely* sea and the sky." Of course, the students see right away the rhythm of song lyrics, but you could save this until later. For now, acknowledge that "just as some poetry has a specific rhythm pattern, so do the lyrics or words of some songs you know."

A second way to look at the music of poetry is to consider the rhyme, which occurs when words with similar sounds are used in an observable pattern. The rhyme may occur at the end of a line or within a line.

Students can discover the pattern of rhyme by using letters of the alphabet to indicate repeated sounds. For example, begin writing with the letter *a* at the end of the first line of poetry. If the second line ends with the same sound, write *a* again. If it ends with a different sound, change to *b*. Continue throughout the poem to determine if there is a pattern and what the pattern is. The narrative poem "The Cremation of Sam McGee" by Robert W. Spruce makes particularly interesting reading when you are teaching internal and end rhyme. The macabre story is intriguing, too.

Point out that free and blank verse poetry has no systematic rhyme pattern. This kind of poetry may be discussed later in your unit, but you should point it out now, particularly if students bring in examples of free verse poetry or notice it in their class anthology. This is why it is good to begin the unit with the definition of poetry that mentions structured meter or natural cadences. Your discussion of the music of poetry gives space to talk about blank and free verse without having to provide another definition or having to backpedal when students point out that some poetry is unstructured in terms of rhythm and rhyme.

Song Lyrics as Poetry

Now is an optimal time to ask selected students to read aloud the lyrics of their favorite songs. Most of them have a steady beat and many of them rhyme, making more concrete the connection between poetry of music and poetry in books much easier to comprehend. Be prepared for students to show more interest in what they bring to the class. Show your enthusiasm as you look at and listen to what they bring. They are providing you a window into their worlds, and what you learn reveals what they know and indicates what you may need to teach or reteach as you continue planning learning experiences for your poetry unit. Combine the familiar with the new by encouraging your students to use the vocabulary of poetry as they talk about poems they choose themselves.

If you have the nerve of most middle school teachers, you can "prove" the link between poetry and music by singing the "I'm Nobody" poem to either the tune of "Yellow Rose of Texas" or "America, the Beautiful"! Even if you are a very good singer, the students will probably laugh at you, but they also remember the lesson. Is that not the goal of teaching?

A third way to talk about the music or sound of poetry is to point out onomatopoeia, words that are spelled to imitate the sound they describe. Middle school students love making peculiar, sometimes shocking and vulgar noises. One way to harness that particular pleasure is to have the students write poems that capture the sounds of everyday experiences. Warren, a seventh grader, wrote "The Kitchen" about the sounds at home. Like Shakespeare, Warren enjoys making up words, too.

> With a cling clang
> Not a bang or dang
> a swish and a wish
> all the dishes are in the sink

screech creach
open
close
scuffles ruffles
a sea of bubbles and water
a crounging rounging
with a turn of the knob
all the dishes are clean
then click click click
whoosh.
Are you hungry for lunch yet?
("The Kitchen")

Another way to address sound as you discuss the music of poetry is to consider repetition of vowels (assonance) or consonants (consonance or alliteration). Most middle school students recognize tongue twisters as examples of alliteration.

Students are intrigued to learn that the sound of words suggests certain emotions. For example, a poet who wishes to convey the emotion or sense of experience in a calm, peaceful way is likely to select soft-sounding consonants like, *l*, *m*, *n*, and *s*. If the emotion is harsh or bitter, the poem is likely to pick hard consonants that must be forced through the lips and teeth to be formed like *p*, *t*, *f*, or guttural sounds like *k*, *g*, and *j*. A graphic way to illustrate this can be pointing out that most obscene words in English include these harsh, guttural, and dental sounds.

Of course, you need not say them aloud or write them down. Students know the word if you refer to "the F word" or "the S word." Students smile and smirk, and your point is made. If many of your students speak other languages, and if you can maintain control of the class, you may ask these students if profane words in their language follow this pattern of harsh sounds. Again, let them think, but not speak, the words. The point is made.

The Letter *E*

The *E* stands for the emotion of the poem—the emotion expressed by the poet and the emotion experienced by the reader. How do students discover these emotions? By paying attention to the kinds of images (comparisons to positive or negative things), and the music, rhyme, rhythm, and sounds of the words the poet chooses to use to convey the experience of the poem. The students may find examples of emotions expressed such as pride, love, grief/distress, fear, joy, jealousy, or shame/embarrassment. They may experience similar feelings as they read or hear the poems. But, the emotion expressed and experienced often is not the same.

If the students are ready, go ahead and teach them that the "tone" of a poem refers to the author's attitude or feeling about the topic or experience related in the poem. On the other hand, "mood" refers to

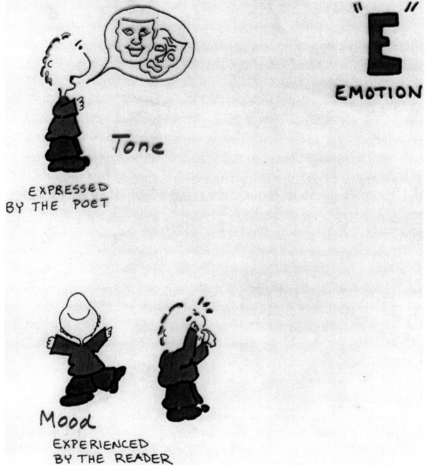

Figure 7.7.   Poetry E = Emotion

the way the poem makes the reader feel when he or she reads or hears a poem. (See figure 7.7.) To help make the link more personal, you can draw their attention to the *m* in mood and say, "Mood means the way the poem makes ME, the reader, feel." That usually is sufficient instruction at this time. As you teach these poetry terms, continue to encourage students to use them regularly when talking and writing about poetry. Such use raises the level of their conversation and expands their working vocabulary. Makes them feel oh so sophisticated!

USING T.I.M.E. TO READ WIDELY ON THEIR OWN

One way for students to practice reading on their own without feeling undue pressure is to ask them to continue bringing in poems and to point out the ways their self-selected poems reflect the various elements already studied. This subtly entices them to read more widely. They are likely to return to the books skimmed before and come across poems that speak to them differently this time. Giving this assignment again also reveals to you how students' choice of poetry is being modified by the series of lessons you are teaching. Invite them to post their choices on your class wiki, remembering to include the title, author, and source. Or, they can print out copies and staple those on a bulletin board set aside for this purpose in your classroom and labeled "Poems We Like."

As they seek out poems, encourage your students to interview their family members to learn about their favorite poems. It's surprising how amazed middle school students are to learn that their moms, dads, aunts, uncles, and even grandparents had to memorize poetry as a regular part of their literature course work! If your students speak languages other than English at home, invite them to bring in poems by favorite poets in those languages and read them aloud to the class. This affirms their heritage and expands the cultural experience for you and their classmates as well.

Allow plenty of class time for students to immerse themselves in the poetry you have assembled in the classroom, in their anthology, and on the websites listed in this chapter. Those students who have not done so may now choose to bring in lyrics from their favorite songs. Appropriate

---

Box 7.2.   Questions to Ask about Poetry

Who could be the speaker? Indicate clues in the text to support this supposition.

Who could be the audience? Indicate clues in the text to support this
supposition.

What literary devices/techniques has the poet used?

How do these elements work to create the total impact on the reader?

What do you imagine is a message or theme of the poem?

What clues in the text support this assertion?

---

ones, of course! Consider including an assignment for students to recite
an appropriate poem of their choice.

As always, alert your students to the fact that the poems address an
array of topics in a variety of ways. And remind your eager young teens
to use their judgment on which poems would be appropriate to share in
class. Thankfully, by this time in the school year, you have established a
classroom milieu for sensitive reading and sensible selections. However,
reminding them at this time is still a good idea.

Notice in box 7.2 that the use of "a message or theme" is to keep the
poem open for the students to draw from it what the poem says to them.
As soon as you suggest the "meaning," your students begin guessing and
hoping they come up with the "right" answer. With self-control, you can
let the poems speak for themselves.

As you plan to teach poetry in a more formal way, schedule time to assign an extensive poetry project such as those described in Teacher Resources on the companion website for this book. There are two outlines
for poetry units in which students collect and share poems they find
and ones they write. Both poetry units require students to write original
poems in which they practice the various poetic devices you study. Most
students choose to include a metaphor poem similar to the one Kristen
writes about looking at photographs in a family album.

> Pictures are memories
> They evoke emotions unexplainable

Remind you of your past,
Giving clues for your future.
They make some people remember
Long Forgotten Friends
Or
Never Forgotten Enemies
For others they are
Excellent Parties
Or
Horrible fights
Either way
Pictures are still Memories.
("Memories")

CONCLUSION

Few readers deny either that poets tend to write cryptically or that it takes more effort to discover what poets have to say to their listeners and readers. When you teach your students to tell the T.I.M.E. of a poem, you give your adolescent readers a golden key they can use for life. Using this key, they know to look systematically for different aspects of the poem on each reread. They experience the delight of discovery and empowerment when you give them T.I.M.E. to study this genre of literature. Through the guided practice you offer, your squirmy adolescents slow down and pay attention to the words, the form, the sounds, and eventually to the messages in poetry. They may even astonish you when their careful reading leads to interpretations similar to those that published critics write about the poems!

By the end of your formal instruction, your students feel far more confident about studying this challenging literary genre. They may not have the ease of Huck Finn's friend Emmeline Grangerford and be able to "slap down a line . . . just scratch it out and slap down another one,"[7] but they now are able to read, write, and talk more confidently about poetry in their own way. Your young teens can respond to those "prodigiously stirring words" and feel comfortable putting pen to paper to capture the "viscerally urging words" that become poems of their own.

BOOKS AND WEBSITES TO SUPPLEMENT THE TEACHING OF POETRY

Books

Joshua Blum, Bob Holman, and Mark Pellington, *The United States of Poetry* (New York: Henry N. Holt, Inc, 1996).

Committed to Memory, John Hollander, ed. (New York: The Academy of American Poets, 1996).

Sharon Creech, *Love That Dog* (New York: HarperCollins, 2001).

Stephen Dunning, *Reflections on a Gift of Watermelon Pickle* (Glenview, IL: Scott Foresman, 1995).

Sara Holbrook, *By Definition: Poems of Feelings* (Honesdale, PA: Boyd Mills, Press, 2003).

Inner Chimes: Poems on Poetry, Bobbye Goldstein, ed. (Honesdale, PA: Boyds Mills Press, 1992).

A Poem of Her Own: Voices of American Women Yesterday and Today, Catherine Clinton, ed. (New York: Harry N. Abrams, Inc, 2003).

Poems That Sing to You, Michael Strickland, ed. (Honesdale, PA: Boyds Mills Press, 1993).

Poetry in Motion: 100 Poems from Subways and Buses, Molly Peacock, Elise Paschen, and Neil Neches, eds. (New York: W.W. Norton and Company, 1996).

Revenge and Forgiveness: An Anthology of Poems, Patrice Vecchione, ed. (New York: Henry Holt and Company, 2004).

Seeing the Blue Between: Advice and Inspiration for Young Poets, Paul B. Janeczko, ed. (Cambridge, MA: Candlewick Press, 2002).

Truth and Lies: An Anthology of Poems, Patrice Vecchione, ed. (New York: Henry Holt and Company, 2001).

Voices: Poetry and Art from Around the World, selected by Barbara Brenner (Washington, DC: National Geographic Society, 2000).

Words with Wings: A Treasury of African American Poetry and Art, Belinda Rochelle, ed. (New York: Amistad HarperCollins, 2000).

Websites

The Academy of American Poets
American Poems

Favorite Poem Project (founded by former poet laureate Robert Pin-
sky)

Poems Daily

Poetry 180: A Poem a Day for American High Schools (the 180 poems
Billy Collins chose the year he was poet laureate)

8

VERSING LIFE TOGETHER

Robert, Bobby, Bob
Fast, fleet, flown
Baby, boy, grown

—Anna Roseboro, "Our Son"

Even if your students are initially excited about reading poetry, they may soon face a roadblock when you ask them to write it. Why? Perhaps it is because reading poetry can be such a challenging experience. Students may not think that they are "deep" enough to write poetry. True, some students are naturally talented poets, but others learn by seeing how others write, being inspired by what they learn, or simply by patterning the work of others. This probably is the best reason to read and study a variety of poetry before assigning all your students to write it. Once they understand the unique characteristics of poetry and experience the joy of word play by others, they eagerly accept the challenge to try versing, writing poems of their own.

Like many English teachers, you probably have been reading poems and having students write poetry as part of other lessons already. You may have students write poems in response to literature as recommended in chapter 5 on the modern novel. You understand what a fine vehicle poetry is for showcasing young writers' understanding of the literature and its connection to their lives. Now, in this chapter, notice that the purpose of writing poetry is different. It is for your students to experiment and conscientiously apply some of the elements of poetry to recreate experiences of their own.

This chapter offers suggestions for trying out different approaches to poetry writing. So, feel free to let the students play with the language before evaluating the quality of their writing. Choose from the following activities, those in your own textbooks, or those you have found useful in the past. They all are designed to help your students compose a variety of poems that reflect their own personal experiences and observations and to encourage these young teenagers to dig deeper into quality literature.

PATTERNS AND EMULATIONS

Want a compelling way for your reluctant writers to jump into poetry writing? Imitation. Modeling what others write. This is nothing new. Patterning and copying the work of others are traditional ways to teach difficult skills. Consider the painter and musician, the dancer and athlete. In each case, these novices try to duplicate the strokes and colors, the sound and technique, the form and movement of the masters. You can give your students similar opportunities during this poetry unit.

Lead the way and model for them, first—choose a poem that you love and, with your curious young teens, show how you work through the process of figuring out the pattern, then of imitating that pattern. Ask them to look for rhyme and rhythm; draw their attention to sentence structure; entice them to imitate the kind of imagery; or challenge them to recreate the emotional impact through sound and choice of words.

Perhaps you already are familiar with the poem "Where I'm From" by George Ella Lyon. Use this verse to begin, and then let the students pick one or two of their favorite poems from the unit and write a poem that emulates the structure, style, techniques, and rhythm of their chosen poet. See the companion website for this book for specific assignment handouts.

Structured poems may be your choice to introduce this kind of poetry writing. The limerick, haiku, and sonnet are traditional patterns of poetry—each with a specific rhyme or rhythm pattern. Many of your students already are familiar with these patterns from elementary school. Here are a couple traditional patterns to trigger their memory:

Limerick: a five-line poem, usually funny, that follows an aabba structure.

> There was an Old Man in a tree,
> Who was horribly bored by a Bee;
> When they said, "Does it buzz?"
> He replied, "Yes, it does!"
> "It's a regular brute of a Bee!"
> (Edward Lear)

Sonnet: a poem of fourteen lines that follows a strict rhyme scheme and specific structure. There are different types of sonnets, the most well known being the English sonnet as shown below:

> Let me not to the marriage of true minds (a)
> Admit impediments, love is not love (b)
> Which alters when it alteration finds, (a)
> Or bends with the remover to remove. (b)
> O no, it is an ever fixed mark (c)
> That looks on tempests and is never shaken; (d)
> It is the star to every wand'ring bark, (c)
> Whose worth's unknown although his height be taken. (d)
> Love's not time's fool, though rosy lips and cheeks (e)
> Within his bending sickle's compass come, (f)
> Love alters not with his brief hours and weeks, (e)
> But bears it out even to the edge of doom: (f)
> If this be error and upon me proved, (g)
> I never writ, nor no man ever loved. (g)
> (Shakespeare, "Sonnet 116")

Or you may refer them to the ballad "Barbara Allen," as modeled in chapter 7.

While you definitely want to spend some time modeling the different poems with or for your students, save plenty of time for them to experiment independently. Remember, your goal is to provide the classroom structure and cultivate a nurturing environment that makes for a safe and comfortable setting in which to learn. Slowly, but steadily release some of that control as the students become comfortable with the classroom routines. The way you spend time shows what is important. During this portion of the unit, play and practice are important. Soon, you can persuade them to perform self-selected or written poetry for their peers. And just as athletes and dancers who practice a lot feel more confident performing, your maturing teens feel more assured when they have practiced.

Pantoums

One pattern that yields successful poems in middle school is a version of the less-familiar pantoum, a poem consisting of eight nonrhyming lines where each are used twice. A pantoum is less intimidating for reluctant poets and works well because it is based more on repetition than on rhyme or rhythm patterns. It also can be used as an alternative book report to capture key events, a memorable scene, or a favorite character from a literary work or from a life experience. You may have noticed a student sample in chapter 5 about the twentieth-century novel. Here is a sample poem written when a seventh-grade class finished reading *A Farewell to Manzanar* by John Houston and Jeanne Watasuki Houston, an autobiographical novel about Japanese internment during World War II.

Begin by writing four original lines:

(1) When I was seven
(2) My family was evacuated.
(3) We rode a bus
(4) To Manzanar.

Repeat lines two and four, and add lines five and six to expand ideas introduced in lines two and four, like this:

(2) My family was evacuated.
(5) Only forty-eight hours to prepare, then
(4) To Manzanar.
(6) We rode in shock, but together.

Repeat lines five and six, and add lines seven and eight to expand ideas
mentioned in lines five and six, like this:

(5) Only forty-eight hours to prepare.
(7) Mama, stressed and frustrated, broke all the dishes.
(6) We rode in shock, but together.
(8) Together, except for Papa.

Finally, repeat lines one, three, seven, and eight in this order:

(7) Mama, stressed and frustrated, broke all the dishes.
(3) We rode a bus
(8) Together, except for Papa.
(1) When I was seven.

The final poem, then, reads

> When I was seven
> My family was evacuated.
> We rode a bus
> To Manzanar.
> My family was evacuated.
> Only forty-eight hours to prepare, then
> To Manzanar.
> We rode in shock, but together.
> Only forty-eight hours to prepare, then
> Mama, stressed and frustrated, broke all the dishes.
> We rode in shock, but together.
> Together, except for Papa.
> Mama, stressed and frustrated, broke all the dishes.
> We rode a bus
> Together, except for Papa.
> When I was seven.

The result is a lovely poem that captures the essence of the story. If you try this pattern yourself you can see how much grammar students must review to make sure pronouns are the right number and gender and that the verbs are the right tense to make sense as they add more lines!

Lazy Sonnets

Here is a simple structured format that works well with ninth-grade students and gutsy young ones. You may assign these "lazy sonnets" after a formal study of poetry that included study of the traditional fourteen-line sonnets, after teaching Shakespeare's *Romeo and Juliet* or another play that includes sonnets. The students use this exercise to practice poetry and also to summarize their thoughts about the play. The only rules are to use fourteen words and to follow the rhyme pattern of an Elizabethan (Shakespearean) or Italian (Petrarchan) sonnet.

As a culminating activity, following a study of *Romeo and Juliet*, the assignment was simply to encapsulate a key idea, to show the characters, conflicts, or a theme of the play using just fourteen words and to end with a rhymed couplet. You could divide the class into five groups, one per act, or a number that fits the play you are studying, and have students in each group write about their assigned act. Here is one Kaveh wrote based on act 5 of *Romeo and Juliet*.

Paris
slain
by
Romeo.
Romeo
then
slew
himself.
Later
Juliet
slew
herself.
Madness
Sadness.
(Kaveh)

What is particularly fun about writing these lazy sonnets is that they are manageable for a range of students. Students who are frustrated by writing other poetry likely can compose a lazy sonnet successfully. Some even include a rhyme or rhythm pattern as well as the couplet! Your creative students may write quickly enough for you to enter their sonnets on the computer and print out these unrevised sonnets by the end of the period. Quick. Fun. Enlightening for students. Revealing to you.

CAPTURING PERSONAL EXPERIENCES IN POETRY

Much writing is autobiographical, portraying personal experiences. But it can be more. Joseph Epstein writes, "The personal essay is, in my experience, a form of discovery. What one discovers in writing such essays is where one stands on complex issues, problems, questions, and subjects. In writing the essay, one tests one's feelings, instincts, and thoughts in the crucible of composition."[1] This self- discovery is also true when writing poetry.

For their poetry assignments, encourage the students to use their personal experiences and observations as they imitate the structure and pattern of published poetry they enjoy. In keeping with the training in the National Writing Project, write along with your students. This keeps you attuned to what it feels like to write "on demand" and also gives you an opportunity to reveal to your students a little of who you are when you are not teaching. The poem opening this chapter is one written about a son's growing up and leaving home.

Initially, you may be uncomfortable writing about your personal experiences in front of or along with your young teenagers, but it is well worth any risk of discomfort. Be prepared; you and your students may be surprised by what comes out in this kind of writing. Occasionally several of you may decide not to show it to anyone or read it aloud. Honor these decisions. You can pass; allow them to pass.

You saw in the last chapter the poem written when one class read and patterned the narrative ballad "Barbara Allen." Later in the school year, when one class was modeling the sentence structure, rhyme, and rhythm pattern of Robert Frost poetry they were asked to recreate an experience of their own. You probably recall from attending poetry readings yourself that poets often explain the incident that gave rise to particular poems. Invite your students to do this and model such an introduction yourself. That was done before reading the draft of the poem evoked by the Robert Frost poem "I Have Been One Acquainted with the Night" read that day. Here is what I gave as background for the poem.

In 1996, I was part of a team of teachers who, sponsored by Rotary International, served as ambassadors of education to Kenya, Uganda, and the French island of Mauritius. I had never been to Africa and was thrilled about the opportunity, but a little apprehensive at the same time.

Families who were curious about us and about our country often volunteered to be our hosts. On our last evening in Mombasa, Kenya, our new friends had a lawn party and invited members of the local Rotary groups and their families to attend. After dinner, they asked each member of our team to speak about our time in Mombasa. When I arose to speak, trying to compose myself and gather my thoughts, I looked up. Seeing the brilliant night sky, it all of a sudden struck me that I could be standing on the soil of my ancestors; they could have stood in this same place and witnessed such a sparkly navy blue night.

As a fifth-generation descendent of African slaves, I don't know where exactly in Africa my family is from. Nevertheless, standing there in the Kenyan night moved me deeply. Tears leaked from my eyes; primordial memories arose and clogged my throat; I couldn't see; I couldn't speak, but somehow I began to sing the old Negro Spiritual "Sometimes I Feel Like a Motherless Child." To this day, I have no idea why that particular song came to me. Nor did I realize how deeply lodged in my memory that experience had become—until I began patterning Robert Frost's poem "I Have Been One Acquainted with the Night." It was then that I understood Epstein's point that writing is a form of discovery.

Describing my African experience did help my students understand that we humans often do not know what we think or feel until we read what we write. I encourage you to write with your students, too. You, too, may unlock something memorable about an experience you have had and may write a poem you are willing to share with your students. Here is mine:

I have been one acquainted with that song.
I've sung the song in tune—and out of tune
I have held that high note oh so long.

I have sung the song—clear like a loon.
I have kept within the music's beat
And swooped down low, yet staying right in tune.

I've sung that song and let my voice just soar
While deep within my soul the words brought tears
That slipped right down my cheeks; my heart just tore.

That song, reminding me of trials sore
Experienced by people who did so long
For freedom, justice, rights, and so much more.
Freedoms they'd awaited for too long.
I have been one acquainted with that song.
(Anna J. Small Roseboro, "Acquainted with That Song." Patterned after
"Acquainted with the Night" by Robert Frost.)

WRITING ABOUT POETRY

Responding to poetry through essay writing is an important component
of poetry study. You can combine writing poetry and writing about poetry in the same unit. If so, it would be beneficial to begin with a quick
review of poetry T.I.M.E. Then select and project on screen an appropriately challenging poem and have the students conduct a T.I.M.E
analysis of it. Projecting the poem can be better for the whole class work
because all must focus their attention up front.

As in earlier class lessons, you follow this format: ask the students
to read the poem silently; read the poem aloud; have students in the
class read according to the punctuation following the jump in reading described in the previous chapter. By the fourth readings students
begin noticing the elements of imagery and music and they also may
sense some emotion—either expressed by the author or experienced by
themselves, as readers.

If you provide students with copies of the poem, also give them a
couple of colored pencils. In this case, you have the students underline

what strikes them as they read the poem to themselves. On the first reading, encourage the students to underline appealing or thought-provoking words and phrases. Then, before the second reading, ask them to exchange pencils for another color, and mark what attracts them on this second reading. It is fine to underline the same word or phrase in a second color. Then, conclude this version of multiple readings by asking students to read aloud the words or phrases they have underlined. If one student reads a line first, it is all right for another student to repeat it. It is likely that the repeated words and phrases reveal the theme or main ideas of the poem.

Next, after whatever opening reading strategy you choose, have students complete their T.I.M.E. worksheets on their own, answering questions about the title, thought, and theme; and imagery; music; and emotion (see Teacher Resource F). Then have them talk about their observations with a partner. Finally, conduct a full-class discussion of student reactions and responses. Remind them to use the P.I.E. format—oral practice for writing an analysis of the poem. Ask them to state their point/observation about the poem, illustrate that observation with a direct quotation from the poem, and explain the significance of that illustration.

For homework or during the next class meeting, assign the students to write a three-part essay in which they write an analysis of that poem or one of their own choosing. They should use the information they gathered while "telling the T.I.M.E" of the poem (see box 8.1).

Another way to have students write about poetry is to invite them to make connections based on their own experiences, a text-to-self response. In the Gordon Parks poem "The Funeral," Parks writes about returning to his hometown after years of absence. Instruct them to consider how a place they knew as a child seemed different when they returned as a young teen. Warren's response follows.

Warren's response to Gordon Parks's "The Funeral":

> When I was younger I would go the YMCA and for the camp we would go to Discovery Zone. Everyone I knew would go down this slide that was called the black hole. Now I was about 6 then and still disliked the dark and it wasn't just the dark that made the slide scary. It was that I would always create so much friction that it would spark and pop on my skin. I was much shorter then also, so the slide seamed much larger that it realy

---

Box 8.1.   In-class Writing about Poetry—Telling the T.I.M.E.

Carefully read the assigned poem noting the structure, imagery, and meaning or message for you. Then write a complete essay in response to the poem that includes the following:

- Summary of the poem—What is it about?
- Structure of the poem—What poetic devices does the poet use?
- Personal response to the poem—What poetic devices help create this personal response?
- Thesis statement that indicates the kind of poem it is and your personal response to it.
- Body paragraphs that explain ways the structure of the poem influences your response.
- Quotations that support your observations.

You may write on the copy of the poem and use the space below it for your notes.

---

was. 3 years later one of my friends had a birthday party at Discovery Zone and amazingly I had gone throw a couple of growth spirts so I was much taller. I went up to the "Black hole" which apparently wasn't so dark as I had previously found. So when I went down it had seemed to extremely short as well.

ASSIGNING THE POETRY PROJECT/NOTEBOOK

An effective way to reinforce the interests raised and skills developed during a poetry unit is to have the students assemble a poetry notebook. The collection should include poems students have read and enjoyed as well as poems they have written themselves. Decide how much time you have to devote to this project and select activities that may be organized around the students' choice of one or more of the following topics:

- Poems by a single poet
- Poems written on a single theme (love, family, hobby, season, etc.)

- Poems employing common poetic devices
- Poems reflecting a specific culture

It is imperative to inform your students at the beginning of the poetry unit that they are to create this poetry notebook. In this way they can think about and collect poems throughout the weeks you spend on formal poetry study. Encourage students to use twenty-first-century technology to save their poems, and also to create video, digital, or audio components of their poetry notebooks that can be shared live or online.

Assigning a poetry project is a good way to incorporate a research component into your instruction, too. Your school librarian can help students find background and biographical information on their selected poet and, if the access to the Internet is available, refer students to preselected websites. Your youngsters may prefer to create an electronic version of this notebook and post it for sharing with other middle school students around the country and around the world. In your planning for the project, check online sites with safe environments for students to post their writing. Your colleagues may be familiar with such sites or you can ask online teacher communities such as the NCTE Ning for recommendations. You may even decide to connect with students in other areas of the world through e-pals.com.

The choices students have to make for this project, conducting research, writing and selecting poems, deciding formats, creating order, using technology, collaborating with classmates all are part of an authentic assessment where students are showing what they know and are able to do based on skills they bring and those they learn under your carefully designed tutelage.

Poetry Out Loud in Choral Form

Invite local poets to come read or perform for your students and include time in class for students to prepare and perform poetry for one another. This can be a powerful experience for speakers and listeners as evidenced by the opening poem to chapter 7, called "Words, Words, Words." That is a poetic response to a performance of student poets.

When teaching *Romeo and Juliet*, for example, you could require students to memorize the prologue to act 1. To aid the students in learning these fourteen lines, on the day you introduce the play, perform the sonnet yourself, and then have the students echo it back to you, line by line. On subsequent days, begin the class period by having the class stand and recite the sonnet together. Since the prologue previews the plot of the play, this oral, auditory activity provides a regular reminder of what happens as the drama unfolds.

Performing poetry is an occasion to use hand gestures to help the students see and remember the lines and the ideas. Think of the line "A pair of star-crossed lovers take their lives," which you could begin by holding up the pointer finger of each hand and then bringing the fingers together, forming an X, by the time you reach the end of that line of the poem. Logically, when you reach the closing couplet, "which if you with patient ears attend / What here shall miss, our toil shall strive to mend," just point to an ear.

Some days, conduct the chorus of students by beginning the first stanza as a solo, direct one side of the room to recite the next stanza, then have the other side speak the next one, and conclude by saying the closing couplet together. On other days, you might divide the poem into parts and organize speakers by gender. By the second week, when most of the class knows the sonnet by heart, invite individuals to recite a line alone, or with a student "director" while you stand aside or sit as their audience. On the test for the play, offer extra credit for the students to write as many lines of the prologue as they can. Most are able to write the whole sonnet!

You should not be surprised either if you see students you taught this way standing around challenging one another to perform this sonnet . . . with the hand gestures! Repetition and physical movement are powerful reinforcements to learning.

In other classes, assign a poem and then ask small groups to develop their version of a choral reading to perform for the class. A classic performance piece is "The Highwayman" by Alfred Noyes. For a chilling end, suggest that the closing line be spoken by a single soft-voiced student.

A contemporary favorite is Maya Angelou's "On the Pulse of Morning," which she recited at the Presidential Inauguration Ceremony for Bill Clinton in 1993.[2] Not surprising, no two groups develop the same script. That is just fine. Seeing and hearing different "versions" of this poem expand the students' understanding of and appreciation for the ideas, sounds, and images of diverse people groups Angelou mentions in her memorable masterpiece.

Your colleagues may even welcome this opportunity to have their students witness poetry out loud. So, on performance day, have each class decide which group gives the most powerful or interesting performance and then commission this group to represent the class and go "on the road," reciting their rendition of the poem to other classes that meet in your hallway. What pride students feel performing poetry for classes of older or younger students!

CELEBRATING POETRY

By this time you and your students have read, written, and performed poetry in class; you are ready for a special Poetry Celebration. See Teacher Resource G for ideas for student preparation. It can be simply a special time during the regular class period or a bigger event to which family and friends are invited to meet in the cafeteria, auditorium, or library.

For the celebration, invite all the students to memorize and perform a selected poem—one that they have read or one that they have written. If you have multiple classes celebrating together, you could hold an "open mike" time where volunteers come forward to perform their chosen poem. To assure that someone volunteers, ask students to sign up ahead of time. On celebration day

- Have all students display their notebooks on tables like a science fair exhibition.
- Have a student master or mistress of ceremonies welcome the guests.
- Have a second master or mistress of ceremonies call on the volunteers to recite their poems.
- Invite everyone in attendance to share the light refreshments.

Be prepared for on-the-spot volunteers who see the joy of performing and want to share the spotlight. All of this means planning ahead to reserve the space, to have microphones in place, and to have refreshments bought or brought and laid out. Students should be recruited to help set up and clean up.

If you work together with other teachers, you may be able to turn this into a schoolwide event. Post student poetry in the halls. Write it with colored chalk on the sidewalks (with permission of the principal, of course). Encourage the students to enter their writing in local, state, and national poetry contests in print, audiovisual, or electronic formats, or to perform it in age-appropriate poetry slam venues.

The Poetry Celebration is the perfect time to invite students to recite poetry of their nationality, culture, or home language. Since poetry is written to be heard, it does not matter whether everyone in the audience understands every spoken word. Just invite these students to recite a favorite poem and let them bask in the pleasure of sharing themselves in a language close to their hearts. To enhance the experience of the listeners, though, encourage those students who are comfortable reciting the poem in a language other than English to first give a synopsis of the poem.

Figure 8.1. Poetry Little Key

CONCLUSION

Poetry writing need not lead to student defeat or frustration. Your creative, well-structured lesson planning and nurturing instruction can create an environment in which students compose and recite poetry with pleasure and poise, with personality and pride. You can invite professional groups like Poetry Alive to come perform at your school. You can confirm the fine work of your students and encourage them to submit their poetry for publication in print or on safe Internet sites. Of course, support students who decide to enter local poetry slams and attend them if you can.

Celebrate poetry with your students and watch how what they learn about the power of careful word choices, deliberate crafting, and attention to organization and appearance carries over into their reading and writing about other fiction and nonfiction. With your help, they look forward to "versing" their lives in poetry, the way I learned to turn my prose thoughts about my son, Robert, into the verse that opens this chapter.

⑨

OPENING THE PAST IMAGINATIVELY:
TEACHING HISTORICAL FICTION

I will always be grateful to her for one thing. She taught me my letters. My mistress, I realize now, like many women of her class, had very little education. She read slowly and laboriously, and it always took her several tearful afternoons to compose a letter to her family in Portugal, or to her nephew in Madrid, a young man who was a painter. Yet Mistress had a great deal of practical wisdom, and she knew many things because she trusted her judgment and cultivated her memory.

—*I, Juan de Pareja*[1]

Five sentences. A mistress, a slave, a painter. Tearful afternoons, practical wisdom, and judgment. From Spain to Italy—and beyond. All brought alive through the magic of one work of historical fiction that transports twenty-first-century teens to Renaissance Europe. Five sentences and thousands of miles spanning hundreds of years. There is an entirely engaging education in one novel of historical fiction thanks to a splendid writer like Elizabeth Borton de Treviño. With the ideas here and this accessible work of fiction, or one from your list or from those mentioned at the end of the chapter, you can have a great time exploring the past, meeting the academic needs of your modern-day students and the goals of your school.

Not only is teaching historical fiction fun, but it also is an excellent way to integrate English language arts with other subjects like social studies, science, and the arts. Consider collaborating with colleagues in another department. In this case, choose a literary work that introduces or reinforces a historical period or explores some scientific concept your shared students are learning in one of those content areas. You can create together a course of study that meets the requirements of both content areas for state and national standards and presents integrated lessons so critical to a successful program for adolescents. Such cross-curricular study helps adolescents to see and make connections across the disciplines. It also is an enriching experience for you.

WONDERING WHY THIS HISTORICAL NOVEL?

I, Juan de Pareja, by Elizabeth Borton de Treviño, is written as an autobiography from the point of view of Juan, an African slave inherited by Diego de Velázquez, the court painter for King Philip IV of Spain who reigned in the seventeenth century. Juan became the assistant and friend to Velázquez and later an accomplished painter in his own right. One of Juan de Pareja's paintings hangs in the Prado Museum in Madrid, Spain, and Velázquez's painting of Juan is in the New York Metropolitan Museum of Art. See images of both paintings at art sites on the Internet.

If you are looking for an engaging book to expand your reading lists to include works from and about other cultures, this one works. It may be an immediate favorite to teach if you are inspired by someone like Suzanne Federico who had been a closet art historian. She pointed out that Velázquez's work reflects four schools of European art. Descriptions in the book introduce readers to specific fifteenth- and sixteenth-century painters' artwork and the distinctive characteristics of chiaroscuro, baroque, realism, and idealism. Borton de Treviño writes so clearly students hardly realize how much they are learning. But you can ensure that they do so from the very beginning. Let them help build the foundation and research some of the historical period themselves.

The novel, *I, Juan de Pareja*, is set during the Renaissance, an epoch of people, places, and incidents that impacted art, science, and exploration. In the novel, Rubens (1577–1640), the famous Flemish painter, visits the Spanish Court, and Velázquez travels to Italy to purchase art for King Philip. Imagine the budget! This novel also talks about friendships—a topic that middle school students also love to talk about. The characters are faced with ethical issues that can elicit lively student conversations about issues of right and wrong.

The premise of the story is the fact that the painting *Las Meniñas*, in which Velázquez includes a portrait of himself, shows the Cross of Santiago painted onto his garment in a style quite different from his own. Ms. Borton's tale attempts to explain who painted this cross and why anyone would do so. That is a good reason to display a copy of *Las Meniñas* in the classroom while you and your students study this particular historical novel. Images of famous artwork like this are readily available on a range of websites and in books on Renaissance art found in most libraries.

GETTING INTO THE NOVEL

Begin by explaining to students the features of historical fiction and the fact that they are going to be reading one. Share with them that historical fiction may include real people, real places, and real events. Following Louise Rosenblatt's reader-response approach, encourage the students to look for the familiar, even in a piece of historical fiction. Susan Zimmermann and Chryse Hutchins use different terminology but also urge teachers to have students make connections when reading literature.[2] These educators advocate such relationships as

- Text to self (between the novel and their own lives)
- Text to text (among the people, places, and incidents in the novel)
- Text to text (between this work and other literature students have read)
- Text to world (between this book and historical or current events)

If you chose a novel in collaboration with a colleague from another content area, add text to study in history or text to study in science, or whatever the other content area is.

When you teach a work of historical fiction, it is important to set the scene. For *I, Juan de Pareja*, give a brief overview of the Renaissance period, an era whose style in art history began in Rome, Italy, and spread throughout Europe during 1450–1600. Following the dark ages, this was a period of intense revival in all areas of math, science, arts, and humanities.

The Renaissance is often referred to as the rebirth of the classics, as the participants looked to the texts and monuments of the Greco-Roman civilizations for inspiration and direction.[3] This could be a good time to do a quick word study on the prefix and root of Renaissance! Teaching vocabulary in context makes it easier to remember.

BIOGRAPHICAL ORAL PRESENTATIONS GIVE AN OVERVIEW OF PEOPLE AND EVENTS

To help set the stage for students to acquire a richer sense of the historical period and practice their research skills, let them look for information about the real people, places, and events of the period in which the novel is set and report out to the class what they learn.

Consider assigning them to use the Internet or an encyclopedia to learn about the people of the golden age that Borton de Treviño mentions in her foreword, like Galileo, Rembrandt, and Sir Walter Raleigh. Most of the names on this list are so well known that students have little difficulty locating facts for a brief two- to three-minute informative speech. The same is likely to be true for the novel you choose since historical novels tend to be written about famous times, places, or people.

Depending on your students' access to resources, you may decide to spend a week on this assignment, allowing in-class time for research, writing, and practice. You may wish to include minilessons on note taking, summarizing, and documentation, making citations to reduce innocent plagiarism. And, it is a good idea to assign students to use time at home to practice their delivery, perhaps in front of two adults who sign a confirmation form that they have heard the speech. This also is a way to let families and friends know what their child or friend is learning.

This mini-assignment you are giving your young adolescents provides a real purpose for conducting simple research, collaborating with a peer, practicing speech writing, and giving oral reports. If it is not realistic to expect your students to complete this assignment at home, allot in-class time for pairs of students to give their speeches to each other or recruit faculty and staff at your school to be listeners. You may be surprised how many school support staff members are delighted to play a part in the academic education of the students they serve as secretaries, janitors, bus drivers, and cafeteria workers.

Preparing for Oral Presentations about People of the Renaissance

As you prep for teaching this novel, notice in the foreword of the novel, *I, Juan de Pareja*, that many of the names in the reading (such as Galileo, Rubens, and Shakespeare) are familiar, but none are women. But, as you conduct background research on artists of this period, you do learn that two female artists should be included: Artemisia Gentileschi and Elisabetta Sirani. Both were talented artists whose work is equal to that of their male contemporaries. Add their names to your list along with other noteworthy names of women of the Renaissance.

Women of the Renaissance

It may be a little more difficult for your students to locate information about women of the Renaissance, other than Joan of Arc.[4] Nevertheless, students should be able to locate online information about:

- Elisabetta Sirani—the lightning-quick painter who opened an all-female art school and became an international sensation.
- Grace O'Malley—the mother of three who ruled the high seas as Ireland's pirate queen and freedom fighter.
- Artemisia Gentileschi, a colleague of Elisabetta Sirani, was the first woman to paint large-scale history and religious pictures. She was known for her inventive use of techniques developed by the Italian artist Caravaggio, who once worked with Raphael in Rome.[5] Susan

Vreeland's *The Passion of Artemisia* is told from the point of view of Artemisia Gentileschi.

- Christina of Sweden—the eccentric Swedish monarch who awakened her country to the wonders of Renaissance art, science, and literature.
- Gracia Mendes Nasi—the Spanish humanitarian and philanthropist whose "underground railroad" during the sixteenth century saved the lives of countless persecuted Jews.[6]

For ease in assigning topics, simply have the students pull for numbers one through eighteen or more (based on the number of names on the list). Those who have the same number can research the same person, and then those students can work together to decide how to best make their presentation. Each presentation should include the following information based on the five W's and an H: Who, What, When, Where, Why, and How. Whatever list of people you offer your students should reflect both genders, as well as cultural, and social, economic and political incidents representative of the historical setting of your book.

Sample Assignment Sheet for Oral Presentation
Based on Renaissance Personages

1. Use a print or online encyclopedia to find the answers to the following questions about the person you are assigned to give an oral report on:
   - Who is the person?
   - What is he or she famous for doing?
   - When was he or she born?
   - Where was he or she born? Locate the country on a world map.
   - Why is his or her work, invention, discovery, and so forth important in contemporary society?
2. How was his or her work, invention, discovery viewed during his or her lifetime?
3. Record the information that tells where you got your facts. Include:
   - Author (if one is listed)
   - Title of article or encyclopedia entry

- Title of encyclopedia and volume number (if applicable)
- Number of volumes (if applicable)
- City where published
- Publisher and city where published
- Year the book was published
- URL where you found information
- Date you accessed URL

4. Write a one-page summary that highlights what you learned to make an engaging informative speech. (A written summary of 250 words takes about two minutes to speak.)

Validating Student Research

To expand their knowledge, extend their recall, and to validate the significance of their classmates' research, assign students to keep notes as their peers speak. At the end of the unit or semester, include questions from these reports, an opportunity to demonstrate on an exam what they have learned during their study of the historical novel. While the students are researching and once they have presented their oral reports, keep the list of names visible, either written on the board, on a poster, or projected on a screen when they enter the classroom. Because students are likely to encounter these names as they study history, science, and art, the assignments in this unit support many interdisciplinary curricula. Keeping such a word wall with these names is just another effective way to reinforce valuable new information.

Symbols help students remember details. In the journal section set aside for notes about this historical novel, ask the students to create a chart in which they list the names of the Renaissance personages with space to include five W's and H facts as well as a column in draw in symbols. During the presentation by classmates, have your students write in their journals facts they hear. At the end of the presentations, as you review this information, invite students to recommend appropriate symbols to serve as memory aids.

For example, for Galileo, someone may suggest a telescope; for Moliere, the happy and sad face drama masks; for Isaac Newton, a stick figure sitting under an apple tree; for Joan of Arc, a woman with a sword. Deciding appropriate symbols is another way to teach to the multiple intelligences your students have. Consider asking one of the more artistic ones to draw the symbols for the class to copy. This can be a fine time for you to stand aside and let them shine.

Reinforcing Learning

During the first couple of weeks that the class reads and discusses the novel, schedule a four- or five-minute review of the historical personages at the beginning of each period. One day, you could project or show the symbol(s) for ten or more of the historical figures and have students name the person(s) and something for which each is famous; another day read the names and ask the students to draw the symbol or write a fact about the person. To avoid having to collect and grade these quickie quizzes, you could conduct "honor" checks. While the students are writing their responses, pick up your grade book and have it ready to record how they did immediately following the quiz.

Since the purpose is to give the students a daily opportunity to show that they are learning about these famous Renaissance personages, you want to make this a low-key activity. Therefore, immediately following the quiz, go over the answers and ask the students to indicate to you how many they missed, using their fingers held close to their chests so that only you can see them. Then, just record a check-plus, check, or check-minus instead of a letter grade. If someone misses more than five, enter a minus sign. Commend them all for their fine work, and move to the next activity for the day. Your daily checks encourage them to study their notes and by the second week most of the students are able to identify these famous figures and recall a pertinent fact about each one.

Occasionally, some of your students extend the assignment on their own and bring in articles or ads from the newspapers or magazines that allude to or mention the people on your list or show some symbol of the times. Depending on where you are teaching, you may ask the students to search through the telephone book, the local newspaper, or an online source to see how many products and companies carry these Renaissance names, or names of people or places in the book you are studying.

Set aside a space in the classroom, hang up a blank poster board, and encourage students to bring in examples of these ads and articles. They can add these examples to a poster that all can view during your historical novel unit. For *I, Juan de Pareja*, you could label the poster "Renaissance Today" and watch as a collage of student contributions emerges. Or, you could have students add their findings to a gallery you set up in a class wiki just for this purpose. It's just another way to have students paying attention to the world around them, thinking about what they are reading, and contributing to the learning environment they share with you.

OFFERING EXTRA CREDIT—YES AND NO

Yes, it's fine to offer extra credit when students find the names of the people mentioned in your text in their history or science texts or in the newspaper. Yes, you want to ensure that the students are making connections, not simply finding the names and earning unwarranted extra credit. So, to help control dependence on the extra-credit option, limit the percentage of extra points students may earn each marking period to about 5 percent. These extra points can help a student who has had a slow start make up for homework points missed earlier in the marking period, or to make up for a test or quiz taken when the student had been tired, ill, or distracted by some personal issue. With young adolescents, it doesn't take much for them to have an off day!

Extra points should not be so weighty, however, that they make it unnecessary for students to earn passing grades that demonstrate proficiency in the required curriculum content. It is important to resist assigning or encouraging students to do extra projects that take time from that which they should be giving to learning basic course content materials or skills. Most important, extra-credit points should not require extra work for you, the teacher.

All extra-credit points should be recorded in your grade book at least a week before the marking period ends. This early cut-off date reduces the temptation for students to misdirect their attention from learning and showing knowledge of required course content and skill acquisition just to raise their quarter grade. And enforcing this early cut-off date preserves time for you to grade those assignments needed to determine the student grades for that marking period.

WORKING THROUGH THE NOVEL

If possible, teach the historical novel in the spring. By this time, your students already have studied the structure of fiction and several short stories that illustrate the elements of fiction and they know the literary devices authors use to enhance the storytelling. Your maturing young teens know to set up a section in the journals for this new kind of novel, and to write notes as you present facts about the period in which this particular historical novel is set. When you begin your unit, just remind them that historical novels are fiction, with plot lines arranged in much the same way as short stories.

By spring, your students pay attention to facts revealed in the exposition, but you may need to review ways to mark their texts or to take notes in their journals. For example, you could have them use a pencil to circle the name of each character the first time each is encountered in the reading. Then, underline the words or phrases that identify that character.

If students are not allowed to write in their texts, they can list the names of new characters in their reading journals and include the page numbers and a few words or phrases the author uses to identify those characters. Then, ask them to pay attention, as they continue reading, to see if or how the author rounds out the characters through direct and indirect characterization. By this time in the school year, your students know that the protagonist is a dynamic character, so they are watching to see what brings about the change in this character from the beginning, through the challenge of the conflict, to the falling action and resolution.

The students can identify the setting by putting a rectangle around words and/or phrases that indicate time and places; or students can record this information in their journals. This kind of marking and writing forces students to slow down a bit. It also helps them get to know the people and places in the book, and these readers are less likely to be confused as the action intensifies and conflict increases. Because *Juan* is written as an autobiography, the students quickly notice that the point of view is first person and can predict that the major problem to be solved is that of growing up and surviving the challenges Juan encountered during his lifetime.

As with all direct instruction of reading, according to Carol Jago, your ongoing challenge is "to help students refine how they examine a piece of literature without destroying their confidence as readers."[7] Teaching students to be active readers increases their reliance on their own ability to understand whatever they read, whenever they read, and for whatever purpose they read.

STIMULATING INTEREST IN STYLES OF PAINTING

After reading chapter 5 of *I, Juan de Pareja*, "In Which Rubens Visits Our Court," you can introduce the students to four styles of art reflected in the book and prominent in the Renaissance: chiaroscuro, baroque, realism, and idealism. This prepares the students to understand later book-related discussions about art. Keep in mind that art often reflects the social, economic, and political milieu of the times in which the artists live. So, even if you are teaching a different novel, it is still worthwhile to bring in photos, art work, or articles. They all can give a richer sense of the history of the period in which your novel is set. The school media center likely has many resources your librarian is delighted to have you check out and use in your classroom.

You could adapt your presentation of art terms like this. Prepare a handout for the students with the information such as that below. Use PowerPoint to present visual examples of each style. During the PowerPoint presentation, read some of the narration that defines and illustrates key terms: chiaroscuro, baroque, realism, and idealism. In Teacher Resources on the companion website for this book is the *I, Juan de Pareja* PowerPoint presentation prepared for this section of the unit.

- *Chiaroscuro*—"treatment of light and shade in a picture."[8] Caravaggio, an Italian artist, is known to have used this style.
- *Baroque*—a "style of art and architecture that prevailed in Europe from about 1550 to the late 1700's, characterized by the use of curved forms and lavish ornamentation."[9] Rubens is a key baroque painter; be careful about showing paintings of his nude (not "naked") models.

- *Realism*—(in art and literature) "the picturing of life as it actually is."[10]
- *Idealism*—(in art and literature) "the representation of imagined types rather than of exact likeness of people, instances, or situations."[11] The students may be disappointed when they learn that Velázquez seemed to stray from his philosophy to paint what is "truth."

Showing the works of such artists as Murillo, Michelangelo, Titian, and Raphael helps students understand references about the art that Velázquez and Juan saw during their trip to Rome.

If you and your students are enjoying this adventure with art, consider letting them demonstrate their new knowledge of art. Create a scavenger hunt during which students find examples of various paintings and styles in the library books with collections of Renaissance art. Websites like the Art Archive and the Artcyclopedia are additional resources for a range of artworks. The National Archives at archives.gov is a good source for information on American artists. Invite students to post what they find on the class wiki or create a PowerPoint presentation that they show one day in class.

If you are teaching a different historical novel and would like to incorporate a visual arts component, do so. Among the historical novels that work well for this kind of study are *Across Five Aprils* by Irene Hunt, *Bud, Not Buddy* by Christopher Paul Curtis, *Esperanza Rising* by Pam Muñoz Ryan, and *Girl with the Pearl Earring* by Susan Vreeland. The Library of Congress website (loc.gov) and numerous open access websites provide historical photographs to enhance your study of each of these titles. The loc.gov site also has sound recordings of real people from American history. Including auditory resources helps those students who learn best by listening and hearing real people talk about their lives and times and helps make these historical personages come alive for all your students.

CONNECTING GEOGRAPHY AND MAP STUDY

Velázquez and Juan make two trips from Spain to Italy; the story gives their itinerary. Ask students to locate the places on a map and follow

---

Box 9.1.   Search It!
Using Google Maps for Historical Literature

If you have access in the classroom or media center to the Google Maps website you can view the following with students:

- Current street-view images of historical sites
- Traditional, satellite-image, and topographical maps of locales
- Website previews of sites about historical buildings, events, and people

---

the journey by marking the places they visit. You could ask the history/social studies teacher for a blank map that includes outlines of Europe with France, Spain, and Italy, or the places mentioned in your book. For those reading *Juan*, this map work gives the students a sense of the distance between towns and the kind of topography the two characters had to cross to get to the Mediterranean Sea, and then on to their destinations in Italy. Since map reading is a skill most adolescents are expected to acquire, asking them to refer to and use maps while studying in your class provides opportunities to practice that skill as they expand their understanding of what is going on in the novel they are reading with you. (See box 9.1.)

EXPLORING FRIENDSHIP: A MULTILAYERED THEME

Elizabeth Borton de Treviño artfully describes friendships between King Philip and his court painter, the court painter and his slave, the apprentices and a slave, a dwarf and a slave, and a male and a female slave. So, these relationships are ready-made springboards for discussions about the nature of friendship. You could get the discussion off the ground by writing the word *friend* in the center of the whiteboard, on a poster, or on an overhead and then asking the students to brainstorm for words to describe a friend. Without commenting, list their answers around the word *friend*, forming a weblike cluster.

Next, ask them to open their journals to the section on this novel, and do a quick write on friends or friendship. Set your timer and write along with them. Having them write nonstop for three or four minutes to describe their concept or experience with friends usually elicits a level of honesty that may be missing in more prepared writing. They may write about a friendship that went well, one that dissolved, or one they wish existed. Then invite a few students to read aloud what they have written, honoring their privacy if they choose to decline. Unedited writing sometimes reveals emotions too raw to share in public. So, again, honor the choice to pass.

Round out the lesson by asking the students to write about the friendships they notice are developing in your novel. Which surprised them? Which do they think will develop, continue, or end? Why? Why not? To help the student to go beyond a simple listing of facts in their speaking and writing, encourage them to continue using P.I.E. paragraph format—where they answer the questions by stating their point, using specific incidents from the text to illustrate that point, then explaining the reasons they believe the incidents show that the friendship identified begins, continues, or ends.

Because the P.I.E. writings are more objective than their quick-writes, the students often are more willing to share them. In fact, students might disagree and even debate their differences about friendship. To keep them focused on the text, and to practice considering perspectives of others, challenge your students to take an opposing stance that they can support with evidence from the book. In doing so, they experience what it is like to give serious consideration to a different point of view. This is good practice for developing open minds about others.

WRITING AND DISCUSSING ETHICAL ISSUES

The National Middle School Association (NMSA) recommends that teachers address ethical issues while developing curricula. An NMSA publication even argues that any "curriculum design that does not provide opportunities and support for student to do 'right things' along with the significant adults in their lives is sadly incomplete."[12] A unit of study based on novels like *I, Juan de Pareja* provides such opportunities. Juan and the other characters in the book are faced with a number of ethical choices related to slavery, honesty, and loyalty.

The word *ethics* normally refers to defining and using standards of right and wrong, moral and immoral conduct. Ethics also involves analyzing situations in which people have to address moral conduct, duty, and judgment—making right, but often tough decisions. Several of the characters in this autobiographical novel are faced with just such choices. As your students read about them, they may identify with these situations even if they disagree with the characters' choices having to do with conducting slavery or using mentally and physically challenged persons to entertain one's children. Very likely equally rich topics arise in the book you choose to teach. Some raging debates may arise among students when you challenge them to consider the actions and attitudes expressed in the stories they read.

Responding Holistically to Literature

Fran Claggett says that teachers often dissect literature so minutely that students lose sight of the work as a whole. She recommends using art and graphics to give readers an opportunity to "make it whole" again.[13] Here is another opening to assign art, music, or poetry writing for that purpose: to help students reassemble the parts of the story, to see the novel as a whole work of literature. One assignment asks the students to write a narrative poem, similar to a ballad, in which they tell the whole story in quatrains. In this case, have the students include at least five, four-line stanzas to account for the exposition, rising action, climax, falling action, and resolution of the story.

If you choose to teach historical fiction at the end of the school year, your students already have had an in-depth poetry unit during which they learned that writing can be a poem—even if it does not have a set rhyme or rhythm pattern—as long as the writing "convey[s] a vivid and imaginative sense of experience, especially by the use of condensed language."[14]

Amanda's six-stanza narrative about *I, Juan de Pareja* follows:

> I am Juan de Pareja
> A black man living in Spain in the seventeenth century
> I once was a slave
> To Mistress Emilia and Master Diego Velázquez

Mistress Emilia died of a plague
It nearly took my life too
But a caring friar saved me
Who I called Brother Isidro

I was taken to Master Diego
By Don Carmelo, a terrible gypsy man
He made me beg and steal for my food
And then in turn stole things from me

I finally got to Master Diego
A very talented painter
I made his paints and was
His one and only helper

I was his slave for many years
Until he saw my painting
And then he freed Lolis and me
And we married

My dear wife and I
Live now in Seville
Master is long gone
But he is still alive in my hand and my heart.

Amanda captured some of the elements of the exposition, plot events, and even minor conflicts between Juan and Don Carmelo that may have arisen because Juan was a slave. However, when she concluded with a subtle hint of the theme of the unlikely but friendly relationship that grew between master and slave, Amanda reflects the essence of poetry with "But he is still alive in my hand and my heart." One would expect "my heart," but the "my hand" suggests an artistic, poetic bent reflected in Amanda's other work. She found a simple image to embody the love and talent that grew during Juan's years with Diego de Velázquez. See Teacher Resource E for an idea for Book Report #3, writing a narrative poem.

ALTERNATING END-OF-NOVEL ASSIGNMENTS

The following are particularly useful kinds of creative, open assignments at the end of a unit. It allows you to see what the students have learned in ways that may not have been revealed in response to earlier assignments. The students are free to choose their idea and structure to demonstrate what they know. Possibilities include:

- Create a melody for each of three or four of the main characters (à la Darth Vader from *Star Wars*).
- Bring in samples of music that reflect key scenes (like mood music).
- Bring in three or four different published songs that have lyrics that could have been sung by three or four different characters.
- Create original music for any of the three previously mentioned situations.

You can ask the students to write a page or two in which they explain the reasons for their choices and to indicate the page(s) of the text that support their choices for music.

One parent complained that I was "dumbing down" the curriculum when I allowed students to use artistic projects to show their understanding about the characters and their relationships and roles in the literature. However, after visiting my classroom to see the students' artwork, he noticed and acknowledged the sophisticated levels of comprehension they reflected. He was so impressed with the depth, breadth, and creativity of the work that he asked if he could sit in the class for the remainder of that unit!

You can be sure your alternative assignments are well designed and serve as successful alternative assessments if you

- Determine in advance what you want to learn about the student
- Tell students the knowledge on which they are being evaluated
- Give students options to show that knowledge in their dominant intelligence

WRITING ASSIGNMENTS TO EXPAND AND EXPLORE VISUAL ART

Ask students to choose a painting by one of the artists in *I, Juan de Pareja* or another historical novel or period based on the book you are studying. Selections may be by artists you have studied together or chosen because they reflect artistic styles similar to those students already have seen. The goal is to offer a variety of paintings for students to view and make connections between experiences the students have had reading the literature or just living life.

The following activities are based on notes taken and from handouts received during the workshop "Entering Art" led by Terry and Jenny Williams at the Detroit Museum of Art.[15] Variations on these suggestions work to inspire student poetry as well as essays because any work of art invites imaginative entry into its drama, mood, theme, locality, texture, and space. Both representational and abstract art can entice viewers into the artist's original act of creation.

This imaginative entry evokes all five senses, memories, and dreams as students look and allow themselves to feel and imagine. Allow a full period for this assignment to give time for an experience that is personal and uniquely their own. Putting experience into words enriches both their own viewing and the work of art itself. And, so you can take part in the writing, set the timer to ring five minutes before the end of the period to allow time to debrief.

1. Have a large, sharp copy of the artwork projected when the students arrive in the classroom.
2. Play soft lyric-free instrumental music in the background as they take their seats and you complete your beginning of the period record keeping.
3. Invite the students to join you, and all of you view the artwork silently for three minutes.
4. Then distribute the handouts with the prompts you chose for the art you have.
5. Read each step aloud slowly and softly, pausing between prompts to allow time for students to look at the art and mentally to respond.
6. Finally, invite the students to choose the kind of "entry" they would like to write about and let them write till the end of the period. Join in the experience and do the assignment along with your students.

Invite your students to work with a partner and read what they have written. It is revealing to have two students who have viewed the

---

Box 9.2.   Entering Art

Step inside the artwork. Let its space become your space. What does it feel like as you journey into the painting? Where are you? What do you hear? Smell? What do you notice under your feet? Imagine you can touch something in the painting. What would that be? How would it feel?

1. Write about the artwork as if it were a dream. Bring the scene to life and leave us in that moment. Use "In a dream, I . . ." or "Last night I had the strangest dream . . ." or simply, "I dreamed . . ."
2. Write about the scene as if it is happening now, using present tense and active verbs. Begin with "I am . . ." Move around inside the work and make things happen. Begin a line with "Suddenly . . ." in order to create surprise, moving into something unexpected.
3. Write about the work as if it is a memory. List short, separate memories or one long memory. Both invent and remember as you write.
4. Imagine the art as something you see outside a window. Begin with "From my window, I see . . ."

---

same picture read what they experienced as they entered the work.[16] (See box 9.2.)

> Art illuminates
> lessons we teach our students
> and they understand.
> (Anna Roseboro)

CONCLUSION

Elizabeth Borton de Trevino's *I, Juan de Pareja* is a rich source of multidisciplinary material for teaching in middle school. Like other works of historical fiction, you could teach it simply as fiction. Assignments accompanying this particular novel not only give your students opportunities to refine their research skills, hone their speaking abilities, discover Renaissance people, places, and events, view art by renowned painters, write about and discuss issues of friendship and ethics, but also meet the majority of the English language arts standards recommended by the National Council of Teachers of English and the International Reading Association.

Like the mistress described in *I, Juan de Pareja*, your students may at first find that they read slowly and laboriously and that they have to spend tearful afternoons writing. But once they have the pleasure of getting to know about people and places, delving into another time period through reading, writing, viewing, and discussing ideas to which they can relate today, they feel more confident and competent in meeting both the personal and academic challenges they face in the twenty-first century.

NOVELS TO CONSIDER FOR TEACHING HISTORICAL FICTION

Al Capone Does My Shirts by Gennifer Choldenko

It's 1935 and Moose Flanagan has just moved to Alcatraz Island with his family so that his father can work as an electrician. Not only is Moose now living in the same place as such notorious criminals as Al Capone, but he's had to leave his baseball team and is quickly tangled up in the schemes of the warden's mischievous daughter, Piper. Even more difficult, however, Moose has to help with his autistic sister, Natalie, who has been rejected from a special school. Throughout the book, Moose learns much about responsibility and growing up, and even meets Al Capone's mother! Well-developed characters and an unusual setting make this a great choice for middle school readers. Use the book for lessons on character development, voice, and setting.

Grades: Sixth through seventh
Caution: None

Catherine, Called Birdy by Karen Cushman

This hilarious novel is written as the diary entries of fourteen-year-old Birdy, daughter of an English nobleman in the twelfth century. Impeccably researched, the book includes wonderful (and often disgusting) details of life in the Middle Ages. The crux of the story is Birdy's efforts to scare off all potential suitors through creative practical jokes. Even boys appreciate Birdy as she is definitely not the classic "damsel in distress" of most medieval tales. This is a great book to study characterization, setting, and dialect.

Grades: Sixth through eighth

Caution: None

Crispin: The Cross of Lead by Avi

Crispin: The Cross of Lead is a great book to accompany a study of medieval England. After his mother dies and he is accused of murder, thirteen-year-old Crispin flees from his home. Armed with only a lead cross as a clue to his father's identity, Crispin seeks to uncover the truth of his past. He ends up traveling with Bear, a juggler whose gruff personality hides a big heart. Not only is this a fantastic adventure story, Crispin is also a tale of the developing relationship between two lonely people and the quest for identity. Students are caught up in the story and do not even realize how much they're learning about the Middle Ages or the art of good storytelling.

Grades: Sixth through seventh

Caution: None

Nightjohn by Gary Paulsen

In the 1850s slaves in America were beaten or dismembered if they attempted to learn to read. Why then would a man who had managed to escape from slavery return in order to secretly teach other slaves how to read? Through an unsettling and powerful look at a terrible time in American history, Gary Paulsen forces his readers to consider the answer to this question—and the true importance of learning to read. Students become enthralled by the story of Nightjohn as he teaches brave twelve-year-old Sarny her letters. *Nightjohn* is a wonderful story to show students the value of the written word, but don't expect a light read. Paulsen's novel is brief but gritty and gives an accurate portrayal of slave life in the 1800s.

Grades: Sixth through seventh

Caution: Violence, Racism

Number the Stars by Lois Lowry

In the mostly troubling genre of Holocaust fiction, Lois Lowry chooses to tell an uplifting true story. Without diminishing the terror of one of the worst times in world history, Lowry focuses on the bravery of the Danish people who helped more than seven thousand Jews escape to Sweden. The story is told from the perspective of ten-year-old Annemarie Johannesen whose best friend is among the Jews hoping to escape. Bravery and justice are central to this tale about the importance of doing what's right no matter the cost. The book could be paired with a study of another darker Holocaust book, like *Night* by Elie Wiesel, to show that even in the worst of times there is hope.

Grades: Sixth through eighth

Caution: Racism

Island of the Blue Dolphins by Scott O'Dell

Well-known historical fiction writer Scott O'Dell won a Newbery medal for this breathtaking novel. Based on a true story, *Island of the Blue Dolphins* tells the remarkable tale of a twelve-year-old Native American girl, Karana. When her home island, Ghalas-at, located off the coast of California, is evacuated, she jumps the boat to stay with her little brother who has been left behind. After her brother dies, Karana must survive on her own for eighteen years. This is a story of bravery and perseverance enriched by beautiful descriptions of natural living. Despite Karana's survival adventures, the book may be a bit slowly paced for some reluctant readers. It is also a better choice for girls than it is for boys.

Grades: Sixth through seventh

Caution: Minor violence

The Ruby in the Smoke by Philip Pullman

Sally Lockhart has none of the "important" skills that young women of her Victorian English home are expected to have. But when she is thrust into the mystery of her father's untimely death, her unusual talents prove to be invaluable. Accompanied by a photographer, his actress sister, a messenger boy, and an orphaned girl, Sally unravels the connections between her own childhood, the treacherous Mrs. Holland, the opium trade, and an invaluable ruby. This baffling mystery is part satire of the "penny dreadfuls" of Victorian England and would serve well as part of a study of literary genres. The BBC production of the book is very well made.

Grades: Eighth through ninth

Caution: Includes some violence and references to sex as well as descriptions of the effects of opium. Pullman's His Dark Materials trilogy turned him into a very controversial author, and some conservative school districts might not approve of including any of his books in their curricula.

10

PLAYING IT RIGHT: READING, PERFORMING, AND WRITING DRAMA

I order you to be silent! And I issue a collective challenge! Come, I'll write down your names. Step forward, young heroes! You'll all have a turn; I'll give each of you a number. Now, who wants to be at the top of the list? You, sir? No? You? No? [Silence] No names? No hands? . . . Then I'll get on with my business.

—Cyrano speaking in *Cyrano de Bergerac*[1]

Cyrano's rousing speech may not have been as successful as he would have liked, but he certainly delivered it with enthusiasm and passion. You need the same passion to draw your students into reading and writing drama. In this chapter are techniques that can produce a far better response than poor Cyrano elicited.

Drama permeates teachers' and students' lives via TV, movies, school productions, YouTube, and so many other venues. This pervasiveness makes it a challenge to teach dramatic literature simply by reading it. But that is just the way some drama is taught in middle school English classes. That need not be the case with you.

Middle school students need to stretch their dramatic creativity, imagining what words could sound like spoken onstage and what characters and scenes could look like onstage. Teaching a work of drama is a superb opportunity to broaden your students' experience with literature and to expand their understanding of the unique features of this literary genre. This chapter describes ways to help your young teens further develop their own expressive, oral reading as well as their creative writing skills. Here are ideas from lessons on *Cyrano de Bergerac* for seventh graders, *Romeo and Juliet* for ninth graders, and playwriting for eighth graders. Even if you select other plays traditionally taught in middle school like *The Diary of Anne Frank* by Frances Goodrich and Albert Hackett or *A Midsummer Night's Dream* by Shakespeare, you can adapt these ideas for your setting. The list at the end of the chapter gives you other ideas of plays to consider teaching your students in addition to or in place of what already is in your curriculum.

READING DRAMA

Drama, like other narrative literature, is written to tell a story of characters facing conflict. In this genre, dramatists create their narrative to be performed by actors who assume the roles of characters in the story. In drama, however, the setting—the time and place—are revealed primarily through sets, lights, props, and costumes, and readers must rely more heavily on the dialogue to reveal character and to advance plot. Unfortunately, middle school students are tempted to skip those important stage directions; inexperienced readers tend to jump directly to the dialogue. Then they become confused, even frustrated when they do not understand what is really happening. Consequently, the aspects of drama to teach first are its unique features. Begin the unit by pointing out those distinctive elements as you remind them of characters and conflicts that are common to fiction in general.

Planning Ahead

Plan your assignments so students can read aloud each day, and so all who want to, have an opportunity to read one of the major roles at least once. If students can be depended upon to study the scenes ahead of time at home, assign parts as homework so students can practice reading aloud. Otherwise allow class time for silent reading so your students can be familiar with the lines, able to read the parts expressively in character. Few things dampen enthusiasm for studying drama more than poor oral reading. To interpret the roles effectively, your young actors need to know what is going on and what the lines portend.

Keep in mind, too, that plays are written to be viewed in a single theatrical sitting (perhaps with intermissions). Therefore, if you stretch out the initial reading over too many days or weeks, you lose the essence of the drama. So, keep the action alive. Once the class has read the exposition of the play and the students are familiar with the main characters and the problem(s) to be solved, move as quickly through the play as possible. And then, after you have read the entire play, go back and have students practice and present scenes.

This doubling back reinforces and clarifies what may have been missed on the original reading. Even as skillful a reader as you are, you are not likely to have come to the level of understanding you have on just a single read of the play. To enhance the conversations and enrich the discussion, assume a complete first reading is needed and allot time for rereading and time for small groups to perform selected scenes.

As students begin working in groups to make decisions on how to act out the play, anticipate the four natural stages of development: forming, storming, norming, and performing. Be prepared for students to grumble that their part is too large or too small; encourage them to decide on staging that includes simple costumes and/or props; consider naming as the director "whoever is creating the biggest stink"! Most of all, keep in mind during this time of middle school students preparing to present scenes that the best-laid plans often are better modified than forced.

The keys for success are to have a goal, explain the goal, and then let the students plan how to implement it. However, they still need you there. Be observant; step in firmly so students use more of the class time practicing than bickering. Setting your kitchen timer to ring ten minutes before the period ends helps. Then, use these final ten minutes to rearrange the room, to reflect on what went well, and to remind the students of the next day's assignment. But, the sooner they begin planning and practicing, the more likely your young thespians are to learn and enjoy drama. Oh yes, this is a noisy activity!

Using Props and Making Masks

Young people are more inclined to assume a persona when they have something to hold or feel they are disguised. Begin with a brief talk about which props or items of clothing would be appropriate for each character. If bringing props from home is unrealistic, ask to borrow some from the drama teacher or provide them yourself. You know to keep props simple and to avoid realistic-looking weapons. Just much too tempting for shenanigans from mischievous adolescents.

To get the students to reflect more deeply on the personalities of the characters, have them make character masks using inexpensive paper plates and colored markers or crayons. Once you assemble all the materials, they can complete the assignment in a single period, choosing colors and symbols that reflect the specific traits of their assigned characters. This creative artistic assignment reinforces learning and appeals to those who show what they know by drawing and those who learn by seeing.

This assignment also sends students back to the text. When they show their masks to the class, each student should quote the lines that substantiate their choice of color, symbol, or the pattern of images on their mask. Students often are surprised when peers choose the same color to symbolize different personality traits. With textual support, those choices are validated.

For example, with the play *Romeo and Juliet*, one student may choose red to reflect the love between Romeo and Rosalind, his lady love before Juliet. Another may use red to show the fiery temperament of Mercutio. A student may use black to represent Juliet's despair while another uses black to represent the stubborn stance the Montagues and Capulets take on keeping their children apart.

The same holds true for symbols. When students support their choices with the text, most results make sense. One student may decorate her mask with birds to represent literally the swan and crow mentioned in the script and also to represent figuratively the flightiness of the characters. Another may use dog food bones to reflect Mercutio's speech about "a dog" and the "house of Montague." Neither the colors nor symbols students select are important, but the reasoning they offer based on the text is. So much is revealed to them, their peers, and to you.

ATTENDING LIVE PERFORMANCES

Check to see if a local theater company is scheduled to perform the play your students are studying. If so, try to attend it. Preparing to go see the performance provides another opportunity to talk about the difference between reading a play and seeing it performed. Even if it is not convenient to take a whole class to a play, you may be able to invite members of the cast to visit your school. If a play appropriate for young adults is being staged, but is different from what you plan to teach, still consider taking your students to see it. Experiencing good live theater performance enhances your teaching and extends their learning.

Many community theater groups have educational outreach programs that are established to introduce students to live theater. You may have local actors who would count it a privilege to come to your school and talk about their profession with students. You may even find a live performance in another version for students to see, such as a ballet or an operatic staging of *Romeo and Juliet*. If you begin planning early enough, you should be able to coordinate your lesson planning with one such scheduled local production.

What if performance prices are high or your school is not near a college or civic theater program that may offer lower rates? Ask around. Consider local community theater groups. Put out the word that you are looking for someone in the area with stage experience; you might find a terrific and inexpensive guest speaker thrilled to come. Also, investigate organizations that might help underwrite the cost of bringing in a touring group; service organizations like the Kiwanis, Rotary, Lions, and Optimist clubs; local foundations and arts associations are possibilities, too.

Planning the Field Trip

If you are new to your school or district and you decide to plan an outing to the theater, consult with your administrator and seek advice from other teachers who have experience with field trips. Trips can take weeks of planning: coming up with the finances, raising the funds for those who cannot afford tickets, arranging transportation, finding chaperones, and securing permission slips. But, do not be dissuaded by naysayers. Attending a live performance can be an eye-opening experience well worth the effort you expend. Careful planning can make it a pleasure.

Young students enjoy being known as a respectful audience. You can help them become one. You see, ushers at school-age performances of plays held at local theaters know which schools and which teachers at those schools have well-mannered students. You can inspire commendable behavior even in rowdy young teenagers. Believe it or not, what they wear makes a difference, but no need to tell them how important it may be to you. Instead, urge students to dress for the occasion with special attire appropriate for your community. When teenagers are dressed well they seem to behave better.

The public talks. So, do what you can to prepare your students to confirm your school's good reputation or to surprise others that your particular class is better behaved than expected. For some students this may be their first experience with live theater. It is exciting for them. Some will be awed by the ambience. You can allay their anxiety and reduce their squirrelly behavior if you can show them pictures of the interior and a layout of the facility. This will increase their curiosity and prepare them for what to expect. Encourage them to talk about the experience before, during, and afterward. For young teens, this entire process may be a highlight of the school year.

GETTING INTO READING THE PLAY— STAGING TABLEAUX

But, the best preparation to attending an off-site performance is a good in-class experience with a play. Start right with the list of characters and the author's description of setting, and stage directions. Encourage students to predict. For example, if there are family members, ask the students what conflicts they anticipate among them considering the age and gender of the characters. Think about the setting. What is likely to occur in the time and place the playwright has chosen? Based on the stage directions, where should the characters be positioned when the curtain opens? (See box 10.1.)

If the students previously have studied the elements of fiction, they anticipate from these opening observations, even predict that the play

---

Box 10.1. Project It!
Establishing Visual Historical Context for a Play

Dramatic scripts tell the readers as well as the director when and where the action takes place. If the time and place are unfamiliar to students, show them photos or video clips to help them visualize the setting as they read the dialogue. Websites like YouTube and Vimeo, along with video archive sites sponsored by the American Film Institute and the UCLA film archives, provide tens of thousands of short clips that were: (1) shot in historical locations, (2) recreate historical settings and locations, and (3) illustrate both costuming and dialogue for historical periods. These sites are not always easily searchable by key word, so it's best to search concretely by the names of films that you have already linked to a period. Preview everything.

---

will follow the now familiar plot elements with exposition, rising action, climax, falling action, and resolution.

To help students get a feel for drama, ask students to read the opening scene silently. Then, with no explanation from you of what they have read, invite one student to come silently to the front of the class and stand where a specific character would stand if he or she were onstage. Then, one at a time, beckon other students individually to assume the persona of particular characters and to take their places in relation to those already positioned there in the front. Ask the rest of the class to observe silently until all of the scene's characters are positioned. At that time, call for a freeze to create a tableau, montage, or representation of that scene.

Now, ask the class its opinions of the character placement. Before those in the tableau lose their concentration and begin squirming or melting, unfreeze them so they can return to their seats to join the discussion. Invite participants from the tableau to identify lines from the play that support their own choice of position. Other students can look at the text of the play to determine the passages that justify the tableau just presented or to propose an arrangement more accurate to the text. Of course, those who disagree should be asked to quote from the text to show why an alternate placement seems more accurate.

Your well-taught students know to pay attention to what happens in the opening sections of any work of fiction whether short story, narrative poetry, or novel. As they continue reading the play on their own, they are able to follow the plot line, answering in their journals such questions as

- Who are the protagonist and antagonist(s)?
- What is the conflict?
- When does the main action occur?
- Where does the main action take place? (other than onstage)
- Why do characters act the way they do?
- How does the writer have the characters solve the problems raised in the play?

Assigning this writing activity during act 1 focuses students' attention on the main characters as they are being introduced, as well as on the conflicts, which playwrights reveal early in the exposition of their works. Yes, the script lists the names in the cast of characters; some dramatists even mention the relationship among the characters, but the reader/viewer usually does not know the personality or motivations of these characters until the play begins. Since you want your students to be able to follow the play without having to go back too often to figure out who's who and what's what, assign this five W's and H journal entry right away.

Begin the play slowly enough for them to get a firm handle on these relationships; it makes the rest of the reading go more smoothly. Then you can spend your time inviting students to read aloud, in character, and to discuss their understanding of the plot while paying attention to character development, plot advancement, and theme revelation.

However, after closely reading act 1, trust the author to show what is going on among the characters so the members of the audience can understand the personalities and conflicts themselves. This approach to quick reading is in keeping with the idea that plays are written to be viewed in one sitting or at least a single theater visit.

As when beginning other works of fiction, during the first few days of reading a play, remind students to mark their texts, use their sticky notes, or to record in their journals the words or phrases that reveal specific facts about characters, especially motivation. By this time, most of your students already are active readers, so there is no need to plod through the entire play, stopping to identify this basic information. But, answer questions as they arise.

Taking Notes While Reading

While a quick read is usually best for overall narrative comprehension, because they cannot see them, many film-oriented students have difficulty tracking characters. These students may benefit from a simple graphic organizer. If your students are not permitted to write in their books, ask the students to keep character-related notes in their reading journal. They can make three columns:

Column one: Character Name
Column two: Character Traits
Column three: Page Number

You may find that some students visualize better when they draw a diagram of the set, or create charts with arrows, boxes, and circles. Periodically, invite your young students to share with their classmates the strategies they devise themselves to help them make sense of the text. These shared peer perceptions increase peer comprehension.

These notes and drawings can prepare students to participate actively in discussions about ways the playwrights unveil the personalities and motivations of the characters. Writing and graphically representing these facts and impressions slow the readers and they pay attention to the crucial information the dramatist reveals in the opening scenes, thus reducing confusion and frustration later. Once these details are firm in their minds, students can read more confidently and understand more deeply. Nevertheless, you probably have to remind your students that reading a play is different from watching one. As readers, they must use all the clues the author gives in the dialogue and in the stage directions to imagine what the characters look like and what movement they may be making onstage.

GETTING THROUGH THE PLAY—ART AND ACTING

Some teachers ask students to draw pictures or bring in pictures from magazines or newspapers to represent the play's characters. Others ask students what movie or television actors and actresses should be cast for certain parts. Of course, the students should be asked to find evidence from the text of the play to support their choice of picture, actor, or actress. They may even design a playbill or suggest music for the dramatic work you have them read. If this play were a musical, what style of music would be appropriate? Why? If it were a ballet, what would it look like? These assignments call upon students' imagination, and help students to connect and to contribute to the discussion inspired by their own creative ideas and their own artistic skills.

Further involve students and invite their input by suggesting that they bring in childhood toys and dolls to represent characters or spend a class period making sock puppets to use when reading a scene. What about using children's building blocks to re-create sets? Remember, these are young teens, bridging the gap between childhood and adulthood. Playing with appropriate toys that they bring while studying a play may be just the thing to bring the literature alive for them.

Such activities reinforce learning by doing, seeing, and hearing. Because students have written in the journals the words from the text and discussions, have experienced reading and hearing parts read, and have seen the visuals (photos or drawings in their text), they are more likely to remember the particulars of the plot and theme and to make connections between the actions in the plays and their own lives. These visual depictions also provide memory aids students may recall during written assessments.

Deciding to Show or Not to Show

To supplement the study of a play, you may decide to show video clips. You could use clips of the same scenes from different productions—such as different versions of Shakespeare's *Romeo and Juliet*, or an English production and French version of *Cyrano de Bergerac*.[2] In addition to using clips to give more insight into the setting, show a video clip of a conflict similar to one dealt with in the play you are reading. Afterward, ask the students to compare the way each set of characters responds to the conflict. The key for you is to decide why the video clip is being shown and to determine whether it helps or hurts their reaching the standards for reading, viewing, and critical thinking laid out for the course.

Showing video of the play you are studying may be a good time for an in-context talk about the grammar of film. See chapter 11 for more extensive suggestions for incorporating media grammar in language arts instruction.

Comparing and Contrasting Film Versions of Plays

When you study *Cyrano de Bergerac*, for example, you could show video clips both from an English version of the play and also the French version of the play starring Gérard Depardieu. The French version can be advantageous even if students don't speak that language; students can pay attention to the action that is implied by the dialogue they have been reading. The fact that this version is performed "in the field" and "on location" and not onstage provides an opportunity to discuss how stage and screen communicate differently—especially with lighting, close-ups, scene transitions, and audio/sound.

Then ask students to discuss or write about the differences they note between the two media. Some students are disappointed when they have imagined the people, places, and scenes to be different from what is shown in the video. Use this as an opening to talk about the power of language to create images in our minds and the pleasure of reading widely and independently.

Literary Devices and Vocabulary in Drama

During the classes' study of a play is an excellent venue for expanding or reinforcing the list of literary terms taught about the elements of fiction and of poetry. For example, during the study of *Cyrano de Bergerac*, this list could include those elements that Rostand used brilliantly, such as

allusion
ballad

dramatic irony
mood
verbal irony

If the play is in your anthology, you may rely on the literary terms and vocabulary featured in the text. The editorial staff usually does a fine job of selecting words middle school students need to know to understand the play, along with some that would be good for them to add to their speaking and writing vocabularies. Of course, take time for them to look up and talk about any other words that interest them or trip them up when they are reading or discussing the play you have chosen. By the second semester when many course outlines suggest teaching drama, the students are comfortable with each other and with you and are open to acknowledging gaps in their understanding, and accustomed to looking of words they do not know.

KEEPING THE PEACE WHILE ENJOYING THE PLAY

As the students get further into the play, they are eager to read aloud and act out the scenes. And, because they are adolescents who have a strong sense of fairness, it is important for you to be perceived as such. To be fair, arrange it so each one who wishes to read a "good" part has the opportunity to do so; keep a chart of who reads which part each day. At the end of each class period, you write on the board or project a list of characters they are to meet in the next day's scene(s) and then ask for volunteers to prepare for the reading.

Those who have had small parts should have first choice for choosing the character they would like to read the next day. Those who are scheduled to read ought to understand that they are expected to practice reading their lines aloud at home so they can read in character, without stumbling over unfamiliar words during class. Holding this casting session at the end of each class period is a subtle way of tantalizing them to keep reading to find out what happens next and anticipating how well their classmates are going to interpret the upcoming scenes.

If practice at home is not realistic in your school setting, invite the readers to come before or after school and practice in your room. Young teens abhor embarrassment, so they take seriously their responsibility of bringing alive the characters in front of their peers. And meetings like this can be a great opportunity for you to have one-on-one time or get to work with a smaller group of students.

Acting Scenes and Creating Tableaux

Allotting time to act out the scenes is particularly important to ensure that your teaching appeals to multiple intelligences—especially your visual, auditory, and kinesthetic learners. To demonstrate the ways that dialogue demands certain action and activity, you could give the same scene to multiple groups and ask them to do a dramatic reading that includes some staging and movement. If your class tends to be noisy, talkative young teens, how about assigning them to present scenes silently, with pantomime only! Still, after they present the scene, ask the group members to justify their choices for acting or reacting.

Creating tableaux again, of the later scenes in the play, further reinforces student understanding of the relationships of characters one to another. This time, raise the level of reflection and observation and ask students to pay attention to posture as well as position in relation to another character. One may have a dominant character standing, a neutral one sitting, and a subservient one kneeling. Students may decide to have one character standing farther away from the audience and another nearer depending on the mood of the scene. In a quiet scene, ask the students to decide what gestures would be appropriate during a particular speech. What would the nonspeaking characters be doing during that speech? Why?

You can maintain more consistent control in the classroom during acting scenes by planning backward—clarify for yourself what you expect to accomplish when you schedule lessons for the students to act out scenes. First, consider the dynamics of each class: how have the students interacted in prior situations? Next, give clear directions before "letting them loose," and then circulate among them as they work. Finally, set your timer to signal about five minutes before the end of the period. That way, you can call the students back to order and conduct a short oral reflection on what they learned by acting out the scene. When students know what is expected, what is allowed or not allowed, and know that you are nearby to help them behave themselves, they usually live up to your expectations. You can achieve your goals and retain your sense of humor.

Keeping Up with Literary Devices

By the second semester, your middle school students are at ease identifying, discussing, and writing about most of the literary devices except theme and irony. So, when you plan lessons for drama study, design activities to help them develop greater confidence with these features of literature. You could quiz them with quotations from the play and ask students to identify the speaker, the situation, and the importance of that speech to characterization, plot advancement, or setting. These informal assessments measure their retention of this knowledge.

To understand and identify literary themes in plays, students must understand the plot line, so students may find it useful first to refer to their one-paragraph summaries of the five W's and H questions. Just as you taught during the short story unit, ask the students to write thematic statements in which they identify the universal situation based on the conflict, and the universal response to the situation, based on the character's response to the conflict.

It may help them write these theme statements by reminding them of what they learned in the short story unit. For those who need it, provide a sample formatted sentence with missing words:

When people _____ (the students fill in the situation), they _____ (the students fill in the response to the situation).

For one homework assignment, ask students to try writing some of these sentences in their reading journals or spiral notebooks. After students write the theme statements, they can later convert the S.W.B.S.T. phrases (Somebody Wanted, But, So, and Then) into simple sentences that generalize the concept captured in their preliminary drafts. Students soon recognize the universal quality of plays in much the way they saw them in other literary works studied this school year. (See box 10.2.)

> **Box 10.2.   Kristen's Statements about**
> **Theme in *Cyrano de Bergerac***
>
> - When people have a crush on someone, they show off for their crush.
>   (In some neighborhoods "crush" is also slang for the object of one's
>   affections.)
> - When someone dies, their loved ones mourn for them.
> - People respond to tense situations with brave action.
> - People are willing to battle physically or emotionally to get what they
>   want.
> - People with physical flaws try to impress others to avoid rejection.
> - People are attracted first to external features.

WRITING PLAYS AND CROSS-CURRICULAR COLLABORATIONS

Middle school students learn well when they see a link to other topics or subjects that they are studying in other classes. Collaborating teachers who take time to create such lessons tend to have more success in getting their students to engage. One activity that lends itself well to cross-curricular collaboration is playwriting. For example, in many schools eighth graders study physical science, which includes units on geology, weather, and the planets. Many eighth-grade literature lists include the study of mythology. What a wonderful opportunity to write plays based on those myths that attempt to explain early man's rationale for the way the earth is formed, what causes weather, and why the planets exist.

The same kind of teaming could work with colleagues in the history or social studies department. The students could write plays about historical people and events. Invite a teacher in the other department to work with you to design a joint assignment for which your students write a play that is set in the same historical period or features the real people the students may be studying in one of those other classes. Think about working with a colleague in history, science, art, or even music.

Then, you can share the grading. Consider using the features of the familiar six traits rubric or one that teachers from both departments create together. For example, one of you could read the student-written plays for accuracy of facts and ideas, for voice and sentence fluency. The other could read for organization, word choice, and conventions of drama writing as well as for mechanics, usage, and grammar. Such sharing could half the labor and double the pleasure of working together on a project that enhances authenticity of assessment in both areas of study.

Or, after studying a group of short stories, you may be ready to introduce students to playwriting instead of short story writing.[3] Small groups could choose different short stories already studied and then create a script based on one of the short stories and incorporate the elements of drama they learn in this drama unit. See Teacher Resource H for a sample playwriting checklist.

Depending on the students you have, assign each student to author his or her own personal play or assign them to work as a group. By second semester, when you teach play writing, you have a better feel for what works best for the classes you have any particular year. If possible, arrange for a final performance of the best two or three plays your students write. This may be a practiced reading performed for other classes or a full performance in your theater space for an invited audience of families and friends.

If you begin planning early enough in the first semester, your drama teacher may have time to join forces with you and plan time for the drama classes to perform selected plays your eighth graders write. You can imagine how gratifying it would be for these middle school authors to see their words come to life! And, knowing their work is to be seen by their peers, families, and friends encourages the students to do a better job on the assignment. Win. Win. Win.

GRADING DURING PLAY WRITING

During the preliminary stages of playwriting, just give credit for completing each step, making note of participation instead of giving letters or percentages. It works better to keep the students focused on the process rather than the grades, so any student who completes the step in the assignment on time should receive full credit. Although students who do not complete a particular step receive no credit for that step, encourage them to participate fully in each group meeting and earn partial credit. Their contributions can enhance the final script and they are likely to stay involved knowing they have not lost all by missing one assignment.

Observations—No-Stress Assessments

As the students work together, use the opportunity to add to your notes about their behavior and contributions. You may have photocopies of seating charts on which to record these comments. Or have student names printed on large address labels to remind you to make notes for each of the students by the time the group playwriting meetings are finished. If you do not maintain individual student record sheets, you still can keep these notes in a folder to consult when needed. Your documenting of student learning with these anecdotal assessments helps you to plan subsequent lessons and to prepare reports to parents or administrators should the need arise.

At the end of such a group project, have students evaluate their own contribution to the task. It is not necessary to ask them to comment on what others have done. Everyone in the group already knows if each has been supportive and cooperative, so you do not want to create situations for them to "tattle." You want to avoid creating schisms among classmates, which can damage the fragile egos of adolescents, even those who hide them with bluster.

ADDITIONAL ASSESSMENTS

At the end of the unit, you need to assess student learning by having students demonstrate their understanding of relationships among the characters, or the author's use of literary devices and the newly taught elements of drama. You could include options for which they can choose to

- Summarize their learning by writing a poem about the play
- Write an additional scene describing what happens next with characters who have survived

- Write a one-act play with the same conflict set in a contemporary time or place
- Take a test
- Write a paper
- Produce a video
- Create an animated video to post on your class website

CONCLUSION

The study of drama can be an enriching experience for students and teachers because it incorporates six language arts skills (reading, writing, speaking, listening, representing, viewing), the use of technology, and a reason to practice cooperative learning. Moreover, while reading drama, students see how previously learned literary concepts are used in another genre of literature. Finally, drama is just fun because it appeals to a wide range of students across the range of multiple intelligences, especially those who like to talk, to move, and to act up. Whose left?

Yes, by the time you have completed a series of lessons with drama, you may find yourself quoting Cyrano's line, "I order you to be silent!" With your careful planning, your students become so excited about playing their parts that you may need to "write down their names" and they each will want to be "at the top of the list." When you issue the challenge to "Step forward, young heroes!" even the shyer students volunteer to be a part of the fun and are ready to "break a leg."

WORKS OF DRAMA TO TEACH

A Doll's House by Henrik Ibsen

The most well known of Ibsen's realism plays, *A Doll's House* boldly addresses the issue of women's rights. Nora Helmer is a seemingly empty-headed wife, only around to be a pretty object in her husband, Torvald's, perfectly run house. As the play unfolds the audience learns that Nora is not happy and longs to live her own life. The play is easy to follow and not weighed down by difficult language or excessive cultural references. It is a good choice to teach about the social implications of literature, as it was such a shocking story for early audiences. Try sharing two movie versions, or one movie and a live performance of the play, to have students compare the representations of Nora.

Grades: Seventh through eighth

Caution: None

The Mousetrap by Agatha Christie

The Mousetrap had the longest initial run of any play in the world. The play is a murder mystery, famous for its twist ending. The story is about a couple that starts up a new hotel and is soon snowed in with five guests. The plot thickens when a detective arrives on skis and tells the group that he believes a murderer is on the way to the hotel. The play's unique performance history and exciting plot make it a great choice for study. Unfortunately, there are no movie versions of the play as copyrights prohibit production until the West End production (which began in 1952) has been closed for at least six months.

Grades: Sixth through eighth

Caution: Discussion of a murder scene

The Diary of Anne Frank by Frances Goodrich and Albert Hackett

Set in Holland during World War II, this perennial favorite is a dramatization of a real young girl based on a diary her father found at the end of the war. The play is of a Jewish family and their friends who are hidden from the Nazis by their Dutch friend Miep Gies. Middle school students of all ages are drawn to the musings of a girl their own age that describe the conflicts between sisters in their teens, the hoarding and arguing among those in hiding, and the longing of an adolescent for friendship, love, and freedom.

Grades: Seventh through eighth

Caution: Sexual innuendos. Story ends with family taken to a Nazi concentration camp.

The Monsters Are Due on Maple Street by Rod Serling

This dark tale begins innocently with what appears to be the passing of a meteor that causes a power outage. Very quickly, in an attempt to explain why the power to their gadgets ceases, the neighbors on Maple Street give in to mob psychology. One young boy, Tommy, says that he has read in his comic books about monsters that send a family ahead of their invasion to take over the town. Each one wonders who could be the monsters' emissary family?

This television script of an episode from *The Twilight Zone* series includes camera cues and lots of stage directions and is a good companion piece to read with *To Kill a Mockingbird* by Harper Lee or *Anne Frank: The Diary of a Young Girl* by Anne Frank. Check YouTube for a video clip of this Serling drama.

Grades: Seventh through ninth
Caution: Story includes a murder

A Raisin in the Sun by Lorraine Hansberry

This Pulitzer Prize–winning drama is fully accessible to middle school students primarily because it tells a story with which many of them can identify—the struggle to improve the living conditions of a family. In this play, an urban African-American family bickers and quarrels trying to decide how to use insurance money the matriarch inherits. Should it be used to start a new business for the son, pay college tuition for the daughter, or make a down payment on a house for them all in a better neighborhood?

Grades: Seventh through ninth
Caution: Language

These Shoes of Mine by Gary Soto

This short play is about Manuel, a young man who resents the too-large shoes his mother has bought for him at the thrift shop. She relents and gives him his birthday gift early, a new pair of penny loafers. The play unfolds with Manuel's adventures sporting his new shoes, growing out of them, and wearing them anyway just to impress the girls.

He finally has to choose what is important when a relative arrives who needs a nice pair of shoes to wear for a job interview. Spanish dialogue is translated making it accessible to all readers.

Grades: Sixth through seventh

Caution: None

Trifles by Susan Glaspell

This short mystery play explores gender differences in a way that amuses middle school students and leads to lively discussion. When John Wright is murdered by his wife, the sheriff and other men attempt to figure out why. At the same time, their wives examine Mrs. Wright's kitchen and discuss her life, uncovering clues that the men think are simply "trifles." In the end it turns out that the "trifles" are what lead to the truth about the Wrights. Interested students could easily put together a performance of this simple play.

Grades: Sixth through eighth

Caution: Descriptions of a murder scene

11

SPEAKING OF GRAMMARS: PUBLIC SPEAKING AND MEDIA ARTS

The mark of an effective speaker is "the ability to adapt to a variety of audiences and settings and to perform appropriately in diverse social situations."

—Clella Jaffe[1]

A dear friend is an accomplished welder and a talented musician, who can skillfully navigate a luxury tour bus through dense urban traffic and parallel park it with only inches to spare. And, she is pathological about talking in public, except in casual conversation. She believes people judge her intellect by her speech; given her accented regional dialect and limited experience reading and writing Standard English, she doesn't want to appear ignorant, so she self-muzzles. She seldom writes anything formal and only writes an informal note in an emergency. She believes people generally judge her education by her writing. So she corrals her speaking and writing, keeping herself to herself.

True, my friend left school early, married young, and soon became the sole wage earner for her family of three children. Even though she is gifted mentally and manually, she still feels hampered, unable to advance on any of her careers paths primarily because she lacks proficiency communicating in Standard English. So sad. So frustrating.

This story of a dear friend illustrates just one of the reasons for this chapter. How one speaks, how one writes, and how one uses technology matters. The ideas that follow can help you fulfill the charge, meet the obligation, and ensure that the middle school students you teach do not have to live like this, stifling their thoughts because they are ashamed of their oral and written skills, or their ability to navigate using twenty-first-century technologies as receivers or senders. Teachers have to help students realize that their future success may be thwarted if they know and use only nonstandard grammar and avoid learning the grammar of the media. Share your own stories with the young teens you teach and inspire them to take full advantage of the opportunities provided in school for them to read, hear, and speak Standard English, and to write in a style or version of English appropriate for the setting and to use current technology for communicating in a range of situations.

WHY TEACH STANDARD ENGLISH?

It is important, in the middle school, to teach students the rules of Standard English and to hold them accountable for following the rules when doing so is beneficial to them. They should know that in the national and international communities, English is the language of commerce, technology, and diplomacy. You can substantiate these claims by showing them "An English Speaking World," part of the video series *The Story of English*.[2] Hearing from others in a resource such as this one narrated by respected journalist Robert McNeil can help your students to understand the history and development of the English language, but also convinces them of the value of knowing how to write and speech English well.

Your young teenagers, like most humans, want to be understood and respected for their mental acumen, and you can build on this basic drive. Design classroom activities to review and teach the basics of English grammar, plan writing workshops in which students hear comments on the effectiveness of their writing, and structure guided discussions in which students receive feedback on their oral presentations. These lessons raise their awareness and demonstrate the impact of their choices, and your students soon see that using nonstandard grammar can obscure their own written and oral communication and that using

Standard English grammar can clarify both. The challenge for you is to honor their home language and, at the same time, to give them the knowledge to be able to code-switch.

SKETCHING TO CLARIFY THE FUNCTION OF PARTS OF SPEECH

Even though many students study some grammar in elementary school, you still can start this direct instruction lesson by showing students the function of "parts" of speech in everyday communication. This first example is to demonstrate that grammar is not just about rules, but about effective communication. You can show students what this looks like by using visual symbols to represent the shared understanding of ideas and images. If you were to visit a classroom to "see" and "hear" what this lesson would look and sound like on the opening day of direct instruction of formal grammar, like the paragraphs that follow, your notes may have recorded what happened in that particular teacher's classroom.

Draw a stick figure to represent the speaker; draw a second stick figure to represent the listener. Then draw balloons by the heads of each figure, with small bubbles connecting the balloons to each head. Try to draw, as exact as possible, the same image, say, of a bird flying over a bush, in both the speaker/writer's balloon and the listener/reader's balloon. The images are not precisely identical, but neither are shared messages. Explain that clear and effective communication occurs when you can transmit your ideas effectively to your listener or reader. Now, sketch on the board another stick figure with a very large cartoon balloon that represents verbal communication—either written or spoken. Next, divide that balloon into eight segments to represent the eight common parts of speech. (See figure 11.1.)

Of course, there is no need to use the exact words you hear when you visit this imaginary classroom, but you may find this to be an effective way to review these basic parts of speech with seventh graders who may not have thought about grammar in this way. Write or draw while explaining why languages have different parts of speech. So, here goes . . .

"When we want to name people, places, things, and events and activities, we use nouns. A noun is one part of speech. Nouns name. When we

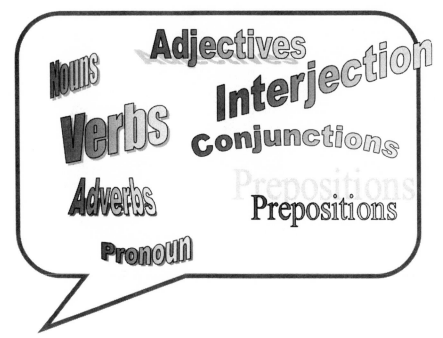

Figure 11.1.   Parts of Speech Balloon

want to talk about what those nouns do, we use verbs. They are another part of speech. Verbs can express action as well as indicate when the action takes place. There are other functions of verbs we'll talk about later.

"Now, occasionally, we want to clarify what the listener/reader imagines, by modifying the mental image of a noun. Adjectives modify or limit nouns."

How Do Modifiers Work?

Continue in this fashion and give examples of ways that adjectives limit or modify nouns. One incident: "When I was eight years old, I got a ball for my birthday. On the opening page of the grammar section of your journal, draw the ball I received." Invariably students draw different types and sizes of balls. Now, add adjectives that limit the image of the noun by telling what kind ("rubber"), what size ("little"), and what color ("purple" with red diamonds around the circumference). By adding adjectives, thus creating a shared mental image, you communicate an image ever-closer to the ball received.

Reiterate this concept and use any noun that elicits a wide variety of images and enables you to limit the meaning of the noun simply by adding adjectives indicating kind, size, and color. Modify the example to fit your students' backgrounds. Consider the example of the dog, a horse, or a sweater. Begin saying just "dog." Let the students write the kind of dog they imagine. Then you add modifiers and ask how mental images come closer and closer to the dog you really received. Students begin to understand the value of linguistic precision.

Point back to the cartoon bubble depicting parts of speech, add the three you've described so far, and continue on to the next part of speech, the modifier for verbs. Remind students that speakers and writers often want to limit or modify others' mental image of an action. In this case, the writer would use another part of speech, an adverb. An adverb modifies verbs by telling when, where, how, and to what extent. If students bring up the fact that adverbs also are used to answer these questions about adjectives or other adverbs, acknowledge this fact and move on.

In the presentation, you may illustrate your explanation with the verb *walk* and then ask the students to suggest adverbs that tell where the action could take place (outside, inside, around, out, and so on). Usually the students suggest prepositional phrases, too, like "around the corner" or "in the mall." Go on to tell them that they are correct, sometimes phrases (or groups of words) can modify a noun or verb, and that you will talk about these kinds of modifiers later. You can expand your discussion about the verb *walk* by asking When? (early, late). How? (quickly, slowly).

Conjunctions and Interjections

The lesson presentation continues, "Sometimes speakers and writers want to combine words, phrases, or clauses, so they need another part of speech to do that—a conjunction. A conjunction joins words, phrases, and clauses." (Remember to include a simple definition of each of the parts of speech as you introduce the concept of "parts of speech.")

Going on, "When speaking or writing, we sound repetitive or boring if we keep saying the same noun repeatedly to refer to the same person, place, thing, activity, or event. So we sometimes replace a noun with a pronoun. A pronoun replaces or stands for a noun. Pronouns change form to indicate whether the noun being replaced is masculine, feminine, or neither, and to indicate whether we're talking about one noun or several."

By this time, as you have been adding the names of the parts of speech to the balloon drawing, most of the students are getting the picture and they can offer correct examples of the different forms of pronouns, showing that though they may not know the rules of grammar, many of them know how the language works grammatically! Some of your English language learners may perk up and comment that in their language the forms of pronouns change in much the same way. This is good, because the next part of speech often throws them a curve—the preposition.

Continue with the lesson. "Sometimes speakers and writers want to show the relationship between a noun or pronoun and some other word in a sentence. They want to indicate the place or position of the other noun or pronoun. To communicate this, they use yet another part of speech—the preposition. A preposition shows the relationship between a noun or pronoun and another word in the sentence.

"Look at this marker I'm using. Suppose I want to communicate to others that the marker is *in* my hand or *on* my desk, or *under* the table. Notice that some of these words show the relationship or place of the noun, the 'marker,' in relation to my hand, the desk, or the table. Those words are prepositions (notice the root *position*). Suppose I put the marker here (hold the marker above the head)? What word tells the position or relationship of the marker to my head (*above* or *over*)? Suppose I move it here (behind the back)? What word shows that relationship or position (*behind*)?" By now, students usually understand the concept or function of the preposition.

Now, deal with the interjection. "This last common part of speech does not name, show action, modify or limit, join, replace, or show relationship or position. But because it serves another function in communicating, it is another part of speech. This eighth part of speech identifies those words that interrupt a flow of thought to express mild or strong emotions. This part of speech is called an interjection."

An interjection exclaims emotions and has no other grammatical connection in the sentence. The word *interjection* comes from a Latin prefix *inter*, which means "between" and a root word *ject* that means "to throw" (as in "project" to throw forward or "reject" to throw back). Speakers and writers sometimes "throw" in words to show emotion, like *wow, darn, ouch,* or *hey*! For this eighth part of speech, invite students to suggest those words that speakers and writers throw into their communication between other ideas as interjections. Be prepared for them to get silly and try to throw in "no-no" words.

Pulling the Parts Together

Finally, a classroom dénouement: by this time, you have completed the drawing with the names of the eight parts of speech all within the balloon graphically illustrating that speech is made of different parts, each serving a specific purpose to communicate clearly exactly what we want to get across to our listeners or readers. And so, you conclude . . .

"These, ladies and gentlemen, are the eight common parts of speech. Each has a different function in communicating what we speak or write. The more precisely you use parts of speech, the more likely the ideas you have are transferred clearly and accurately to your listeners and readers.

"As you continue studying grammar, you'll learn how parts of speech are used in different ways in sentences. You'll soon learn that groups of words—phrases and clauses—can function as a unit the same way as single-word parts of speech function.

"The key for you to remember is the part that each of these single words or single units of words plays in communicating ideas. As you learn these functions and put them into practice in your own speaking and writing, each of you can become a better speaker and a better writer, getting across to the listener/reader, the exact idea you want to communicate."

Introducing or reviewing the parts of speech according to their function in the sentence prepares for an easy transition to teaching phrases, verbals, and clauses. When students see a prepositional phrase that modifies a noun, answering the same kinds of questions that single word adjectives answer, they can understand adjective phrases. For example, "Please bring me the box *in the closet*, not the one *under my bed*." Or when the students see a sentence in which a prepositional phrase answers questions about verbs in the same way that single word adverbs do, the students get the idea of adverb phrases. For example, "Ahmad reached *into his pocket* to get his cell phone."

The same transfer of conceptual understanding seems to flow when students encounter verbals that name actions (gerunds). "*Walking* is good exercise so my grandfather gets up early and walks three blocks just to get his first cup of coffee." Similarly, they can understand when they see verbs describing nouns (participles). "My grandmother still has the *carving* knife her mother received as a wedding gift." You get the point. Taking the time to teach parts of speech as functions of communication makes it easier for students to see the patterns in the language, even in more sophisticated settings.

WHY SYNTAX MATTERS

In the eighth grade, the curriculum usually moves beyond parts of both speech and sentences to phrases, verbals, clauses, and confusion-causing dangling modifiers. One of the ways to help students understand how much they use syntax (the order of words) to make sense of what they hear and read is to have them draw what they hear or see. Your grammar book probably includes a section on dangling modifiers, so you can ask the students to draw as precisely as possible just the sentences that you verbalize, or project the sentences one at a time. Or you may use the examples that follow:

- A group of students was watching the show in their cars.
- The track star twisted his ankle with the green sweatshirt.
- I learned about the cat that was lost on the Internet.
- Punctured by a nail, I had to repair my bike tire.
- Reading my CD insert, my cat crawled into my lap.
- Locked in the trunk, my sister found my diary.
- Our class gave gift bags to all the children filled with raisins.
- Growing in the garden, I picked a bushel of green beans.
- We saw a mountain lion hiking along with our binoculars.
- I noticed an accident turning the corner.

You are right. Doing these drawings evokes snorts and sniggles. That is just fine. Your youngsters wonder about their own work and fear this may be the response others have to their speaking and writing. Thankfully this activity demonstrates emphatically that sentence syntax does influence communication, and afterward your students become more conscientious writers and work harder to avoid that confusion of imprecise language and sloppy grammar.

IN OR OUT OF CONTEXT—
FORMAL OR INFORMAL INSTRUCTION

By the ninth grade, teachers expect students to be familiar with parts of speech, parts of a sentence, and verbals. They also expect students to write using consistent agreement between subject and verb, pronouns and their antecedents. Most curricula for this grade include lessons on a range of sentence structures, various sentence starters, and appropriate punctuation for these more complex sentences. Sometimes formal grammar lessons are taught and students take tests on identifying grammatical structures and correcting errors in sentences or paragraphs. Other schools teach grammar entirely through student writing. In either setting, when a problem arises, you should teach the rule and give students exercises to practice the rule.

In fact, both approaches to teaching grammar eventually work, but lasting learning seems to occur when you hold students responsible for correct grammar in their own, everyday writing. When they see grammar merely as a game of memorization or identification, students soon lose interest and they seldom apply grammar rules beyond the classroom. Hold your students accountable and encourage them to become better speakers and writers.

After a concept is taught, add the correct use of that concept to the evaluation standards on subsequent graded writing assignments. Consider adapting rubrics from your text or those found online, like the Six Traits® rubric published by the Northwest Regional Educational Laboratory.[3] Most published rubrics include grammar as one criterion for evaluating speaking and writing in formal and informal setting, in and out of school.

GRADING FOR GRAMMAR—NOT ALWAYS

After teaching a new concept, you could give a short writing assignment to see how well the students can apply that new concept. The National Writing Project calls this "primary trait" grading. An alternative way to have students practice a newly taught or reviewed concept is to assign journal entries. At the beginning of the class period while you take attendance or collect homework, you could assign the students to write a few sentences about a piece of literature they are studying at the time. The twist, in this situation, is that you could require them to write using the newly taught grammar or syntax concept, such as using only active voice, or using three different kinds of sentences, or beginning each sentence with a different grammatical structure. Your grammar text has ideas and sample sentences for students to pattern.

These five- or ten-minute writing assignments allow students to practice, to demonstrate the variety of forms one can use to communicate clearly, and to produce for discussion examples of problems that can arise when writers do not follow the rules. These kinds of writings should not be collected or graded. Instead, simply have the students exchange journals, read them, and comment to their partner about what meets the assignment and what does not. Encourage students to discuss what changes need to be made to make the sentences better meet the assignment requirements. Then move on to the lesson of the day. Easy. Quick. Writing. Reading. Talking. Reviewing. Reinforcing.

PATTERNING TO TEACH SYNTAX

Another way to make grammar come alive for students is to examine sentence patterns in the writing of published authors—fiction and nonfiction. Sometimes, to demonstrate to the students that they can write similarly powerful sentence styles and grammatical patterns, ask them to model a piece of their own prose after a short passage from the literature they are studying. You could select specific sentences and have all the students pattern the same sentences. Better yet, ask students to locate in a recent reading assignment two or three sentences they, themselves, find interesting. Next, ask them to pattern those on a topic of their choice and then to tell what makes the sentences appealing and if patterning them is a challenge.

Think about the evocative paragraphs students could write based on the Elie Wiesel's memoir, *Night*. Consider using the "Never shall I forget"[4] passage, which describes his first night in the concentration camp. Similar remarkable writing occurs when students pattern the sentence structures from literary works by Hemingway, Twain, and Fitzgerald. Paying close attention to the way published writers organize their sentences helps students understand the power of order and word selection.

Middle school students often hold sophisticated ideas but cannot easily write comparably complex grammatical structures to convey these thoughts. You can help them express themselves more fully and more adeptly. Design lessons that help them slow down, pay attention, practice, and use the appropriate grammar as they attempt to write in precise prose. Patterning can help achieve this standard of communication.

One helpful book is Harry R. Noden's, *Image Grammar: Using Grammatical Structures to Teach Writing*.[5] Noden offers students a variety of sentence starts, modifying strategies, and sentence endings to pattern. Doing activities from *Image Grammar*, your students can practice varying their structure and creating more interesting sentences as they write fiction and nonfiction in English and other classes across the curriculum.

PATTERNING CAN JUMP-START ENGLISH LANGUAGE LEARNERS

You likely have heard the admonition to students editing their papers, "Just read it aloud." That works in some cases, but your ELL students may not have developed "an ear" to recognize Standard English even if they are intellectually sharp with fascinating ideas to share. Reading their writings aloud may not be enough to give students with an untrained ear the helpful clues they need for revision.

You can help them jump-start their English composition and avoid feeling hampered even by simple English language vocabulary or sentence structures they have already learned. How? By encouraging them to pattern sentences. They become more comfortable writing on their own if they are following the syntax of writing passages that you recommend. For some reason, paying close attention to the way that published authors structure sentences can speed the process and increase the confidence limited English speakers have in writing freely.

Another idea for ear training comes from Dr. Arlene Mulligan who uses drama to help her new English speakers improve their sentence syntax. She writes, "Because second language learners, by necessity, must be acute listeners, they already have developed . . . ears sensitive to differences in diction, dialect, and speech patterns. Most of these young people are very bright and are attentive to the spoken word."[6] Mulligan invites her new English speakers to write drama and to incorporate considerable dialogue in their writing. This invitation inspires these writers to attune their ears to the rhythms of spoken English and to imitate these patterns in their writing.

TEACHING GRAMMAR WITH RECORDED BOOKS

The oral language students hear in informal situations is not likely to be entirely Standard English. By encouraging them to attentively pattern the spoken word we can help them train their ears for linguistic rhythms. This would be another reason to use audiobooks in your teaching. The more often all your students tune in to the rhythm and syntax of spoken English, the sooner they are likely to imitate both in their own speaking and writing. So, conduct some research on your own to locate and create lists of appropriate resources. Then you can recommend that your learners across the board listen regularly to good readers on recorded books on the Internet, or downloaded onto student iPods.

ANALYZING THE GRAMMAR OF MEDIA

For decades English language arts educators have taught students the grammar rules for writing and the grammar rules of literature (plot structure for fiction and text structure for nonfiction), but only recently have they begun to teach the grammar of media. Twenty-first-century students view other print and electronic media many more hours than they view/read traditional books. For this reason, you are beginning to see media literacy among the standards to which you are to teach. You can design lessons to teach your students how to "read the media" found in magazines and film, as well as on websites.

You can find lots of resources on the Internet at such sites as Edutopia.com, which includes interviews about the value of teaching the grammar of media literacy and a variety of video clips to use for classroom instruction. Or you can just use magazines you collect and keep in your classroom. One simple lesson introduces the students to the use of color and layout. Other more in-depth lessons may involve learning the language of film—camera angles, use of lighting, timing of shots, and numbers of cuts; viewing samples; and then in groups, creating short video or webpages that illustrate the concepts you are teaching.

Teaching Media Grammar

Deconstruction is a collection of lesson plans developed by the Center for Media Literacy (CML). Deconstruction includes CML's Five Key Questions and Five Core Concepts.[7]

Five Key Questions:

1. Who created this message?
2. What creative techniques are used to attract my attention?
3. How might different people understand this message differently?
4. What values, lifestyles, and points of view are represented in, or omitted from, this message?
5. Why is this message being sent?

Five Core Concepts:

1. All media messages are constructed.
2. Media messages are constructed using a creative language with its own rules.
3. Different people experience the same media message differently.
4. Media have embedded values and points of view.
5. Most media messages are organized to gain profit and/or power.

You can give these same students assignments to practice communicating in these media, too. Instead of requiring each unit of study to include only writing to show what students know, offer options for them to represent graphically what they are learning. Assign PowerPoint presentations, cartooning, photography, and video as ways to show what they understand about the literature they read and the life they live and observe. With your students, create rubrics that refer to elements of layout, color, and design you teach about the media they view. Becoming critical viewers is just the first step in understanding the grammar of the media. Producing that media is the step that shows that learning is taking place.

GIVING AN ORAL REPORT OR PRESENTING A SPEECH

Are you one of the English teachers who bemoan the fact that you find it a challenge to teach students to give a "good" speech? Like other colleagues in your department, do you acknowledge that students do well on "oral reports," yet something still is lacking? Speech giving really is different from giving an oral report. But how?

Ask your students a few questions and the features become clear. Start your unit on public speaking by asking your savvy young adolescents what they notice about a good speaker. Surprisingly, they seldom comment on the content of the speech, but instead point out aspects of delivery like giving verbal clues to organization pattern, making eye contact, using gestures, rate of speech, clear articulation, varied intonation, poise, and so forth. Of course, middle school students probably do not use these terms, but what they mention shows clearly that how the report is delivered is the feature that makes the speech an effective one.

Therefore, if you expect your students to become effective, competent, and confident speakers, it seems only right that you incorporate into your lesson planning opportunities for students to observe and critique good speaking and also the time to write and practice their own speeches. Ask them to watch television news reporters. Find and show them short video clips of politicians and businessmen and businesswomen delivering speeches. Watch an inspirational speaker giving a talk. Observe their teachers. Encourage students to pay attention to the delivery styles of their pastors and priests, rabbis and imams. After just a few times, your teen monitors can assemble a list of those characteristics of content, structure, style, and vocal qualities that make oral presentations easy to follow and to remember.

Generally there are four basic kinds of speeches, and during the course of a school year you can ask students to prepare and present one of each: to inform, to persuade, to entertain, and to commemorate. So, include in your planning for a formal speech unit of two or three weeks, assignments for analysis of speeches and time for students to complete their presentation. Both elements will prove that the keys to effective public presentations are preparation and practice.

The informative speech could be on what they learn about the author of a book they read. A persuasive speech can be preparation for one of the service club speech contests like those of the Rotary and Optimists clubs or simply to convince their classmates to read a particular book. To help students relax giving the speech, give them the option to present the speech in the persona of a character from a piece of literature you read together as a class. In fact, the persuasive speech assignment could be to persuade a character in one of the stories to read the particular book the student has just finished! The speech to commemorate could be one honoring a special friend, family member, community leader, person in history, or literary character. These commemorative speeches could be somber and serious or entertaining and humorous.

Picking a Topic and Planning a Speech

For older students, you may assign a news-related speech assignment where students are expected to think critically about authentic purposes for persuasive speaking and then to conduct research and practice using citations and documentation for a speech on a current issue. In this case, too, you can link the assignment to a piece of literature you are studying. For example, you could ask the students to select a news-related topic that might interest one of the characters from a novel or article the class has read or is studying. Or write a speech to address a problem in the school or community. See Teacher Resource I for a sample handout for planning a problem/solution speech.

Assessing News Grammar

This news-related assignment requires students to conduct research, practice citation and documentation, and to think more critically about persuasive techniques. During the first two weeks of this month-long assignment they are to select a topic reported in any medium. Then they should bring in copies of four or five written articles; students can also use text transcriptions of television reports available on local and network websites. If your students have access to the Internet, they can follow the news easily. The purpose is to have them follow the news for a month and be prepared to assess ways that nonfiction writing is the same and/or different from the text structure of fiction being studied in class.

After the students have read opening chapters of the book of fiction your class is reading, are through the exposition of the text, and have a solid sense of the personalities of the characters, you could ask students to write a brief rationale to explain why a particular literary character would be interested in the current event and what would be that character's response to those particular news stories. For example:

- Why would Jem in *To Kill a Mockingbird* be interested in a particular trial reported in news media? What would he say about the verdict?
- Why would Mercutio or Benvolio in *Romeo and Juliet* be interested in curfew laws that require teenagers to be at home before 10 p.m.? What arguments for and against them might they use?
- Why would Panchito from *The Circuit* or Esperanza from *Esperanza Rising* be interested in educational opportunities for illegal immigrants? How would they advocate for more?

As you and the class continue studying the novel, the students can be gathering articles to flesh out their persuasive speeches. Or, students could write a speech in your class based on a topic they are studying in history, science, music, or math. Depending on your school setting and the access your students have to resources, you may need to allot in-class time for research as well as for practicing the speeches once they are written.

This kind of multigenre and interdisciplinary assignment, looking at fiction and nonfiction concurrently in both print and electronic media, helps students make text-world connections, seeing that times change and people don't—a universal quality of good literature. Since a portion of the assignment requires the students to justify their reasons for choosing the particular kinds of news articles and relating them to fictional characters, this assignment requires your teen readers to consider the ways their fiction authors reveal the personalities and motivations of characters in the novels. Finally, incorporating a speech based on real news articles in the same instructional unit as the study of a novel gives students a chance to detect the different text structures used in fiction and nonfiction, a critical thinking skill most schools expect middle school students to acquire.

Preparing the Speech

Vital to your planning is allotting time for students to construct the speech and to practice it. Your future orators soon recognize that writing to speak is very different from simply reading an essay aloud. They realize that shorter, less complex sentences make for better speaking. They see they need to state the goal, explain it, and review it in much the way they used P.I.E. patterns in class discussion. Your particularly astute students may even recall and apply what they learned in the poetry unit about choosing and arranging words based on their sound and suggestive power.

Insist that your students get feedback on their speeches. This listener could be a friend or family member, or if that is not reasonable to expect in the setting where you teach, this someone should be a classmate. Practicing aloud is the only way for students to know for certain they are familiar enough with the content of their speech to deliver it with confidence, making eye contact, using gestures, pronouncing words correctly and clearly, varying the pace of the speaking, and maintaining their poise. See Teacher Resource J for a sample peer evaluation form students can use during practice and you can use for grading.

Student Self-Check: Wise Use of a Variety of Evidence Leads to Successful Speeches

Do I provide adequate support for each main section of my speech? (Check the number of times you include each of these supporting materials in your speech.)

_____ illustrations/examples   _____ explanations
_____ definitions   _____ restatements
_____ statistics/numbers   _____ humor
_____ comparison/contrast   _____ opinion of experts
_____ testimony   _____ quotations

Having the students make a script of their speech is a practical way to have them practice the grammar they have been learning, too. Their goal is to communicate clearly both in writing and in speaking in an appropriate grammar, Standard English or otherwise. Their choice of grammar makes the difference in how well they get their ideas across to their audience even if their purpose is to entertain peers in their class commemorating a character in a story, a historical figure in history, or a real friend or family member.

Practice, Practice, Practice

Students sometimes wonder what they should be paying attention to when they practice a speech. So, plan on providing a few guidelines to assure these prospective speakers that they are on the right track. Recommend that they give their speech at least three times standing in front of a mirror, holding their notes on the same index cards they plan to use when they give their speech in public. If they can look up at themselves and keep talking through their speech, they probably are prepared to look up and make more frequent eye contact with their audience.

Help students understand the function of the opening seconds of a speech and provide questions to help them consider what their speech includes or needs.

Get Off to a Good Start

- Does this speech open with an attention getter that will make the audience want to listen?
- Does the introduction include *signposts* that will indicate the order of the arguments to follow?
- Does this speech clearly show that this topic is important to me (personally or as the character)?
- Does this speech clearly show why this topic is important to the members of my audience?

Suggest wearing something special on the day they give the speech, an outfit that is especially neat, comfortable, and appropriate for their intended audience. Choosing what to wear reminds them that people in an audience are spectators, also influenced by the speaker's physical appearance and posture. When resources are available at home or at school, encourage your students to make an audio or video recording and listen and watch to hear and see what others are to hear and see when the students deliver their speeches.

Students who are asked to give a little more attention to observing; assigned to point out the qualities of a good speech; and given the time to research, write, and practice, become attuned to differences in effectiveness, and these young communicators no longer are content simply to give a report, but endeavor to present a speech.

Providing students with probing questions helps them evaluate their speech plans and encourages them to modify them before presenting them in public. For example, if you assign a speech to persuade, ask students to include arguments that appeal to the head, the heart, and the pocket:

- Does this speech make appeals to the head (definitions, statistics, explanations, and comparison/contrast)?
- Does this speech make appeals to the heart (humor, explanation, illustrations, quotations, testimony about people)?
- Does this speech make appeals to the pocket (definitions, facts, statistics, and comparison/contrast about money)?

CONCLUSION

When students have personal reasons for code-switching to communicate in the grammar of Standard English, they usually are amenable to learning how to do so. Whether they are writing for a specific purpose to a real audience, presenting a speech in class, or talking with their peers in middle school, students want to be seen as smart enough to use the right language for the situation. You can help them expand their knowledge and skills by incorporating regular opportunities to learn and use Standard English. Asking them to pay attention to effective writers and speakers raises their level of awareness about how humans make judgments about others based on their skill in using appropriate language in specific settings.

Teaching middle school students to view the media with a critical eye helps them become defensive viewers and thoughtful creators in a variety of media. Students become more sensitive to the impact color, size, and design have on those with whom they wish to communicate. If your middle school students know Standard English grammar, if they have had lots of practice delivering informal and formal speeches, they can access these skills when they want to be perceived positively by those they wish to impress with their improving education.

As your students increase their confidence and competence in selecting the appropriate grammars for a social situation and particular audience, they are less tempted to muzzle their speech like my friend has done for so many years. As they mature and enter the world of work, students you teach are not likely to be passed up for a job promotion simply because they lack the writing, presenting, and speaking skills sought in the twenty-first-century job market.

(12)

CELEBRATING NAMES:
A UNIT ABOUT COMMUNITY
AND IDENTITY

We must wear our names within all the noise and confusion of the
environment in which we find ourselves; make them the center of
all our associations with the world, with man and with nature. We
must charge them with all our emotions, our hopes, hates, loves,
aspirations. They must become our masks and our shields, and the
containers of all those values and traditions which we learn and/or
imagine as being the meaning of our familial past.

—Ralph Ellison[1]

Names are important. They can distinguish one thing from another
and link a person to families, cultures, and communities. For young
adolescents, such as those in ninth grade, names can make them proud
or embarrassed, one with others and separate from others. This paradox
of emotions poses a challenge and an opportunity. This paradox makes
for an engaging unit in communication, community, and identity that
incorporates lessons that also meets a range of English language arts
standards in your school curriculum.

Depending on your school district, ninth graders may be the oldest,
youngest, or only students on campus. In any setting, they are in their
early teens, eager to become independent of their parents or guardians,
often straining against the ties that bind them. These adolescents are

developing their own self-identities distinct from that of their families. For this reason, it is a good time to provide opportunities for these youngsters to rekindle fond relationships with their families, and talking about their names can do just that. These lessons require the students to consult their parents or other family members to complete some of the assignments for this unit of study. Family members may recall their own warm memories of choosing a name for their child, and for a few days both the older and the younger ones can bask in that warmth.

This unit of lessons based on names may become one of your favorites to teach early in the fall, mainly because it is a good way to learn a little more about the students through their writing. Whether the students in your classes have been together for several years or are just meeting each other for the first time, this assignment builds a more trusting learning community in a nonthreatening way. Perhaps it is because the students are to be doing what so many teens like to do best—talking about themselves!

ALERTING YOU WITH WORDS OF CAUTION

This assignment could cause emotional difficulties for some students and their families. You must be sensitive to the fact that some children are unable to get the information for this assignment for personally traumatic reasons. If you learn that any of your students do not live with parents or do not communicate regularly with their parents or family members, simply modify the assignment so these young people can complete it without appearing uncooperative or inept.

Consider the ethnicity of your students. When children are in elementary school, their social studies assignments sometimes require that students trace their history, create and display their family trees. This proves to be difficult or impossible for many students. Because of the practice of chattel slavery in the United States, few African Americans know their family's genealogy; they cannot even talk without anguish about their ancestry.

Prior to the 1860s, the birth records of African Americans included few surnames and, when kept at all, the first names often were recorded among the cattle records. Even in the twenty-first century, few African

Americans can trace their ancestry more than a few generations. Those families that can trace their history may already know that they carry the names of those slave owners. Most know that their families originated in Africa, but few have access to information that can verify the country or the tribe.

Discussing the issue of ancestry proves to be difficult for some students and impossible for others. This may be the case for current new-to-America students whose families may have come to escape political unrest in their own country. Clearly you know to avoid any name-tracing assignments that may cause undue anxiety for students and families. The more diverse your school's community, the more careful you may need to be.

If you teach in a community with a large number of immigrants from war-torn countries, you may discover that some families are able, but unwilling, to discuss their lineage. Ancestors may have changed their names in order to protect themselves from political repercussions. On the other hand, some families appreciate the fact that you are interested in learning more about their cultures and are thrilled with the opportunity to share theirs.

Be similarly on the alert to situations with blended families in which parents and siblings have different last names, and when students have blended or hyphenated names. And know that in some cultures, children have different names from those of their parents simply because it is part of their culture. A teacher new to the school or community knows to confer with veterans at the school and then adapt the unit as needed to gain the benefits and avoid the pitfalls. With this many pitfalls, why bother?

Because, just reading literature about naming and living with names can be a rich intellectual experience for your students. Additionally, the accompanying assignments help meet several of the English language arts standards in interesting and illuminating ways. The following unit includes lessons for

- Reading, discussing, and analyzing literary works in a variety of genres
- Learning name-related vocabulary
- Conducting various kinds of research (online, library, and interview)

- Writing essays, authoring vignettes, drafting autobiographical sketches
- Composing short stories patterned after literary works read
- Participating in peer editing groups

LEARNING THE VOCABULARY OF NAMES

Begin with an overview of a unit you can call simply, "What's in a Name?" One very popular name-related assignment is based on Sandra Cisneros's "My Name," a chapter from *House on Mango Street*, her autobiographical vignette about growing up as a child of Mexican immigrants in Chicago.[2]

As you get to know your students and plan your unit, you can add or substitute other name-related narratives, especially stories and poems about various ethnic or cultural groups reflecting your school population and, each year, determined by the reading level of your particular students. Three selections that seem most accessible to all students are Cisneros's vignette "My Name"; Santha Rama Rau's autographical sketch, "By Any Other Name," set in British colonial India; and "The Name," Aharon Megged's short story, set in modern Israel and describes Jewish naming traditions.

"Hidden Name, Complex Fate," a sophisticated essay by Ralph Ellison, an African American named by his father for Ralph Waldo Emerson, works incredibly well as a springboard for discussing issues of living with a name. Even if your students are not particularly strong readers you still can begin with the Ellison essay. In that case, read it in class with considerable support to aid understanding. Remind them that expository writing uses text structures they may have learned earlier. If necessary, do a minilesson introducing these structures to your students. Ellison's essay inspired some questions you can use for the students' research and writing about their own names. (See box 12.1.)

You might also consider substituting or adding a chapter from Richard Kim's *Lost Names* about Korean families forced by the Japanese government to adopt Japanese names; *Not Even My Name*, an biographical work by Thea Halo about Pontic Greeks in Turkey; or *The Namesake*, a novel by Jhumpa Lahiri, about naming traditions of a fam-

---

Box 12.1.   Search It! Researching Your Names

1. Use a dictionary and/or online resources to find out what each of your own names mean.
2. Interview a family member to learn the sources of your name(s). If you have equipment, audio- or videotape the interview. Who named you and why? Are you named for a friend or family member?
3. Determine the kind of surname or last name you have. Is it a place name, like Hall or Rivera; an occupation, like Smith or Taylor; a descriptive, Brown or Strong, or a patronymic or version of a father's name, like McNeil, Von Wilhelm, ibn Maryam, and so on?
4. Describe incidents you have experienced because of your name, including mispronunciations, misspellings, and misunderstandings.
5. Write about nicknames and related embarrassing or humorous experiences.
6. Identify challenges you feel because of the name(s) you carry.

---

ily from India. Let your own interest and that of your students guide your selections each year. As always, select readings to fit your particular school setting, literature that serves as windows for seeing others, and mirrors for seeing self.

Reading and Researching

During the first couple of weeks of this four-week unit, read and analyze the literature selections to discover their organizational pattern, diction, and sentence structure. Discuss the vocabulary of naming, including concepts such as

surname
given name
nickname
nom de plume
pseudonym
pen name
alias

The assignment prompt that asks them to interview a family member provides enough information to get them started on learning how they have come to have the names they have been given. You may have to review with them the correct way to cite an interview in the text of the essay and the format for their bibliographies.

With expanded resources available on the Internet, most students are able to find enough information to fulfill the basic purposes of the assignment—to consider their own names, to conduct research, and to write about traditions of naming they discover. If students have uncommon names or common names that are spelled uncommonly, they may need a bit of help identifying similar, researchable alternatives. Prepare them for research by showing them alternative spellings of the same name, such as—Anna, Ana, Anne, Ann, Annie, even Hannah.

Students who have online access from home and some parental supervision of the project might benefit from using ancestry.com and similar websites to collect historical information about their family names. By all means, share your name story and write along with your students.

As students consider responses to these prompts, they reflect on who they are in their families, the school, the wider community, and perhaps even the world. Some of the students may learn family history never previously discussed. Other students awaken tender memories of relatives and family friends for whom they have been named. Some may just be embarrassed; others pleasantly surprised.

One student developed a new appreciation for a stepfather and deepened her relationships with her biological parents. This student's first name is a combination of her biological parents' first names. Her stepfather later adopted her and she now carries his surname.

DISCOVERING INTERESTING FACTS ABOUT NAMES

As students read about the name-related experiences during peer response sessions, they discover interesting naming traditions observed in the families of their classmates. They might learn that in some villages in India all the girls in a family may have the same middle name, or that some Thai families carry extremely long, polysyllabic names, like Prachyaratanawooti, for which each syllable represents a generation the family has lived in a particular region. Students might learn that in some families it is the grandmother who chooses grandchildren's names, that the eldest son always is named for his father, or that middle names for all the children is their mother's maiden name.

Your teens may notice interesting combinations of Anglo and Asian or Spanish names. Some students find out that their families' names have been Americanized to avoid discrimination based on ethnicity, religion, or nationality. A number of your students may have saint's day names or hyphenated last names that include both their mother's maiden name and their father's last name. Some learn the spelling of their surnames is simply the result of an error made when their ancestors entered the country through Ellis Island in New York or Angel Island in San Francisco. No one ever bothered to correct the mistake.

One of the assignment prompts invites students to talk about the challenges of living with their names, as described in the essay by Ralph Ellison, "Hidden Name: Complex Fate." Some student writing may reveal that carrying the name of a particularly famous or infamous relative causes them discomfort. One young man named for his father, a prominent businessman in the community, acknowledged in his essay that he felt unworthy to be called Robert and insisted that his peers call him Robbie, a diminutive version of the father's strong name.

Cecilia, a talented singer, was depressed for a few days upon learning that the name she loves means "blind one," but then became jubilant after discovering that St. Cecilia is the patron saint of music and musicians.

Other students may write about the embarrassment of having to correct the pronunciation of their name at the beginning of every school year, and the frustration of having to spell their name everywhere they go. These reminders of how sensitive students are about their names remind us to learn to pronounce and spell each student's name as early in the semester as possible. It is just another way of honoring each one as an individual with his or her own special name.

Springboarding to Writing

Distribute a copy of the vignette "My Name" by Sandra Cisneros and prepare to conduct a "jump in reading" activity to help students get a feel for the style and to think about what the writer may be "saying to them." But first, ask students to read silently, underlining words or phrases that catch their attention. Then you read the vignette out loud, asking students again to underline words or phrases they think are interesting or important. Finally, starting at the beginning again, invite one student to begin reading, stopping at the first mark of punctuation. Others jump in to read, without being called upon, and read to the next punctuation mark. If more than one student begins reading at the same time, urge each to listen to the other(s) and read as one voice. Let the silence between voices resonate.

You may recall from doing this kind of reading of poetry that students are uncomfortable at first, giggle a bit, but soon catch on. The silence between and the sounds of different single voices and combinations of multiple voices leave indelible impressions and elicit powerful results in the next step of this assignment—writing.

To help the students comfortably share their stories, after reading "My Name" by Sandra Cisneros, ask them to do a quick-write based on a phrase or sentence that they select from the vignette. A quick-write is short, nonstop writing on an assigned topic; students let their thoughts flow without censoring them for a brief spurt of time—for example, three to seven minutes. In this assignment, ask students to copy an underlined phrase or sentence from the reading. Then use that phrase or sentence as a jumping off point to write rapidly about their own names for six or seven minutes. Write along with them. The following is a quick-write based on the Cisneros piece:

"My Name," a Quick-Write Inspired by Sandra Cisneros's Vignette of the Same Name

Anna Jamar Small Roseboro. Is this "me"? My name is a combination of my paternal grandmother's, Anna; my maternal grandmother's, Jamie; my dad's name, Small; and my husband's name, Roseboro. Everyone has had my name—made something of it, then passed it along to me. Anna means "gift of God." Is it I who am the gift or my grandmother who is a gift to me? Jamie is short for Jamar. My grandmother, whose full name is Jamar Elna, is named for her four aunts, Jane, Martha, Ellen and Nora—what a burden, what a privilege, to carry the names of so many relatives. Or is it a blessing? Am I standing on the shoulders of those who've come before me?

Small, my maiden name, always caused me trouble. "Small," they'd tease. "You're not small; you're tall!" I was always the tallest girl in my elementary school classes. In high school, however, I used the name to my advantage. I ran for a senior class office. My slogan was "Good things come in Small packages." Finally, success with that name.

Then, I married Bill Roseboro during the years that Johnny Roseboro was a star catcher for the L.A. Dodgers. He'd been in the news because of a fight with Juan Marichal. Everywhere I went, "Are you related to Johnny Roseboro?"

"Yes, but what has that to do with me?"

Who am I really?

The extended writing assignment in this unit on names asks students to select an author's style they like and to pattern that style to write about their experience of living with their own names. Some of the students are comfortable with the familiar, formal essay style of Ellison; others enjoy the storytelling with strong sense of place in Rau's piece or with a series of symbols as in Megged's "The Name" and may choose one of these genres or blend one or two.

One ninth grader, Alexis, of Jewish descent, was drawn to the Aharon Megged story, "The Name," but preferred modeling Cisneros's poetic style with short phrases instead of consistently complete sentences. So, Alexis modeled her essay after Cisneros's "My Name."

"So Much Like Me" by Alexis Rebecca De Sieno

My name is a strong name. In Greek it means "defender of mankind." It was the name of many rulers in the dynasty of Russia. Powerful and re- fined. It is energetic, strong, and beautiful, like a lion. It is not like other names like Kelly or Mary that end in a comma. It ends in an exclama- tion. Like a line, with a beginning and an end. It is like the number 1, or the beginning of the alphabet. The leader. The individual. It is like the finale number at the end of a piano concerto. Like Mozart or Beethoven, it leaves an impression. It has force. A car shares my name, though it is spelled differently, because it displays power and strength. It is durable, it will not disappear. Remembered. It is a name to be remembered. Alexis. My name. So much like me.

My great-grandmother should have been named Alexis because she was strong too. My mother and I are named after her in hope that we could carry on her strength. I wish I could have known her. She was a woman with a strong soul and a caring heart, so caring she had seven children which were all overly tended for. Ana. I think she must have been misnamed, for this names ends in a comma, as though it needs the help of another name, but she needing nothing to help her because she was strong. Alexis would have fit her better. That is why I am not named Ana as is the Askhenozic tradition. It is delicate like the petals of a blooming flower that need the help of the stem to grow. Both my mother's names and my name use the first letter of hers, which is the next closest traditional way, because she died before my mother was born, too. Allyn. Alexis. Names that continue to carry on her strength.

In Hebrew my middle names means to tie or bind. It was my other great-grandmother's name and now it is mine. It is a solid name, thought it was changed in America. Rifka. In Russia, that was her name. But now, it is Rebecca. It is not a common name, though it is known. It is like the color red. Energetic, and not easily defeated. It is bold. It is not plain or boring. It is like the flame of a candle, tame but with hidden strength that not many know about. It dulls the power of my first name. It is like me because I am not always what everyone thinks.

Of Sienna. In Italian that is what my last name means. It has Italian spice, like the peppers they put on their pizza. Solid and smooth. In Italy it is easily said while speaking with your hands. Like Boboli, or spaghetti. It is colorful like the Italian culture. Like the Italian wines. It bubbles. It is like a symphony of instrumental sounds, rhythmic and mixed. In America, it is always misspelled and mispronounced. Spoiled. As if the wine had turned to vinegar and makes you cringe. But in Italy, it is like the color blue. Like the blood of royalty. Free flowing and smooth.

My great-grandfather was the first DeSieno. He was the son of an Italian man of royal blood, and a less prominent maiden. They could not marry. It was against the aristorcracys rules. So he was given to a foster family at an early age, and was given a different surname from that of his father. He became a DeSieno, because he was born in Sienna, and he grew up with a different last name from his foster parents. I have inherited his name, but I am not alone like him.

When I was still playing with dolls, I used to want to change my name. I thought it was ugly. I wanted a pretty name like Samantha or Alexandra, just like the dolls I played with. To me, they were perfect. I used to dream that I was like them, and I lived in a Victorian furnished house in the early 1900's, rest next to central park. But now I am content, and I look back at these memories and laugh. No other name could suit me. Not Alexandra or Samantha. They're just not me. Alexis. Yes, I am Alexis and could be nothing else.

To many, though, I am not Alexis. I am known as something else. I can become "Lexie Poo" or "Lex" or "X," "Xie" and "Lexus." But strangely, I am also "Betty Boop." I like my nicknames. Usually. People often tease me that Lexie Poo sounds like a name that an old lady calls her dog. But I think they are wrong, because Lexie Poo is me. It brings back so many memories, because my first grade teacher came up with that name. She had a nickname for everyone in the class. I was Lexie Poo. There was also Lindsey Tortolleni, Kelly Jelly Ben, and Jake the Snake. My friends created other nicknames. Most of them were "inside jokes." Sometimes, when I am angry with myself, I don't want to be Alexis. I can change my identity and put on my nickname mask. When I am Lexie Poo, I am an innocent first grader. When I am Lex, I am a best friend. When I am Lexus I am someone who is looked up too. My nicknames are not Alexis, but they are me too. They are each a different aspect of my personality.

Alexis Rebecca DeSieno. My full name. A powerful name with many memories. A name with hidden meanings, hidden like my grandmother's treasures in the attic. Though I am rarely called by my full name, without it I would not be me. It is like my personality. It fits me like a well worn shoe. Or an old pair of jeans. Alexis Rebecca DeSieno. Lexie Poo. Me. I could not have been named better.

On the final page of her essay, Alexis wrote each of her names in Greek and Hebrew. The assignment gave her an occasion to learn more about her family. But it also gave her classmates and me the opportunity to learn more about Alexis. Her essay demonstrated her pride in sharing what she learned and experienced living with her name. Alexis is in college now. When contacted about including her essay in the book, I noticed that Alexis uses "Lexie Poo" in her e-mail address. Even nicknames sometimes remain and become a part of one's self-identity, as suggested by Ralph Ellison in the quotation opening this chapter.

Setting up RAG Sessions for Peer Responses

You probably know a number of ways to organize a class session during which students conduct peer editing. One that you may consider for this assignment is one described by Jenee Gossard in Carol B. Olson's *Practical Ideas for Teaching Writing as a Process.*[3]

In Read Around Group (RAG) sessions, students bring a completed early draft to class and sit in circles of five or six students. Review the rubric to remind the students of the criteria on which their writing is to be evaluated. It may be a rubric you create together, an adaptation of one in your textbook, or one you download from the Internet.[4]

The students write their names on the rubric and lay it on top of their drafts. One student from each group collects all the drafts and hands them to you. Now distribute the drafts to other groups so that none of the students in the group is reading the paper of anyone else in their group (Group A gets Group B papers, B gets C, etc.). This way a student is less likely to be distracted by watching how classmates respond to his or her paper. During the RAG, each student reads five or six papers, but responds to only two. Do not allow those without a draft to sit in on a RAG.

Fairness suggests that paperless students sit out and use the time to work on their drafts. First, it is useful to give those who are behind on their own writing class time to catch up. Second, if a student in a group does not have a paper to be read each round, then someone else has to "sit" out because of too few papers.

No need to worry about students coming unprepared the next time. Most will be ready for the next RAG because they want to see what others have written and also want to get peer feedback and suggestions for their own revisions. Curiosity is a great motivator.

Once the groups are formed and have their stack of papers, the group leader distributes the drafts to members in the group, and you set a timer for three minutes, which usually is enough time to read the two to four pages of these early drafts. Students read the first paper until the timer goes off, then pass the paper to the right and read the second paper, and finally the third paper and fourth until the timer goes off again. After the fourth pass, set the timer for six minutes.

This time, the students read and comment on the content of the paper. On this fifth pass, again set the timer for six minutes and the students read and comment on the structure and style. By this time the students have learned a great deal about their classmates, about the ways their peers have responded to the prompts, about the problems that arise when one makes grammar, usage, spelling, and mechanical errors, and equally important, about the quality of the pool of writing in which their own papers are to be read.

While students are reading the first two or three drafts, you can walk around the classroom, rubber stamp the written drafts, and record in your grade book a check for the students who have their drafts ready on this due date. Afterward, during the longer reading times, take a few moments to confer with those who have come unprepared and offer suggestions to get then back on track with their writing.

At the end of the RAG session, each leader collects his or her group's papers and hands them to you. Return them along with the completed rubric to the students who wrote them. Spend ten minutes or so, soliciting from the students what they noticed about the strengths of their papers, and inviting their suggested strategies for improving them.

Use the remainder of the period for students to read the comments from their peers, and then to plan how to revise their papers. If time remains in the period, quickly scan and then stamp the plans the students have made to improve their papers. This simply creates a record that the student has received feedback and has outlined a plan for revising.

Assign the students to have their final drafts ready for you to read two or three days later. During the intervening days, schedule in-class writing time for students to work on their revisions. Then, you can meet individually with students who are not sure what steps they should take to make their next draft better.

Do not feel frustrated if you find yourself adjusting the length of time needed for revisions. Ask the students. If they feel confident and can quickly complete a revision they are eager to have you read, set a short deadline. If they are working diligently, but believe they need more time, extend the deadline. Thankfully, the students become personally attached to these papers and want you to see their best work. Do both them and you a favor. Create a schedule that is flexible enough to allow them to revise. Well-written papers are a pleasure to read and take less time to grade.

If you teach in a setting where it is unrealistic to expect students to word process the final drafts at home by themselves, allot additional class time for students to use school equipment. Especially in writing, it is more important that students complete a few assignments well than to rush through lots of assignments they cannot finish carefully and turn in with pride. This assignment is one in which they usually are willing to invest time. Students are eager to do a good job on this assignment. The subject, after all, is the students themselves.

On the due date, students should submit for evaluation a packet that includes their stamped drafts, the rubric with their plan, and the final draft stapled to the top. This stack of papers substantiates that the process of writing is a lot of work.

VALUING THE WRITING PROCESS AND THE NAMES ASSIGNMENT

These steps in the process of drafting a paper are important for both writers and classmates. The writer has an opportunity to get feedback during the interim stages of the writing and to see how peers are addressing the assignment. For many students this is both a comfort and a challenge. When they see that they and their peers are having similar problems, they do not feel so odd or incompetent. On the other hand, when they see how well some of their peers are doing, individual students realize that the task is possible, and they are challenged to work a little harder to meet the assignment's standards.

Overall, this assignment is an important one whether given at the beginning, middle, or end of the school year because it allows students to write from a personal perspective. During conferences, parents often express appreciation for being consulted as knowledgeable resources. What is more, this assignment creates a positive, supportive atmosphere in class. Young adults enjoy writing about themselves and reading about each other. Perhaps most important, "What's in a Name?" enables students to complete an assignment successfully anytime you give it. You and your students get to enjoy writing that is lively and interesting. Finally, even though students may model their prose after quality published writing, they truly are developing their own, authentic voices.

CONCLUSION

People's names are important for identifying who they are, where they live, and what they might be like. This is especially true for learning about names in middle school language arts classes. Some of the oldest literature uses naming to identify characters and their relationships to one another. In fact, according to Hebrew scripture, the biblical Adam "named" the creatures in the garden. Most cultures have stories of rituals and naming ceremonies for infants and for those reaching a certain age, often when they enter their teens.

So, even if you decide it is better just to read the literature about names, your students are sure to find pleasure thinking about their names as more than labels. Names reveal much about who and whose we are, where we have been and where we might want to be going. Generation to generation, and place to place, names teach us about who we are as diverse communities. To be human is to name. To name is to be human. Naming is an art—a language art.

AFTERWORD

Congratulations and Bon Voyage!

Whether you are beginning your first, second, seventh, or seventeenth year of teaching middle school, you are set to embark on a trip of a lifetime. Each year of teaching can be different, unique, and very much the same—an opportunity to learn and to inspire learning.

You are not alone on this journey even within your classroom. Your students are there to help. You know, they may know the school, the community, and neighborhood better than you, so let them teach you the ropes, but keep in mind that you are the professional. You are the adult hired to see that you all have safe passage through the sometimes tumultuous sea that is a year in the life of teenagers. Keep your eyes on the goal and, using your peripheral vision, keep your adolescents in view, too. They are who you are teaching. Yes, you are teaching kids, not just content. And with patience and persistence, you all can reach the shore safely, secure in the knowledge you have gained and the skills you have honed.

How can you be assured that you can reach the shore intact?

- By carefully planning lessons based on what you know about the curriculum and what you learn about your students each school year

- By observing and documenting what goes on in your classes
- By varying the kind of performance and final product assessment you assign
- By being willing to modify your lessons to meet the needs and interests of your students
- By being firm but fair in your interactions with students, colleagues, parents, and guardians
- By recognizing that help is available—right in this book and right in your classroom and from your students, your fellow travelers on this journey
- By taking time each week to refresh yourself, spending time with family and friends or reading a good book
- By attending, every year, at least one conference, seminar, or workshop for professional and personal enrichment
- By believing that associating with excited, enthusiastic, and experienced educators is the best way to maintain your passion for the profession

Know that as you teach your young students to understand and use the language arts to receive knowledge and to express themselves, you are giving them the golden keys to academic success and personal satisfaction. You, their language arts teacher, have the privilege of guiding and coaching young adolescents along the journey. You, who provide the balance between dependable discipline and appropriate play in a safe, supportive environment, can help raise their self-esteem and increase their confidence and competence in communicating.

Each time you design flexible lessons permeated with rich experiences for exploring fiction and nonfiction in the print and electronic media, writing in a range of modes for a variety of authentic purposes, talking and listening to you and their peers (those they encounter face-to-face and online), and learning to critically view and use twenty-first-century technology, you are cultivating in them vital skills for growth. With diligence on your part and assiduousness on theirs you all will complete a school year inspired by the success of the current year and eager to move on to the challenges of the next. So, bon voyage! Enjoy the journey!

APPENDIX

Teacher Resources

RESOURCE A: COLLAGE ASSIGNMENT:
THE CIRCUIT BY FRANCISCO JIMENEZ

The Task

As an introduction to the study of literature this school year, you are to work with a group of your peers to present your impressions of ways Francisco Jimenez uses various elements of the narrative: point of view, setting, characterization, conflict, symbolism, and figurative language to create a story that is engaging, meaningful, and one that is stylistically unique and effective.

Using whatever poster board, cardboard, paper, fabric, and so forth that your group chooses, create a collage that depicts the aspect of the story that your group has been assigned. The completed collages are to be no larger than 11 × 14 inches. In addition to pictures and drawings, the collage should include words and quotations from the story. All group members must participate in a presentation of the collage to the class.

Preparation and Organization

With your group members, review the story and brainstorm about the people, place, events, and images that come to mind as you think about your group's focus. At home, hunt through magazines and newspapers and bring to class four or five pictures, words, and direct quotations from the story that can best illustrate your group's focus area. Bring your materials to class. As a group, decide which quotations, pictures, and so on can best illustrate the aspect of the novel your collage is to represent. Make the collage; then decide how your group can present the collage to the class. See Presentation below.

Options

Review the options below in preparation for being assigned to a collage group.

Setting: Choose five or six significant settings. Represent the settings in terms of the impact each has on Panchito; consider also the connection of the various settings with the title of the story. In your presentation to the class, be prepared to explain the reasons for your choices.

Characters: Choose five or six important characters. Present or depict them in terms of their relationship with Panchito and the significance of their influence upon him. In your presentation to the class, be prepared to explain the reasons for your choices.

Conflicts: Choose five or six memorable conflicts in the story. Depict the characters involved in each conflict as well as the effect the conflict has on Panchito. (Note: He may have been an observer of the conflict and not necessarily directly involved.) In your presentation to the class be prepared to explain the reasons for your choices.

Symbolism and Figurative Language: Select examples of five or six particularly effective devices (symbols, images, metaphors, figures of speech) that Jimenez uses to illustrate character, conflict, or theme, or to unify the story. In your presentation to the class, be prepared to explain the reasons for your choices.

Lessons Learned: Put yourselves in Panchito's shoes. Identify three or four of the most important lessons that you think Panchito learns and, perhaps, benefits from his experiences growing up in a migrant family. These lessons may be supported by any of the previous elements: setting, characterization, conflict, use of symbolism, and figurative language. In your presentation to the class, be prepared to explain the reasons for your choices.

The Presentation

Plan a six- to seven-minute presentation during which you display and explain your collage. All group members should have equal time to speak. Plan the order of speakers. Feel free to use notes, but please do not read them word for word. Decide where each group member should stand so that the whole class can see the collage as you make your presentation. Practice what you plan to say, then you can establish and maintain eye contact with members of the audience.

RESOURCE B: BOOK REPORT #1— MAKING CONNECTIONS

Step 1. Select and read a novel.
Step 2. Create a diagram of the plot.
Step 3. Write a summary of your novel.
Step 4. Decide on Option A or Option B and write a meaty paragraph response.
Step 5. Share your report with your classmates on the due date _____ .

Part I

Use one side of a 12 × 9 sheet of construction paper. Draw a plot line that shows how the events in your story progressed. If you have a longer exposition than resolution, have the length of the lines reflect that. If you have a shorter rising action than falling action, let your plot line show that.

Show the following in words and drawings, computer graphics, or magazine cutouts.

- Main Characters
- Setting
- Conflict
- Complications/Obstacles in Rising Action
- Climax
- Falling Action/Denouement

- Resolution

Part II

Write a half-page summary of your book that includes the title, author, main characters, and the characterization the author uses; the setting—both time and place; the conflict and the specific kind(s); and the point of view. *Use literary terms we've been learning.* Word process your summary and paste it on the left side of the back of the same sheet of construction paper.

Part III

Write a half-page paragraph response to Option A or Option B (detailed below). Decide which questions best fit your book. (Consider them all, and then write about three or four of them.) Organize your responses so that your paragraph flows smoothly from one idea to the next. Word process your paragraph, then glue it on to the reverse side of your construction paper. Paste it on the right side. (See figure B.1.)

Option A—My response to this book . . . First, answer these questions about your book, and then decide which are more significant

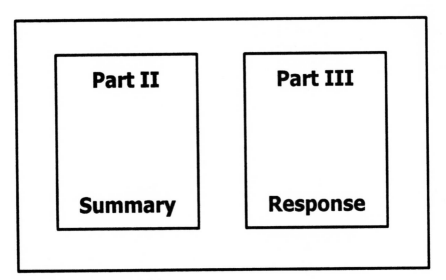

Figure B.1. Book Report #1

to you and pull your responses together into a paragraph that is a unified whole. For example: focus on qualities of character, connection to character, opinions expressed, expectations, and so on.

- What did you like best about the person you read about? Why?
- What did you like least about the person you read about? Why?
- Does this person remind you of yourself? Explain.
- What is the most difficult moment for this person? What does he or she learn from it?
- What is the best moment for this person? What does he or she learn from it?
- Which qualities of this person do you want to develop within yourself?
- Why would you like to develop these qualities?
- Do any of the ideas, incidents, or actions in this book remind you of your own life, or something that has happened to you?
- Do you feel that there is an opinion expressed by the author in this book? What is it? Why do you think this is an opinion? Do you agree with the opinion? Why or why not?
- In what point of view is the book written? How would the book be different if it were written from a different point of view? Which one?
- When you picked the book, what kind of book did you think it would be? Why? Was it the type of book you thought it would be? If not, did you like it anyway?

Option B—This book made me . . . Complete each of the following eight ideas with material from the book you read.

Figure B.2. Pie

This book made me

- wish that . . .
- realize that . . .
- decide that . . .
- wonder about . . .
- see that . . .
- believe that . . .
- feel that . . .
- hope that . . .

Now, decide which questions or ideas are more significant to you, and then write a paragraph that pulls these together into a unified whole. Remember to write a P.I.E. paragraph. Make the point, illustrate it with details from your book, and explain to show the connection between illustration and point.

RESOURCE C: SHORT STORY EVALUATION

You are to read, rate, and rank the manuscripts of the students in another class. Below is the chart with criteria to consider. (See figure C.1.) To get in practice for using these guidelines, read and rate your own manuscript. Fold your evaluation and staple it to the back of the manuscript you turn in to be graded.

1. Manuscript requirements: two printed copies and one posted on our class website.
2. Printed copy #1: Do not put your name on the text of the story. Staple a title page on a separate sheet with your name, class, period, and date.
3. Printed copy #2: Have a complete heading and title on the first page.
4. Website: Name your file, using your last name and period number— Roseboro I or Roseboro III.
5. Upload a copy of your story to our class website, and then submit your story for publication on at least three online magazines,

Manuscript # _____		1	2	3	4	5
Criteria						
Characters	flat, round, dynamic					
Characterization	direct, indirect					
Conflict	unclear, typical, compelling					
Rising Action	single or multiple attempts to solve					
Resolution	anticipated, believable, surprising, but logical					
Setting	sight, sound, taste, touch, smell					
Dialogue	stiff, believable, realistic					
Mechanics, Usage, Grammar	not, somewhat, very distracting					
Vocabulary	flat, adequate, vivid					
	OVERALL RATING (1-5)					

Figure C.1.   Short Story Evaluation Chart

and to our school literary magazine. See class website for suggestions.

Read and rate the stories independently, then, as a group, rank the stories.

Rate the stories on a scale of 1 (low) to 5 (high).

Rank the stories A (first place) through D or E (fourth or fifth).

RESOURCE D: BOOK REPORT #2— SHORT STORY COLLECTION

Due Days 1 and 2 of Next Week

Basic Requirements:

1. Report on three different stories from the collection.

   Write about a story that could complement the short stories in our world literature book. Indicate the title and author of the *World Lit* story and the reason for your choice—similar characters, conflict, theme, literary devices used, and so on.

   Write about another story that you would recommend to a character from *A Day No Pigs Would Die* OR from *A Christmas*

Carol. What is it about the story that the specific character would/should read? Similar personality, similar situation, a lesson to be learned, and so on? Explain the specific reason with details from the short story and information about the character from the novel you've chosen.

Write about a third story that is the one you most enjoyed. Be specific about reasons for your choice.

2. For the body of the report, write three P.I.E. paragraphs with topic sentences, specific references and/or quotations from the stories, appropriate transitions, and conclusion sentences.
3. Include in each paragraph the title and author, a one-sentence summary of the story that includes main character(s), setting, conflict, point of view, and other facts and explanations for each specific story.

Task One—Plan before You Write
1. Determine the kind of collection you've read. Write a sentence or two to explain this. Same author, genre, theme, audience? Use this information in your introduction paragraph.
2. From your collection of short stories, select the three stories you plan to use. Save your favorite.
3. Reflect on the stories we've studied in the *World Literature* book. Choose one of these stories to write about. Which stories from your collection do you recommend to complement that *World Lit* story? Remember to include titles and authors of both stories. Make notes.
4. Reflect on the characters from *A Day No Pigs Would Die* and *A Christmas Carol.* Which of your short stories would appeal to a character from ONE of these novels? Remember to include the titles and authors and explanations in the paragraph about this story. Make notes.
5. Now, make notes about your favorite story from this collection. What is appealing about the story? Characters, conflict, theme, writing style, identification?

Task Two—Draft Your Report
1. Write an interesting introduction that includes title and author or editor of your short story collection and the kind of collection or organization of the collection. Use two or three sentences.

2. Write each body paragraph making certain to include the required information. See notes from planning steps.

3. Revise each paragraph paying attention to using appropriate transition words and phrases.

4. Edit your paragraphs. Check for spelling, punctuation, and verb tense (remember to use present tense verbs to talk about incidents in the plot of fictional works). Have you used quotation marks around words you've quoted from the text? Have you used quotation marks around the titles of the short stories and underlined or used italics for the titles of the short story collection and the title of the novel?

Task Three—Prepare Your Final Paper

1. Include an appropriate title for this assignment—something interesting and inviting.

2. Put the complete heading in the upper right-hand corner of the paper.

3. If time permits, add a computer graphic that highlights the stories you've read and written about.

RESOURCE E: BOOK REPORT #3— NARRATIVE POEM

Practice writing narrative poetry by using the following guidelines to prepare a book report.

Guidelines

1. Write at least five stanzas of about four lines each.

2. Model any narrative poem, such as "Lord Randal" or "Barbara Allen."

3. Follow this outline as best you can:
   Stanza 1—Introduction of main character(s) and setting
   Stanza 2—Conflict and triggering action
   Stanza 3—Rising action to climax
   Stanza 4—Falling action
   Stanza 5—Resolution/conclusion

4. If you wish, use the title of the book as the title of your poem, if not, devise a title that is appropriate.
5. On the end of your narrative poem, write: "Narrative poem is based on [title, author, copyright date, and publisher]."

Grading Rubric

- Adheres to structural guidelines listed above
- Has identifiable rhythm pattern
- Has an identifiable rhyme scheme
- Tells the plot of book in an interesting way
- Is edited for mechanics (spelling, punctuation, capitalization)
- Looks neat on the page

RESOURCE F: PREWRITING PROMPTS FOR TELLING T.I.M.E.

Telling the T.I.M.E. (title) _____
    T = Title, Thought, and Theme

- Who could be the speaker?
- Who could be the audience?
- What is the message in your opinion?

I = Imagery and Figurative Language

- What *kind(s)* of imagery is used?
- What words or lines from the poem support your answer?

M = Music and Sound

- If there is a rhythm pattern, mark the poem: use stressed "/" and unstressed "u" marks to show rhythm pattern.
- What kind of rhythm pattern is in this poem?
- On the poem, use lowercase letters (aabb) to show rhyme scheme.

- What special kinds of words or techniques does the author use to create sound for effect in this poem?
- What words prove your answer?

E = Emotion (expressed/experienced)

- What emotion is expressed by the poet in this poem?
- What words or lines support your answer?
- What emotion do you experience as the reader of this poem?
- What words, phrases, or lines evoke this emotional response for you?
- How well does this poem reflect our definition of poetry? (See your notebook for exact wording.)

RESOURCE G: PERUSING, PICKING, PRESENTING, AND PERFORMING POETRY

Spend some time reading poetry and deciding which poem you like well enough to share with the class. (Please select a new poem; one not done for previous assignments or projects.)

Steps to Selection

1. Select a collection of poems (a collection by the same or by different authors).
2. Start with the first poem in the book. Read the first four lines, and then decide if you understand them.
3. If you also enjoy the poem you understand, stop, and go on to preparing your class presentation.
4. If not, read the next, continue by reading the first four lines of each successive poem until you find one you understand and enjoy enough to share with the class.
5. Keep a record of the number of poems you read before selecting one to share in class.

Preparation for Presentation: Written and Visual

1. In your own words, tell what the poem seems to be saying.
2. Tell why you enjoyed the poem. What about the poem got your attention?
3. Copy out your favorite line from the poem, and tell why it is your favorite.
4. Tell what you noticed about the way the poet wrote the poem— the special way he or she used words, lines, stanzas, sounds, ideas, and comparisons. If you can use the language of poetry analysis, do so.
5. Pattern this poem by writing one of your own using some strategies used by your poet.
6. Photocopy or word process the poem or write it in calligraphy or other attractive print.
7. Mount and illustrate, or select an appropriate border for the poem.
8. Bring your illustrated poem to class the day you are to present your poem. We plan to make an anthology of favorite poems.
9. Memorize the original poem.

Presentation Day

1. Recite the memorized poem dramatically. You can recite it twice. Once at the beginning of your presentation, and again at the end.
2. Your presentation should be about three minutes. During this sharing time, state the title and author of your poem, relate some of the information from your writing about the poem, and perhaps, play some music in the background. (Let me know ahead of time so I'll have the equipment to play tapes, DVDs, or CDs in the classroom.)
3. Let me know if you wish to bring "neat to eat treats" on presentation day.
4. Turn in your illustrated poem and your writing about the poem.

ENJOY!!

RESOURCE H: MYTH PLAY CHECKLIST

- *Who* are the two or three main characters in your play?
- *What* myth is the basis for your play?
- *What* do you want the audience to think, feel, and know as a result of reading or seeing your play?
- *When* does your play take place?
- *Where* does your play take place?
  Simple set requirements?
  Simple lighting required?
- *Why* are the characters in conflict (universal issue)?
  Parent child disagreement
  Sibling rivalry
  Desire for power or glory
  Peer pressure
  Boy meets girl
  Love triangle
- *How* well does your play follow the guidelines for an effective drama script?
  Plot is focused on a single problem to be solved within brief period of time
  Personality of characters is revealed primarily in dialogue; secondarily in action
  Dialogue introduces conflict early in the play
  Dialogue sounds like real conversation—brief, overlapping speeches and some fragments
  Play has an identifiable beginning, middle, and end
  Rising action includes three increasingly more challenging obstacles to solving the problem
  Climax is realistic, but not given away too soon
  Resolution makes sense based on the personality of characters
  Do you avoid the use of narrator and let characters reveal themselves through dialogue?
  Do your minor characters serve as foils or help reveal major characters?
  Do you include suggestions for lighting, sets, and props, but allow dialogue to guide the director in his or her choices?

RESOURCE I: OUTLINE FOR
PROBLEM-SOLVING SPEECH

Topic:

Purpose: to inform my audience that they should listen to me about . . .

Introduction Technique:

Body Organization Plan: Describe *problem* with details from research.

Who is affected, concerned, involved?

   A.

   B.

   C.

What is the nature, significance of problem?

When did it become a problem? How long? Into the future?

   A.

   B.

   C.

Where is problem experienced? Where are solutions planned?

   A.

   B.

   C.

Box I.1

What have you included in your speech to make it a particularly interesting, effective, believable, and winning speech?

- Startling statistics
- Heartwarming, heart wrenching story
- Amusing anecdote (story that illustrates problem)
- Opinion(s) of expert(s)
- Colorful words that sound impressive
- Repetition of key ideas
- A memorable quote or expression
- Transition devices to help audience follow main points or arguments
- Clear picture of reasons audience should listen to you for answers to the problem you describe in your speech

Why should audience be concerned?

    A.

    B.

    C.

How is/can the problem be solved? Says who?

    A.

    B.

    C.

Conclusion Technique: (What are reasons the audience should believe you are worthy of their consideration? See box I.1 for additional questions.)

RESOURCE J: PEER EVALUATION OF TEXT FOR PROBLEM-SOLVING SPEECH

"Optimism Is the Right Stuff"

Speech Writer: _____ Period: _____

Topic: _____

Use a scale of 1–5 (low–high) to indicate how close the speech writer has come to meeting the goal of writing a speech that is an interesting, effective, believable, and winning speech.

Introduction: The opening grabs and holds attention by using

_____ Startling statistics?

_____ Heartwarming, heart wrenching story?

_____ Amusing anecdote (story that illustrates problem)?

Body Organization Plan: Describes *problem* with details from research and answers the following questions

_____ Who is affected, concerned, involved?

_____ What is the nature, significance of problem?

_____ When did it become a problem? How long? Into the future?

_____ Where is problem experienced? Where are solutions planned?

_____ Why should audience be concerned?
_____ How is/can problem be solved? Says who?
_____ Does each paragraph develop/explain the main idea?

Conclusion Technique: (Shows how optimism has helped someone cope with a problem or gives reasons for optimism?)
Grammar:

_____ Fewer than three spelling errors
_____ Fewer than three punctuation errors
_____ Fewer than three grammar errors
_____ Long quotations are indented

Bibliography:

_____ Includes at least three different sources
_____ Conforms to format in Middle School Grammar Handbook

Overall Style:

_____ Acknowledgment of borrowed information within text
_____ Colorful words that sound impressive
_____ Minimum repetition of key ideas
_____ Memorable quote or expression
_____ Transition devices to help audience follow main points or arguments
_____ Clear picture of way(s) that "Optimism Is the Right Stuff" when considering the problem talked about (topic).

Speech Evaluator: _____

NOTES

FOREWORD

1. Don Tapscott, *Growing Up Digital: The Rise of the Net Generation* (New York: McGraw-Hill, 1998).

2. Linda Stone, "Continuous Partial Attention." Linda Stone. www .lindastone.net (accessed 8 September 2009).

PREFACE

1. As Kylene Beers suggests, reading theorists/researchers generally agree that the "point of reading is comprehension." See Beers, *When Kids Can't Read: What Teachers Can Do: A Guide for Teachers 6–12* (Portsmouth, NH: Heinemann, 2002), 59. We could expand Beers's insight, considering that all human communication primarily is for the practical purpose of comprehension, not for the other purposes of personal expression—romanticism, or impact—behaviorism. If humans don't understand one another, they invariably create unhealthy conflicts.

2. Plato, *The Republic*, especially books II, III, and X.

INTRODUCTION

1. Ignacio "Nacho" Estrada, Think Exist. thinkexist.com/quotes/ignacio_estrada/ (accessed 8 September 2009).

2. Chris Stevenson, "Curriculum That Is Challenging, Integrative, and Exploratory," in *This We Believe . . . and Now We Must Act*, ed. Thomas O. Erb (Westerville, OH: National Middle School Association, 2001), 63.

3. Gardner referenced in John D. Bransford, Ann L. Brown, and Rodney R. Cocking, eds., "How Children Learn," in *How People Learn: Brain, Mind, Experience, and School—Expanded Edition* (Washington, DC: National Academy Press, 2000), 109.

4. For further information about Louise Rosenblatt's research on teaching reading, see the article "Louise Rosenblatt and Theories of Reader-Response" by Carolyn Allen published 3 April 2004, 1988, at www.hu.mtu.edu/reader/online/20/allen20.html.

5. Fran Claggett and Joan Brown, *Drawing Your Own Conclusions: Graphic Strategies for Reading, Writing, and Thinking* (Portsmouth, NH: Heinemann, 1992).

6. Quoted in D. Ray Reutzel and Robert B. Cooter, Jr., "Classroom Reading Assessment," in *Strategies for Reading Assessment and Instruction: Helping Every Child Succeed*, 2nd ed. (Upper Saddle River, NJ: Merrill-Prentice Hall, 2003), 26.

7. Anthony W. Jackson and Gayle A. Davis, "Curriculum and Assessment to Improve Teaching and Learning," in *Turning Points 2000: Educating Adolescents in the 21st Century* (New York: Teachers College Press, 2000), 48.

8. Jackson and Davis, 176.

9. Edwards quoted by Suzanne Siegel Zenkel, *For My Teacher* (White Plains, NY: Peter Pauper Press, 1994).

10. Anne King spoke at the Middle school conference on "Teaching the Good Stuff in the Middle," Grand Valley State University, Michigan, February 2006.

11. "NCTE Definition of 21st Century Literacies" (2008), at ncte.org (accessed 15 August 2009); "Writing in the 21st Century: A Report from the National Council of Teachers of English," by NCTE past president Kathleen Blake Yancey, Florida State University, Tallahassee. © February 2009 National Council of Teachers of English. Reprinted with permission. www.ncte.org.

CHAPTER I

1. Oscar Hammerstein, "Getting to Know You." Sound Track Lyrics. www.stlyrics.com/lyrics/thekingandi/gettingtoknowyou.htm (accessed 7 September 2009).

2. For more on observation strategies and record keeping, see "Royce Sadler: Conversations about the Learning Record," *Learning Record Online*, 31 March 2004, www.cwrl.utexas.edu/~syverson/olr/exemplars/intro.html.

3. Most groups progress naturally from forming, storming (arguing over roles), norming (settling down and accepting the skills brought to the group), to performing (getting down to business). See Bruce W. Tuckman, "Developmental Sequence in Small Groups," University of Florida, www.mph.ufl .edu/events/seminar/Tuckman1965DevelopmentalSequence.pdf (accessed 8 September 2009).

4. Mark Twain, *Huckleberry Finn*, www.literature.org/authors/twain-mark/ huckleberry/chapter-23.html.

5. Word Clouds, www.wordle.net (accessed 3 August 2009).

CHAPTER 2

1. Sybylla Y. Hendrix, "Why Our Students Study Literature," Gustavus Adolphus College, gustavus.edu/academics/english/whystudyliterature.php (accessed 8 September 2009).

CHAPTER 3

1. Heather Hansen, "Speak English Clearly and Grammatically, and Boost Your Success!" Articles Base, www.articlesbase.com/communication-articles/ speak-english-clearly-and-grammatically-and-boost-your-success-195745.html (accessed 8 September 2009).

2. "Code-switching is the practice of moving between variations of languages in different contexts. Everyone who speaks has learned to code-switch depending on the situation and setting. In an educational context, code-switching is defined as the practice of switching between a primary and a secondary language or discourse." Heather Coffey, "Code-Switching," UNC School of Education, www.learnnc.org/lp/pages/4558 (accessed 8 September 2009).

3. The poem "The Phone Booth at the Corner" by Juan Delgado is in *Braided Lives: An Anthology of Multicultural American Writing*, published by the Minnesota Humanities Commission and the Minnesota Council of Teachers of English in 1991.

4. Mason Cooley, "Mason Cooley Quotes," Brainy Quotes, www.brainy quote.com/quotes/quotes/m/masoncoole396165.html (accessed 8 September 2009).

CHAPTER 4

1. Edmund Burke, "Quotes and Sayings about Books and Reading," The Quote Garden, www.quotegarden.com/books.html (accessed 7 September 2009).

2. Adapted from diagram in *Literature: Introduction to Short Stories, Drama and Poetry*, Walter Blair and John Gerber (Chicago: Scott, Foresman and Company, 1959), 238.

3. Goran "George" Moberg, *Writing in Groups: New Techniques for Good Writing without Drills*, 3rd ed. (New York: The Writing Consultant, 1984).

4. "Create Rubrics for your Project-Based Learning Activities," RubiStar, 2008, rubistar.4teachers.org/index.php (accessed 5 August 2009).

5. Harvey Daniels and Steven Zememan, "Conferences: the Core of the Workshop," in *Teaching the Best Practice Way: Methods That Matter, K-12*, ed. Harvey Daniels and Marilyn Bazar (Portland, ME: Stenhouse Press, 2005), 182.

6. Although fan fiction is still emerging as a valid educational activity and has not been addressed comprehensively in the educational literature, Wikipedia is tracking the phenomenon with some excellent, user-submitted material on the topic: en.wikipedia.org/wiki/Fan_fiction.

7. Lawrence Baines, "Cool Books for Tough Guys: 50 Books Out of the Mainstream of Adolescent Literature That Will Appeal to Males Who Do Not Enjoy Reading," *Alan Review* 22, no. 1 (Fall 1994): 43–46.

CHAPTER 5

1. Robert Newton Peck, *A Day No Pigs Would Die* (New York: Alfred A. Knopf, 1972), 18–19.

2. Fran Claggett, Louann Reid, and Ruth Vinz with Cammie Lin, *Daybook of Critical Reading and Writing: World Literature* (Wilmington, DE: Great Source Education Group, 2008), 105.

3. California Reading and Literature Project (CRLP) participants, *Literature for All Students: A Sourcebook for Teachers* (Sacramento: California Department of Education, 1985).

4. Adapted from CRLP participants, *Literature for All Students*.

5. Random House offers a free guide to "reaching reluctant readers" at www.randomhouse.com/highschool/RHI_magazine/pdf/scales.pdf. For example, millions of dollars are spent by school districts each year to purchase computerized reading programs; these programs test students on the novels they have read and reward them with points that ultimately lead to prizes and

other incentives. Often, however, there is very little personal attention offered to readers in schools that use such programs.

6. Alberto Manguel, *A History of Reading* (New York: Viking, 1996), 42–53.

7. Adapted from "Using Text Structure," (National Education Association, 2008).

8. Nicholas Wolterstorff, *Works and Worlds of Art* (New York: Oxford University Press, 1980).

9. National Council of Teachers of English, *Standards for the English Language Arts* (Urbana, IL: National Council of Teachers of English, 1996), 31.

10. For background on vocabulary instruction, see Karen Bromley, *Stretching Students' Vocabulary: Best Practices for Building Rich Vocabulary Students Need to Achieve in Reading, Writing and the Content Areas* (New York: Scholastic, 2002), 85.

11. National Council of Teachers of English.

12. See David I. Smith and Barbara Carvill, *The Gift of the Stranger: Faith, Hospitality, and Foreign Language Learning* (Grand Rapids, MI: Eerdmans, 2000).

13. Smith and Carvill.

14. "A Found Poem is a collection of words or phrases quoted from a piece of literature. When read aloud, these words or phrases create a found poem." See "Activity Bank," San Diego County Office of Education website, www.sdcoe.k12.ca.us/score/actbank/sfound.htm (accessed 9 March 2009).

15. SCORE: Language Arts, "CyberGuides: Teacher Guides & Student Activities," www.sdcoe.k12.ca.us/score/cyberguide.html.

16. SCORE, www.sdcoe.k12.ca.us/score/pig/pigtg.htm.

CHAPTER 6

1. Charles Dickens, *A Christmas Carol.* (New York: Viking, 2000), 36–37.

2. Kate Kinsella, "Academic Word List." Hollywood High School. www.hhslibrary.net/PDFfiles/Academic_Word_List.pdf.

3. Sheridan D. Blau, *The Literature Workshop: Teaching Texts and Their Readers.* (Portsmouth, NH: Heinemann, 2003).

CHAPTER 7

1. Naoshi Koriyama, "Unfolding Bud," in *Inner Chimes: Poems on Poetry*, ed. Bobbye S. Goldstein (Honesdale, PA: Boyds Mills Press, 1992), 7. This

poem first appeared in *The Christian Science Monitor* on July 3, 1957, and is reproduced with permission. © 1957 *The Christian Science Monitor*, www.csmonitor.com. All rights reserved.

2. Jump in reading was demonstrated in the San Diego Area Writing Project and in workshops presented by Sheridan Blau, former president of National Council of Teachers of English and director of the South Coast Writing Project in California.

3. *Houghton Mifflin College Dictionary* (Boston: Houghton Mifflin, 1986), s.v. "poem."

4. Poetry T.I.M.E. is not original to me. It's an acronym I picked up along the way, and because it stuck, I've used it with success for more than thirty years when introducing students to poetry analysis.

5. Nancy Genevieve, *NYX—Daughter of Chaos* (Eureka, IL: NOX Press, 2002).

6. Louann Reid and Fran Claggett, *Daybook for Critical Reading and Writing* (Great Source Education Group, June 1998).

7. Mark Twain, *The Adventures of Huckleberry Finn and Related Readings* (Evanston, IL: McDougal Littell, 1997), 121–22.

CHAPTER 8

1. Joseph Epstein, "The Personal Essay: A Form of Discovery," in *The Norton Book of Personal Essays*, ed. Joseph Epstein (New York: W. W. Norton and Company, 1997), 15.

2. The text of Maya Angelou's poem "On the Pulse of Morning" can be found on a number of Internet websites.

CHAPTER 9

1. Elizabeth Borton de Treviño, *I, Juan de Pareja* (Canada Ltd.: HarperCollins, 1993), 6.

2. Susan Zimmermann and Chryse Hutchins, *Seven Keys to Comprehension* (New York: Three Rivers Press, 2003), 50–51.

3. "Renaissance," WordNetWeb. wordnetweb.princeton.edu/perl/webwn?s =renaissance (accessed 7 September 2009).

4. Linda S. Starr, "Outrageous Women of the Renaissance: Warriors, Artists, Rulers, and Thieves," www.education-world.com/a_books/books126.shtml (accessed 6 September 2009).

5. "Artemisia Gentileschi and Elisabetta Sirani—Two Women of the Italian Baroque," newexpressionist.blogspot.com/2009/03/artemisia-gentileschiand -elisabetta.html (accessed 6 September 2009).

6. "Outrageous Women of the Renaissance," www.wiley.com/WileyCDA/ WileyTitle/productCd-0471296848.html (accessed 22 January 2010).

7. Carol Jago, *With Rigor for All: Teaching the Classics to Contemporary Students* (Portland, ME: Calendar Islands Publishers. 2000), 55.

8. *Advanced Dictionary*, Thorndike-Barnhart Series (Sunnyvale, CA: Scott Foresman, 1988), s.v. "chiaroscuro."

9. *Advanced Dictionary*, s.v. "baroque."

10. *Advanced Dictionary*, s.v. "realism."

11. *Advanced Dictionary*, s.v. "idealism."

12. Stevenson, "Curriculum That Is Challenging," 63.

13. Fran Claggett with Joan Brown, *Drawing Your Own Conclusions: Graphic Strategies for Reading, Writing, and Thinking* (Portsmouth, NH: Heinemann. 1992), 5–6.

14. *Houghton Mifflin College Dictionary* (Boston: Houghton Mifflin, 1986), s.v. "poem."

15. Terry Williams and J. Williams, "Image, Word, Poem: Visual Literacy and the Writing Process," National Council of Teachers of English Annual Convention, Detroit Institute of Art, November 1997.

16. Terry Williams and J. Williams.

CHAPTER 10

1. Edmond Rostand, *Cyrano de Bergerac*, trans. Lowell Blair, in *World Literature* (Lake Forest, IL: Glencoe Macmillan/McGraw-Hill, 1992), 472.

2. *Cyrano de Bergerac* (with English subtitles). Starring: Gérard Depardieu and Anne Brochet, Director: Jean-Paul Rappeneau, Format: Color, NTSC Rated: PG, Studio: MGM/UA Studios, Video Release Date: February 21, 2000.

3. You may wish to see the website accompanying this book to see my *California English* article, "An Audience of One's Peers," that describes in more detail writing a myth play, and then decide what kind of play would be best to assign to your class. An extended assignment handout also is there. The play in the article is written in response to a workshop presented by Playwrights Project, a nonprofit arts education organization in San Diego, for its approach to teaching playwriting in schools. Students and teachers at the Bishop's School worked with Playwrights Project for years (www.playwrightsproject.org). The

organization's basic curriculum, written by founder Deborah Salzer, is available as Stage Write, published by Interact (www.catalog.socialstudies.com).

CHAPTER 11

1. Clella Jaffe, "Introduction to Public Speaking and Culture," in *Public Speaking: Concepts and Skills for a Diverse Society*, 5th ed. (Belmont, CA: Wadsworth/Thomas Learning, 2007), 6.

2. Robert McCrum, William Cran, and Robert MacNeil, *The Story of English* (New York: Viking Penguin Inc., 1986).

3. "Six Traits® rubric," published by the Northwest Regional Educational Laboratory, www.nwrel.org.

4. Elie Wiesel, *Night* (New York: Bantam Books, 1960), 32.

5. Harry R. Noden, *Image Grammar: Using Grammatical Structures to Teach Writing* (Portsmouth, NH: Boynton/Cook Heinemann, 1999).

6. Arlene Mulligan, "Opening Doors: Drama with Second Language Learners," in *Promising Practices: Unbearably Good Teacher-Tested Ideas* (San Diego: Greater San Diego Council of Teachers of English, 1996), 72.

7. From www.medialit.org, Share 2007.

CHAPTER 12

1. Ralph Ellison, "Hidden Name Complex Fate," in *Shadow and Act* (New York: Random House, 1964), 148.

2. Brenda Borron offers a similar unit in "My Name, My Self: Using Name to Explore Identity," in *Reading, Thinking, and Writing about Multicultural Literature*, ed. Carol B. Olson (Glenview, IL: Scott Foresman, 1996), 596.

3. Jenee Gossard, "Using Read Around Groups to Establish Criteria for Good Writing," in *Practical Ideas for Teaching Writing as a Process*, ed. Carol B. Olson (Sacramento: California Department of Education, 1987), 148–50.

4. Six Traits® rubric published by the Northwest Regional Education Laboratory, nwrel.org.

BIBLIOGRAPHY

Academy of American Poets. www.poets.org/index (4 September 2009).

Advanced Dictionary. Thorndike-Barnhart Series. Sunnyvale, CA: Scott Foresman, 1988.

Asian Pacific Economic Cooperation. "21st Century Competencies." hrd .apecwiki.org/index.php/21st_Century_Competencies (4 September 2009).

Assembly on Literature for Adolescents. "ALAN Online: The Official Site of the Assembly on Literature for Adolescents." www.alan-ya.org (4 September 2009).

Baines, Lawrence. "Cool Books for Tough Guys: 50 Books Out of the Mainstream of Adolescent Literature That Will Appeal to Males Who Do Not Enjoy Reading." *The Alan Review* 22, no. 1 (1994).

Baker, F. "Media Literacy: One of the 21st Century Skills Your Students Need." *Palmetto Administrator Magazine* (2005).

Beers, Kylene. "The Measure of Our Success." In Beers, Probst, and Reif, *Adolescent Literacy: Turning Promise into Practice*.

Beers, Kylene, Robert E. Probst, and Linda Reif. *Adolescent Literacy: Turning Promise into Practice*. Portsmouth, NH: Heinemann, 2007.

Blau, Sheridan. *The Literature Workshop: Teaching Texts and Their Readers*. Portsmouth, NH: Heinemann, 2003.

Blum, Joshua, Bob Holman, and Mark Pellington. *The United States of Poetry*. New York: Henry N. Holt, Inc., 1996.

Borron, B. "My Name, My Self: Using Name to Explore Identity." In *Reading, Thinking, and Writing about Multicultural Literature*, edited by Carol B. Olson. Glenview, IL: Scott Foresman, 1996.

Bransford, John D., Ann L. Brown, and Rodney R. Cocking. *How People Learn: Brain, Mind, Experience, and School.* Washington, DC: National Academy Press, 2000.

Burke, Edmund. "Quotes and Sayings about Books and Reading." The Quote Garden. www.quotegarden.com/books.html (7 September 2009).

Burke, Jim. "Teaching English Language Arts in a Flat World." In Beers, Probst, and Reif, *Adolescent Literacy: Turning Promise into Practice.*

———. *The English Teacher's Companion: A Complete Guide to Classroom, Curriculum, and the Profession.* Portsmouth, NH: Heinemann, 2007.

Busching, Beverly, and Betty Ann Slesinger. *"It's Our World Too": Socially Responsive Learners in Middle School Language Arts.* Urbana, IL: National Council of Teachers of English, 2002.

Carrasquillo, Angela. *Beyond the Beginnings: Literacy Interventions for Upper Elementary English Language Learners.* Clevedon, UK: Multilingual Matters, 2004.

Carter, James B. *Building Literacy Connections with Graphic Novels: Page by Page, Panel by Panel.* Urbana, IL: National Council of Teachers of English, 2007.

Carter, Myron, and Christie L. Ebert. "Arts Education and 21st Century Skills." community.learnnc.org/dpi/music/AECoordinators.Sept08.CLE revisions.ppt.

Center for Media Literacy. "CML's Five Key Questions and CML's Core Concepts." www.medialit.org/pdf/mlk/14A_CCKQposter.pdf (7 September 2009).

Chabris, Christopher F. "How to Wake Up Slumbering Minds." *Wall Street Journal*, April 27, 2009. online.wsj.com/article/SB124079001063757515 .html.

Claggett, Fran, with Joan Brown. *Drawing Your Own Conclusions: Graphic Strategies for Reading, Writing, and Thinking.* Portsmouth, NH: Heinemann, 1992.

Claggett, Fran, Louann Reid, and Ruth Vinz. *Daybook of Critical Reading and Writing: World Literature.* Wilmington, DE: Great Source Education Group, 2008.

———. *Daybook of Critical Reading and Writing.* Wilmington, MA: Great Source Education Group, 1998.

Clinton, Catherine, ed. *A Poem of Her Own: Voices of American Women Yesterday and Today.* New York: Harry N. Abrams, 2003.

Coffey, Heather. "Code-Switching." UNC School of Education. www.learnnc .org/lp/pages/4558 (8 September 2009).

Cooley, Mason. "Mason Cooley Quotes." Brainy Quotes. www.brainyquote .com/quotes/quotes/m/masoncoole396165.html (8 September 2009).

Daniels, Harvey, and Steven Zememan. "Conferences: the Core of the Workshop." In *Teaching the Best Practice Way: Methods That Matter, K–12*, edited by Harvey Daniels and Marilyn Bazaar. Portland, ME: Stenhouse Press, 2005. www.stenhouse.com.

Dickens, Charles. *A Christmas Carol*. New York: Viking, 2000.

Education Podcast Network. "Education: The What, Why, and How of 21st Century Teaching & Learning." epnweb.org/index.php?openpod=4 (7 September 2009).

Ellison, Ralph. "Hidden Name: Complex Fate." In *Shadow and Act*, Ralph W. Ellison. New York: Random House, 1964.

Epstein, Joseph. "The Personal Essay: A Form of Discovery." In *The Norton Book of Personal Essays*, edited by Joseph Epstein. New York: W.W. Norton, 1997.

Estrada, Ignacio. Think Exist. thinkexist.com/quotes/ignacio_estrada/ (8 September 2009).

Filmore, Lily W. "Aiming High: Academic Vocabulary." www.scoe.org/pub/ htdocs/english-learner.html.

"Found Poem." www.sdcoe.k12.ca.us/score/actbank/sfound.htm (7 September 2009).

Free Dictionary. "Code Switch." encyclopedia.thefreedictionary.com/Code%20 switch (4 September 2009).

Genevieve, Nancy. *Daughter of Chaos*. Eureka, IL: Nox Press, 2002.

Gossard, Jenee. "Using Read Around Groups to Establish Criteria for Good Writing." In *Practical Ideas for Teaching Writing as a Process*, edited by Carol B. Olson. Sacramento: California Department of Education, 1987.

Gregory, Gayle H., and Lin Kuzmich. *Differentiated Literacy Strategies: For Student Growth and Achievement in Grades 7–12*. Thousand Oaks, CA: Corwin Press, 2005.

Gutièrrez, Kris. "Teaching and Learning in the 21st Century." *English Education* 32, no. 4 (2000): 290–98. www.ncte.org.ezproxy.gvsu.edu/library/NCTE Files/Resources/Journals/EE/0324-july00/EE0324Teaching.pdf (7 September 2009).

Hammerstein, Oscar. "Getting to Know You." Sound Track Lyrics. www .stlyrics.com/lyrics/thekingandi/gettingtoknowyou.htm (7 September 2009).

Hansen, Heather. "Speak English Clearly and Grammatically, and Boost Your Success!" Articles Base. www.articlesbase.com/communication-articles/

speak-english-clearly-and-grammatically-and-boost-your-success-195745
.html (8 September 2009).

Hazell, Ed. "21st Century Teaching." *Access Learning* March (2005): 8–9.

Hendrix, Sybylla Y. "Why Our Students Study Literature." Gustavus Adolphus College. gustavus.edu/academics/english/whystudyliterature.php (8 September 2009).

Houghton Mifflin College Dictionary. Boston: Houghton Mifflin, 1986.

How People Learn: Brain, Mind, Experience, and School, edited by John D. Bransford, Ann L. Brown, and Rodney R. Cockin. Washington, DC: National Academy Press, 2000.

Jackson, Anthony, Gayle A. Davis, Maud Abeel, and Anne A. Bordonero. *Turning Points 2000: Educating Adolescents in the 21st Century*. New York: Teacher College Press, 2000.

Jaffe, Clella. *Public Speaking: Concepts and Skills for a Diverse Society*, 5th ed. Belmont, CA: Wadsworth/Thomas Learning, 2007.

Jago, Carol. *With Rigor for All: Teaching the Classics to Contemporary Students*. Portland, ME: Calendar Islands Publishers, 2000.

Jolls, Tessa, and Elizabeth Thoman. *Literacy for the 21st Century: An Overview & Orientation Guide to Media Literacy Education*, 2nd ed. Center for Media Literacy, 2008. www.medialit.org/pdf/mlk/01a_mlkorientation_rev2 .pdf (7 September 2009).

Jones, David K. *Online Teen Dangers: The Five Greatest Internet Dangers Teenagers Face and What You Can Do to Protect Them*. Scotts Valley, CA: Create Space, 2008.

Keene, Edmond O. "The Essence of Understanding." In Beers, Probst, and Reif, *Adolescent Literacy: Turning Promise into Practice*.

Koriyama, Naoshi. "Unfolding Bud." In *Inner Chimes: Poems on Poetry*, edited by Bobbye S. Goldstein and J. B. Zalben. Honesdale, PA: Boyds Mills Press, 1992.

Learning Record. "Royce Sadler: Conversations about the Learning Record." www.cwrl.utexas.edu/~syverson/olr/sadler.html (7 September 2009).

León, Vicki. *Outrageous Women of the Renaissance*. New York: John Wiley, 1999.

Literacy Matters. "Text Structure." www.literacymatters.org/content/text/intro .htm (8 September 2009).

Literature for All Students: A Sourcebook for Teachers. Sacramento: California State Department of Education, 1985.

Manguel, Alberto. *A History of Reading*. New York: Viking, 1996.

Miles, Mike. "Implementing a 21st Century Curriculum." www.hope foundation.org/hope/21st-century-curriculum/implementing-a-21st-century -curriculum.html (7 September 2009).

Mission, Ray, and Wendy Morgan. *Critical Literacy and the Aesthetic: Transforming the English Classroom*. Urbana, IL: National Council of Teachers of English, 2006.

Moberg, Goran. *Critical Literacy and the Aesthetic: Transforming the English Classroom*. New York: The Writing Consultant, 1984.

Mulligan, Arlene. "Opening Doors: Drama with Second Language Learners." In *Promising Practices: Unbearably Good, Teacher-Tested Ideas*, edited by Linda Scott. San Diego: Greater San Diego Council of Teachers of English, 1996.

Noden, Harry R. *Image Grammar: Using Grammatical Structures to Teach Writing*. Portsmouth, NH: Heinemann, 1999.

Northwest Regional Educational Laboratory. "Six Traits Rubric Writing Scoring Continuum." www.thetraits.org/pdfRubrics/6plus1traits.PDF (7 September 2009).

"Outrageous Women of the Renaissance." www.wiley.com/WileyCDA/WileyTitle/productCd-0471296848.html (22 January 2010).

Partnership for 21st Century Skills. "A Report and Mile Guide for 21st Century Skills." www.21stcenturyskills.org/images/stories/otherdocs/p21up_Report.pdf (7 September 2009).

Peacock, Molly, Elise Paschen, and Neil Neches. *Poetry in Motion: 100 Poems from Subways and Buses*. New York: W.W. Norton, 1996.

Peck, Robert N. *A Day No Pigs Would Die*. New York: Alfred A. Knopf, 1972.

Plato. *The Republic*, II, III, and X. classics.mit.edu/Plato/republic.html (7 September 2009).

Professional Development for 21st Century Education. "English Language Arts (ages 11 to 15) Literacy to Learn Standards for Students and Teachers." www.usdlc-l2l.org/ela_mid.pdf (7 September 2009).

Reale, Terry. "A Focused Look at 21st Century Reading English Language Arts." wvde.state.wv.us/teach21/Understandingthe21stCenturyContentStandardsandObjectives.html (7 September 2009).

Reutzel, D. Ray, and Robert B. Cooter, Jr. *Strategies for Reading Assessment and Instruction: Helping Every Child Succeed*, 3rd ed. Upper Saddle River, NJ: Pearson/Merrill Prentice Hall, 2006.

Richardson, W. *Blogs, Wikis, Podcasts, and Other Powerful Web Tools for Classrooms*. Thousand Oaks, CA: Corwin Press, 2009.

Roseboro, Anna J. "Teacher CyberGuide for *A Day No Pigs Would Die* by Robert N. Peck." www.sdcoe.k12.ca.us/score/pig/pigtg.htm (7 September 2009).

———. "Teacher CyberGuide for *I, Juan de Pareja* by Elizabeth Borton de Treviño." www.sdcoe.k12.ca.us/score/juan/juantg.html (7 September 2009).

Rostand, Edmond. *Cyrano de Bergerac*. Lowell Blair. tr. In *World Literature*, Lake Forest, IL: Glencoe MacMillan/McGraw Hill, 1992.

RubiStar. "Create Websites for Your Project Based Learning Activities." rubistar.4teachers.org/index.php (7 September 2009).

Sandel, L. "Literature for the 21st Century: A Balanced Approach." *Childhood Education* (Winter 1998).

Scales, Pat. "Winning Back Your Reluctant Readers." *RHI*. www.randomhouse.com/highschool/RHI_magazine/pdf/scales.pdf (7 September 2009).

Shafer, Gregory. "Standard English and the Migrant Community." *English Journal* 90, no. 4 (2001): 37–43. www.ncte.org.ezproxy.gvsu.edu/library/NCTEFiles/Resources/Journals/EJ/0904-march01/EJ0904Standard.pdf (7 September 2009).

Smith, David I., and Barbara M. Carvill. *The Gift of the Stranger: Faith, Hospitality, and Foreign Language Learning*. Grand Rapids, MI: William B. Eerdmans, 2000.

Southern Regional Education Board. "21st Century Skills Standards." www.evalutech.sreb.org/21stcentury/Standards.asp (7 September 2009).

Standards for English Language Arts. Urbana, IL: National Council of Teachers of English, 1996.

Starr, Linda S. "Outrageous Women of the Renaissance: Warriors, Artists, Rulers, and Thieves." Education World. www.education-world.com/a_books/books126.shtml (7 September 2009).

Stevenson, Chris. "Curriculum That Is Challenging, Integrative, and Exploratory." In *This We Believe . . . and Now We Must Act*, edited by Thomas O. Erb. Westerville, OH: National Middle School Association, 2001.

Stone, Linda. "Continuous Partial Attention." Linda Stone. www.lindastone.net (8 September 2009).

Story of English, The. DVD. USA Home Video, 2001.

Tapscott, Don. *Growing Up Digital: The Rise of the Net Generation*. New York: McGraw-Hill, 1998.

Technology in the Middle. "21st Century Literacy: Basic Literacy." pwoessner.com/2008/11/29/21st-century-literacy-basic-literacy/ (7 September 2009).

"Top 15 Educational Tools/Sites for Middle School Language Arts." techdossier.blogspot.com/2008/01/top-15-educational-toolssites-for.html (7 September 2009).

Tuckman, Bruce W. "Developmental Sequence in Small Groups." Seminar. University of Florida. www.mph.ufl.edu/events/seminar/Tuckman1965DevelopmentalSequence.pdf (8 September 2009).

"21st Century Skills." thinkfinity.org/21stCenturyHome.aspx (7 September 2009).

Vincent, Tony. "Learning in Hand." learninginhand.com/blog/ (7 September 2009).

Warner, Mark. "Enhancing Communication with Edmodo." www.mrwarner.com/2009/03/enhancing-communication-with-edmodo/ (7 September 2009).

Wiesel, Elie. *Night*. New York: Bantam, 1982.

Williams, Raymond. *Keywords: A Vocabulary of Culture and Society*. New York: Oxford University Press, 1976.

Williams, Terry, and Jenny Williams. "Image, Word, Poem: Visual Literacy and the Writing Process." Workshop for National Council of Teachers of English at Detroit Institute of Art, November 1997.

Wisconsin Virtual School. "Middle School Courses: Language Arts." www.wisconsinvirtualschool.org/middle_school_langarts.asp (7 September 2009).

Wolterstorff, Nicholas. *Works and Worlds of Art*. New York: Oxford University Press, 1980.

Word Net Search. Princeton, NJ: Princeton University, wordnetweb.princeton.edu/perl/webwn?s=renaissance (7 September 2009).

Wordle. www.wordle.net (8 September 2009).

Zenkel, Suzanne S., ed. *For My Teacher*. White Plains, NY: Peter Pauper Press, 1994.

Zimmermann, Susan, and Chryse Hutchins. *Seven Keys to Comprehension: How to Help Your Kids Read It and Get It*. New York: Three Rivers Press, 2003.

INDEX

Note: Italicized page numbers indicate illustrations.

ABOUT THE AUTHOR

Anna J. Small Roseboro is widely known for her work with groups like the National Council of Teachers of English (NCTE), the Conference on English Leadership, the California Association of Teachers of English, the Michigan Council of Teachers of English, and the California Association of Independent Schools. A sought-after convention speaker, Ms. Roseboro earned a B.A. in Speech Communications from Wayne State University and an M.A. in Curriculum Design from the University of California, San Diego. With forty years' experience in public and private schools, she is a former National Board Certified Teacher, having earned the prestigious credential in Early Adolescent/English Language Arts from the National Board of Professional Teaching Standards in 1998.

Ms. Roseboro represented Rotary International in a group-study exchange with educators in Africa. In addition to teaching young adolescents in Michigan, Missouri, New York, Massachusetts, and California, she has taught adults at Rochester Theological Institute, Grand Valley State University, and Calvin College, served sixteen years as director of summer session programs for grades five through twelve, coached a National Forensic League competitive speech team for twelve years, and was English Department chair from 1999 to 2005 at the Bishop's School. In 2008–2009, Anna was a faculty leader at the NCTE Affiliates Leadership Conference and served as Master Teacher for the San

Francisco Bay Area Teachers Center in an online teaching environment. In 2009 she was honored with the California Association of Teachers of English 2009 Distinguished Service Award.

Her articles have appeared in journals such as *English Journal, English Leadership Quarterly, Fine Lines: A National Quarterly, Creative Writing Journal, California English, Utah Journal of Teachers of English, San Diego Museum of Contemporary Art Journal*, and the *CAIS Quarterly*. Additional publications include *Black Boy, Autobiographical Guide* (Scott Foresman, 1995), and "Multicultural Literature: A Challenge and an Opportunity," in *Multicultural Voices' Teacher's Resource Book* (Scott Foresman, 1994).

Franklin Pierce University

00188401

Breinigsville, PA USA
08 September 2010
245008BV00001B/3/P

9 781607 096313